Explaining economic policy reversals

Christopher Hood

Open University Press
Buckingham · Philadelphia

Open University Press
Celtic Court
22 Ballmoor
Buckingham
MK18 1XW

and
1900 Frost Road, Suite 101
Bristol, PA 19007, USA

First Published 1994

A catalogue record of this book is available from the British Library

ISBN 0 335 15649 5 (pbk)   0 335 15650 9 (hbk)

Library of Congress Cataloging-in-Publication Data

Hood, Christopher, 1947–
    Explaining economic policy reversals / Christopher Hood.
      p. cm.
    Includes bibliographical references and index.
    ISBN 0–335–15650–9. — ISBN 0–335–15649–5 (pbk.)
    1. Deregulation. 2. Privatization. 3. Economic stabilization.
  4. Chicago school of economics. 5. Government spending policy.
  6. Economic policy. 7. Policy sciences. I. Title.
  HD3612.H66 1994
  338.9—dc20
                                                                        93–36866
                                                                        CIP

Typeset by Graphicraft, Hong Kong
Printed and bound in Great Britain by
Biddles Ltd, Guildford and King's Lynn

Contents

List of tables and figures

Tables

Figures

Preface and acknowledgements

Politics mixed with economics makes a heady and compelling brew. There are so many confident sages who know exactly what *should* be done. Too bad, as the old saw has it, that most of them are so busy driving taxis or cutting hair. And there is the endless parade of attention-grabbing prophets who know exactly what *will* be done, because they have the inside dope or the definitive model or have seen it all before.

Part of the attraction of studying in this area comes from the frequency with which both the priests and the prophets fall flat on their faces. By the 1970s, the predictions of the 1940s of long-term growth in the number of state bureaucrats and of the steady extension of state-owned enterprise, made by such eminences as James Burnham (1942) and Joseph Schumpeter (1944), were clearly coming to rank in the 'wooden-spoon' group of social science prophecies along with Professor Irving Fisher's famous 1928 prediction, on the eve of the great US stock market crash, that 'stock prices have reached what looks like a permanently high plateau'. And it is the 'surprise' arising from the apparent failure of these grand prophecies about economic policy that forms the background for this book.

This book is about the economic policy 'dinosaurs' which apparently went into extinction in the 1980s. These policy reversals were not predicted. How can they be explained? An economist, they say, is someone who can tell you tomorrow why yesterday's prophecy didn't fit today's events (McCloskey 1985: xix). Yet there are few well-developed economic explanations of this process of extinction which go beyond tautology and teleology. Theory remains tentative. Even in political science, accounts of these policy reversals are apt to take New Right ideas as meteorites from outer space, and concentrate on explaining why their impact spread once they had landed.

Having taught undergraduate and graduate classes in this area for over twenty years, I have personally lived through the apparent extinction of the policy 'dinosaurs'. As a child of the 1940s, I was born into the dinosaur age, at a high point of public enterprise, progressive taxation, full employment, hierarchist public administration. In adult life, I have seen its passing. In the endless social science debates which have surrounded this policy shift, I have been struck by how often discussion lapses into the polemical or the tautological when we should be trying to develop something like an 'extinction science' in public policy.

I should stress that this book is only the most modest step in that direction. It is mainly addressed to the general reader and to students of economic policy, particularly in political science and public administration. It aims to pull together material which is not conveniently available in a single source – to 'de-archipelagize', as it were, the present archipelago of scattered policy specialisms within economic policy that need to be brought together to get an overall view of the passing of the dinosaur age. It has arisen from the difficulty which I have faced in finding suitable reading material for teaching in the area. It is not that there is an absolute shortage of literature on any of the topics considered in this book – quite the reverse. But most of the literature that is available is too descriptive, too technical, or simply too hard to find to fit with the needs of students of public policy. If the book has any originality, it lies in the overall treatment and in the range of cases considered.

The book has taken too long – over four years – to write, and I have many debts to acknowledge. In particular, I am grateful to my LSE colleague Brendan O'Leary who offered encouragement and comments on drafts of several of the chapters, and to Desmond King of St. John's College Oxford, and Andrew Dunsire of the University of York, who both read the whole book in draft form and offered valuable comments. Chapter Three draws heavily from what I learned from conversations with David Heald of Aberdeen University during the time that we jointly taught a graduate seminar on public enterprise and regulation at LSE, and I am grateful to David for comments on an earlier draft of the chapter. I am also grateful to Richard Rose of Strathclyde University for comments on Chapter Six. Chapter Five started life as an article in the *Journal of Theoretical Politics* in 1991, building on work that I did at the University of Bielefeld in 1989. I owe a great deal to students at LSE (and also in earlier days in Sydney) who have endured my attempts to put a conceptual framework around subjects like privatization and deregulation and prodded me into discarding ideas that didn't help. In particular, I would like to thank Oliver James, who offered useful criticisms of a draft of Chapter Six. Without the encouragement of successive editors at the Open University Press (Ray Cunningham, Richard Baggaley, John Skelton), the book would never have been written. Finally, I am grateful to my father who read all of the draft chapters and commented on their readability, to my wife for compiling the index, and to Fritz Scharpf and the *Journal of Public Policy* for permission to reproduce Table 4.2.

1

Policy reversals and how to explain them

... to what do the economic policies of the state respond?

(Hall 1986: 4)

Policy extinction and economic policy dinosaurs

Dinosaurs are said to have dominated the earth for nearly 140 million years. Then – some 64 million years or so ago – they mysteriously disappeared. Why this dramatic mass extinction after such a spectacular evolutionary triumph? Was it a long decline brought about by gradual climate change, leading to loss of habitat? Did it stem from some sudden catastrophe such as a meteorite striking the earth or an upsurge of volcanic activity? Or should we blame the victim? Were the dinosaurs really their own worst enemies, themselves causing the climate to change through the effects of their breathing and flatulence? Or was their disappearance perhaps the result of predation, with dinosaur eggs being taken by small mammals? Scientists disagree. But the theorizing and the search for evidence to support goes on.

This book is about some of the 'dinosaurs' of economic policy which apparently became extinct in many OECD countries over the 1980s. Like the stegosaurus, the diplodocus and the tyrannosaurus, they are a familiar group: Keynesian full-employment policy, public enterprise, 'classical' styles of business regulation, progressive income tax structures and traditional public management styles. Only a generation ago, these animals dominated the economic policy landscape. No-one predicted their demise. They were seen as normal and natural life forms. Only a few radicals even questioned their presence. For instance, when Milton Friedman (1977) said, nearly two decades ago, that one civil servant in six should be taken off the public payroll and public enterprises should be auctioned off, the idea could be dismissed as a far-right fantasy (see Foster 1992: 108). Didn't he know that long-term government growth was inevitable and that social modernization required progressive public administration and public enterprise?

How useful is the dinosaur metaphor?

Jurassic Park return to life?

Extinction means unable to reproduce/reappear

Yet Milton Friedman's proposal was actually carried out in the UK in the 1980s; indeed, more than carried out, in that most public enterprises were privatized and more than one civil servant in *five* disappeared from the government's *Staff in Post* count between 1979 and 1990 (see Dunsire and Hood 1989). And many of the other ruling orthodoxies of economic policy in the era after the Second World War seem to have gone the way of the dinosaurs. In their place have come new life forms – the familiar menagerie of deregulation, privatization, neoclassical macroeconomics, flatter taxes and 'new public management'.

If there was indeed a mass policy extinction, why did it occur when it did? Why did it come as such a surprise? Could it have been predicted with better social theories? Was it the underlying *facts* of political life that changed, or the basic theories which were fundamentally wrong? These questions form the starting-point for this book.

Policy 'extinction', of course, is an even less exact science than biological extinction. And the parallel with the dinosaurs, as we shall see, is far from complete. The economic policies that became extinct in the 1980s had a much shorter reign. Some lasted barely a generation. Nor have the old orthodoxies completely disappeared off the face of the earth. Some people say they will soon be back, even that they have started to re-emerge already in the slump of the early 1990s. But still their decline and replacement seems to have been dramatic. And, like the fate of the dinosaurs, there is much fascination in trying to understand why their early evolutionary triumph seems to have turned around. Particularly since, as also applies to the dinosaurs, there is no single accepted explanation of these policy reversals.

The aim, design and focus of the book

The main aim of the book is to examine ways of explaining why the economic policy 'dinosaurs' appeared to die out, to be replaced by other species. Their apparent extinction is an important test for social science theories of public policy. So what are the main explanations of major policy reversals? Which of those explanations seems the most powerful in understanding these changes? What are the strengths and weaknesses of each? Can one all-purpose explanation cover all of them? Or do different theories seem to apply to different areas of policy, such that the most plausible explanation for the disappearance of one type of 'dinosaur' might not be the same as that applying to other types?

In following these questions, the book does not aim to discuss whether these policy 'dinosaurs' *ought* to have died out, or whether they 'deserved' their fate in some moral sense. There is certainly no shortage of writing about economic policy reversals in *that* vein. Nor does the book aim to document the changes in fine detail, for any particular country. That is an important but separate task from what is being attempted here. The focus is on the broad comparative picture and on the general plausibility of the various explanations which political scientists and others have advanced for why the old orthodoxies died out, as against earlier explanations of the rise of the old orthodoxies.

Although major economic policy extinctions are the subject-matter of the book, the orthodox *discipline* of economics has little more than a walk-on part in the pages which follow. Orthodox economics is not concerned with explaining why tastes and preferences (including politicians' tastes and preferences) might change, or with the politics that lies behind economic policy and shapes it in one way rather than another. There are some important exceptions, as we will see, and exciting theoretical developments on the fringes of institutional economics. But in general the answer to the 'policy extinction' problem has to be sought in the study of politics, public policy and less conventional types of economics.

The design of the book is very simple. This chapter looks briefly and very selectively at some different ways of explaining policy reversal. Each of the six chapters which follow are devoted to a particular area of policy reversal, such as the move from regulation to deregulation or from public enterprise to privatization. These chapters are not structured with the mechanical uniformity beloved of so many textbook writers. In each case, the discussion aims to follow the literature specific to that field, trying to see how the old structures were conventionally explained, how much of a 'surprise' the changes of the 1980s were for those traditional explanations of policy development, and whether quite different explanations are needed to make sense of those changes. The final chapter briefly returns to the six cases as a set – to the dinosaurs as a group. Is it plausible to suggest some general or overarching explanation that would account for all of these policy extinctions? Or should we reject the idea of a 'one-size-fits-all' explanation, and accept different explanations for different types of policy?

Four approaches to explaining policy reversals

Since we are focusing here on general policy reversals, we are not concerned with those approaches to public policy which concentrate on explaining one-way trends or the persistence of distinctive national policy styles. Such approaches may be useful in helping us to understand exceptions to, or variations in, patterns of general policy reversal. But they cannot readily explain the phenomenon itself.

If we look for general explanations of policy reversal, there are many possible candidates to choose from. But instead of going through the standard approaches to understanding policy seriatim, as an orthodox public policy textbook would do, the focus here is on four possible types of general explanations for policy extinction, which cut across the conventional academic divisions of the subject (see Kesselman 1992). They are summarized in Fig. 1.1. We distinguish between forces destroying policy from the 'inside' and pressures coming from 'outside'. Out of the 'external' forces, we distinguish between the changes in ideas, changes in interests and changes in environments. Accordingly, the four main candidates considered here are:

But how do you explain without looking at the economic critique or public choice theories?

Figure 1.1   How does policy reverse?

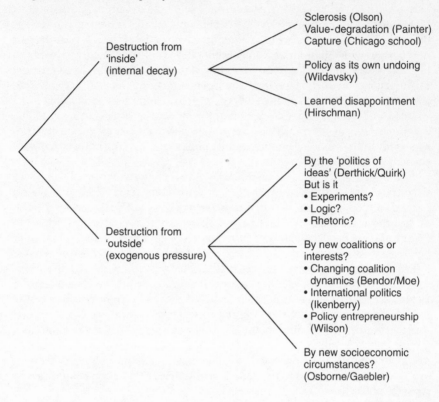

- The idea that policy reversal comes mainly from the force of new *ideas*, which succeed in upsetting the *status quo* in some way (through experimental evidence, logical force or rhetorical power).
- The idea that policy reversal comes mainly from the pressure of *interests*, which succeed in achieving changes that suit their purposes.
- The idea that policy reversal comes mainly from changes in social '*habitat*', which make old policies obsolete in the face of new conditions.
- The idea that policy reversal comes from 'inside', with policies and institutions *destroying themselves* rather than being destroyed from outside.

As we shall see, these explanations are interlinked. For example, processes of institutional 'capture' (in which organizations are colonized or taken over by interest groups) come somewhere between 'internal decay' and 'external destruction'. And, just as with the different explanations of the dinosaurs' demise, it is difficult to find evidence that sharply discriminates among the four explanations. But they do give us different perspectives on policy extinction, and we can at least explore which perspective, or mix of perspectives, seems to be most fruitful in understanding the process.

What about evolution of ideas?
Some environments are more hostile to ideas than others.

Policy reversals and how to explain them 5

Economists' ideas as climate-changing meteorites

One possible explanation of the extinction of the policy dinosaurs is as a result of ideological 'climate change' caused by intellectual developments and changes in the world of ideas. Indeed, it is interesting and apparently paradoxical that economics, supposedly the most 'worldly' of the social sciences, often explains the development of public policy in rather unworldly terms as reflecting the march of economic ideas rather than the weight of interests (see Rhoads 1985: 214). If there is any parallel with the 'meteorite striking earth' theory of the dinosaurs' extinction, the ideas of economists are often portrayed as intellectual meteorites sent from outer space (or whatever planet it is that economists live on) and hitting the world of public policy with sudden and devastating effect.

In a much-quoted passage, the economist Maynard Keynes (1936: 383) argued: '. . . ideas of economists and political philosophers . . . are more powerful than is commonly understood. Indeed the world is ruled by little else . . .'. Indeed, Keynes' theme that 'the economist's pen is mightier than the lobbyist's expense account' received a new lease of life in the 1980s with the apparent extinction of the economic policies considered here. In every case, from the attack on Keynes' own ideas about macroeconomic policy to the attack on classical regulation and public enterprise, new economic theories were coming out of the policy shops to hit the relevant policy communities. In that sense, we could think of key economists like George Stigler, Sam Peltzman, James Buchanan, William Baumol or William Niskanen as 'meteorites' whose impact changed the policy climate and helped to spell extinction for the dinosaurs. For the influential 'institutionalist' school in political science, new ideas can be a key element causing the reshaping of political coalitions and the adoption of new positions by established groups (cf. Thelen and Steinmo 1992: 9 and 22–6). In fact, Martha Derthick and Paul Quirk offered a controversial explanation of deregulation in the USA as a case of 'the politics of ideas' rather than 'the politics of interest', which we will be exploring in the next chapter (Derthick and Quirk 1985; see also Quirk 1988).

In similar vein, Kenneth Minogue (1986) argues that modern liberal democracies are 'loquocentric societies'. By that he means societies in which arguments and ideas, if deployed persuasively enough, can prompt people to act in ways which do not closely fit their own narrow interests and indeed may go against them. Against the 'critical theory' ideas of Jürgen Habermas, Minogue claims that in such societies, 'Politics swings freely subject only to the ebb and flow of persuasion' (ibid.: 342). Giandomenico Majone (1989a) similarly argues that policy change depends heavily on the persuasive deployment of ideas by policy advocates rather than by an inexorable logic of interests.

How might 'ideas' turn policy around? One possibility is that public policy follows the ideas of social science (particularly economics) and that theoretical breakthroughs and 'crucial experiments' can put it into reverse. Indeed, within economics, the story of policy change can often be told in terms of a series of key journal papers which altered received opinion. For instance, in the case of

?!
Keynes (?)
Keynesians

But these ideas were around a long time – why then? timing of the reversal (stagflation of 1970s) discontent.
The doctrine of ripe time. An ideas time has come.

deregulation (as we will see in the next chapter), economists had developed new concepts in the 1960s and 1970s about what made markets 'contestable' and how government regulation could be captured by regulatees.

These ideas undermined the traditional justifications for a particular style of regulation, built on ideas about what made monopoly 'natural' and how regulation worked. The new ideas seemed to be the driving force of the deregulatory movement. By little more than their own intellectual vigour in offering new interpretations of the regulatory world, those new ideas appeared to carry the day over the 'vested interests', all the producer lobby groups which supported the regulatory *status quo* and 'owned' the relevant regulatory bureaucracies. And a similar interpretation of policy change as reflecting theoretical development can be told for many of the other 'extinctions' considered here, such as the apparent triumph of 'New Public Management' over the presumed inertia of public bureaucracies and labour union resistance.

This heroic interpretation of intellectually driven policy 'climate change' is both attractive and convenient. The image of economists as meteorites from outer space, fatally changing the climate in which special interests had flourished by sheer intellectual force, is so flattering to economics professors that it is not surprising that many adopt it so readily.

Others, however, stress the role of *packaging* rather than content in explaining how economic policy ideas become persuasive. For instance, Donald McCloskey (1985: 31) cites some witticisms circulating in the (US) Council of Economic Advisers in the early 1980s, which express the scepticism of 'insider' economists about the idea that policy is the product of crucial experiments in a hard-science mode. ' "Mankiw's Maxim: No issue in economics has ever been decided on the basis of the facts." "Nihilistic Corollary I: No issue has ever been decided on the basis of theory either . . .".'

To those who share such heretical views about policy and economics, change in the intellectual climate surrounding policy does not occur through scientific experimentation. Indeed, to McCloskey himself, persuasiveness in economics is not explained by 'crucial experiments', but rather by economists' success in deploying age-old rhetorical skills to make essentially contestable arguments seem persuasive, and hence close the debate. In rhetoric, success in argument does not lie in systematic examination of cases ('hard data') or formal logic, but in how successfully disbelief can be suspended by making an argument fit a particular social context as a key fits a lock (cf. Hood and Jackson 1991). We should not look for convincing 'crucial experiments' to explain why a particular policy argument triumphed, nor should we be surprised by reinventions of the wheel. It is often said that a 'hit' in popular music typically consists of 90 per cent recycling and 10 per cent originality (if that). Some would claim that the same applies to successful policy argument.

Once we start to see the 'primacy of ideas' in public policy reversal in terms of rhetorical skill rather than in terms of systematic experimentation and formal logic, the distinction between 'ideas' and 'interests' starts to blur. Can anything be 'packaged up' for any audience, given enough rhetorical skill? Can any sort of policy argument be made to appeal to any kind of people? Such is

Suspension of professionalism by economists – like quacks

rise and fall of ideas rather than extinction
learning → modification

the professional creed of the public relations consultant and the 'spin doctor'. Social scientists are apt to be more sceptical, expecting different groups and institutions to vary in terms of the sorts of policy arguments they are 'programmed' to accept, and expecting underlying social changes to constrain the possibilities of what can be 'spin-doctored'. Accordingly, the further we move from 'harder' to 'softer' versions of the 'primacy of ideas' approach, the harder it will be to distinguish 'ideas' from 'interests'.

Emergence of new competitors and predators

Second, the policy dinosaurs' demise could be explained by the development of competitors, predators and parasites, as in the theory that small furry mammals – our own distant ancestors – evolved to prey off dinosaur eggs. Some biological species seem to have been hunted to extinction. The analogy in social science is to put the dynamic of political interests into the centre of the theoretical stage, and to explain policy development by the formation of new interest coalitions which stood to benefit from policy change.

If we take this perspective, we will be sceptical of the notion that the force of ideas alone is enough to explain why some policies become extinct and come to be replaced with new species. We will look for something else to explain why some policy ideas remain out of favour while others attract attention and research grants, resulting in their amplification through refinement, publication, appointments, promotions and intellectual empires. Unless those outcomes are put down to pure luck, pure merit or pure marketing skill, there must be some inherent bias in the political system which selects some ideas as received doctrines and dismisses or downgrades others. Is the development of economic science really independent from the interests and power structure in the society which provide the attention and the funding? Do rising interests generate or at least reward the development of the kind of ideas which are favourable to them?

Once issues of this kind are raised, Keynes' thesis about 'the power of ideas' in public policy might start to look like only part of the story. For Marxists, it is second nature to interpret policy change as a discovery of new policies or structures which work better than the old ones in protecting big business and underpinning the development of capitalism, and to interpret received ideas as those which serve those interests. But you do not have to be a bred-in-the-bone Marxist to suggest that when ideas or institutions change, interests must be at the bottom of it somewhere. Indeed, theorists of the economics-of-politics school tend to have exactly the same expectation. For Patrick Dunleavy (1986), a 'policy boom' has to be a product of a successful conjuncture of ideas and interests. The implication is that each on its own is not sufficient.

If policy reflects the successful exercise of power by some groups over others, a reversal of policy must presumably be explained by changing dynamics of interests – such as the formation of new coalitions of forces or the mobilization of previously unorganized groups. For example, senior public servants in Denmark whose real pay had been eroding over more than a decade by the late 1980s, sought to change their pay structure towards an individualized 'New Public Management' model in the hope of breaking out of pay sclerosis and doing better (see Christensen, forthcoming). Fashionable management ideas may offer a useful cover story for such purposes, but many argue that it is interests which ultimately account for changes in public policy.

But if policy reversal is driven by interests, where exactly does that change come from? Does it simply reflect underlying social changes or is there an autonomous dynamic of politics which causes the relative power of interests to shift? If it is the former, we need to look for changes in policy 'habitat' to explain change, and we shall come to that in the next section. But if it is the latter, where could the autonomous change come from?

There is a long tradition of thought in political science, epitomized by orthodox Marxism, which interprets political change as a product of 'contextual' social and economic change. But some political scientists see politics *itself* as an inherently dynamic, self-destabilizing process. At least three sources of dynamism are conventionally identified, but they closely overlap. One is the dynamics of coalition behaviour in the domestic political sphere. A second is the dynamics of international politics as states compete, forming and breaking up alliances. A third is the process of 'policy entrepreneurship', as policy entrepreneurs put together support for new policy packages in a process somewhat analogous to the activity of entrepreneurs in business.

Most formal coalition theory in political science has been concerned with the way that political parties combine to form governments. But public policy can also be viewed as a product of particular coalitions of interests in a broader sense, and economic theories of policy-making increasingly look at policy outcomes in such terms (see Peltzman 1989: 38). Policy coalitions can be fragile and liable to change as action sparks off reaction, mobilization promotes counter-mobilization and groups break up as malcontents defect. An early path-breaking approach in this vein was William Riker's (1962) ideas on the inherent dynamics of political coalitions, which has led to a generation of later theoretical and empirical work aiming to refine and modify the original propositions. Riker argued that the underlying logic of rational self-interest in politics means that grand coalitions tend to dissolve in the direction of 'minimum winning coalitions'. 'Grand coalitions' are groupings which include all affected interests and which can command overwhelming numbers in decision-making bodies such as committees, councils and legislatures. 'Minimum winning coalitions' are groupings which are *just* strong and numerous enough to control such bodies and vote down rival groups, and no more.

For example, if a company is run by a nine-person board of directors, an alliance composed of all nine of them is in a sense 'wasteful'. Eight can divide the available spoils between them, and so take the share which would otherwise go to the ninth, who can easily be outvoted and marginalized. But exactly the same argument applies to the eighth, seventh and sixth members of the voting bloc. Five is enough to dominate the board, and each of the five dominant members will enjoy a fifth of the spoils and power available to the board rather than the ninth share which is all they would get as part of a grand coalition.

However, the search for the smallest possible winning coalition is perilous. Unexpected spills are likely to occur as a result of incentives to dissimulate and to take strategic positions. Moreover, there are strong incentives for 'maleficiaries' (those excluded from the spoils of power by the coalition of beneficiaries) to counter-mobilize against the dominant coalition in some way (see Bendor and Moe 1985, 1986). Hence there can be inherent instabilities in ruling coalitions, which can topple as a result of splits, defections and the growth of rival coalitions. Perhaps such processes might help to account for Bertrand de Jouvenel's (1963: 107) observation that 'in time, emergent authority always wins' in politics, and may help to explain why policy reversals occur.

But public policy, at least as viewed from the perspective of 'realist' theories of international relations, is not simply produced by the pulling and hauling of interest groups in the domestic marketplace. Just as important as those domestic interest group struggles is the process of competition among states for military and economic power and the power of one state or group of states over others (see Waltz 1979; Strange 1988). And many accounts of the disappearance of the policy 'dinosaurs' lay stress on international pressures and diffusion, as we shall see. So the international dimension introduces another aspect of coalition behaviour. In addition, it provides a dynamic in which individual states have an incentive to innovate in policy (or to follow a trend begun elsewhere) to maintain their international position, even if it means doing battle with entrenched domestic interest groups to change course. As we will see in later chapters, privatization, deregulation, the shift from Keynesian to monetarist economic policy, 'flat tax' reform and even public management reform have all been interpreted as processes by which states seek to maintain or increase their international economic competitiveness. And there is a sense in which, once one powerful player changes course with at least apparent success, others come under pressure to follow suit.

A third possible source of inherent dynamism in politics, which is also closely related to the other two mentioned above, is 'policy entrepreneurship'. A literature on policy entrepreneurship has developed in political science which has extended into the political sphere the idea of 'entrepreneurship' as expounded for the business world by Joseph Schumpeter and his followers (see Baumol 1968). In Schumpeter's famous model, entrepreneurs innovate by recombining resources in ways which result either in new products or making existing products in a different way. In developing analogous ideas for public policy, some political scientists argue that public entrepreneurship is an active process of rebalancing coalitions and repackaging policies, with the effect of upsetting existing structures and policies (see, for example, Walker 1974; Marmor and Fellman 1986; Lewis 1988). Hence public policy tends to be 'self-exciting' rather than simply a response to exogenous pressures coming from sociotechnical change or interest-group demands. Entrepreneurial bureaucrats, politicians and specialized policy 'operators' in particular arenas (such as Jean Monnet, the 'father' of the European Community, or the US consumer activist Ralph

Nader) carry out the 'creative destruction' function of entrepreneurship. In some accounts (e.g. Wilson 1989: 77–8), policy entrepreneurs are like 'class action' attorneys in the USA, who mobilize new social forces, challenging powerful interest groups by aggregating the small claims of many individuals, who would not act collectively in the absence of entrepreneurial action. William Riker (1982) argues that the task of such entrepreneurs is to identify and exploit ways of challenging established policy.

Such ideas are frequently applied to the sort of policy 'extinctions' which are considered in this book. The heroic or catalytic role of particular individuals, for example in US deregulation, is often stressed in accounts of how policy turned around. But, as with the idea of rhetorical skill as part of the 'primacy of ideas' (to which it is possibly related), the notion of policy entrepreneurship straddles the distinctions between 'ideas', 'interests' and 'social contexts' as sources of policy dynamism. And, as with all leadership-focused explanations, it raises the issue of how far we need to take 'proper names' into account in order to explain satisfactorily policy extinctions and what are the limits of what can be 'entrepreneured'.

Changes in policy habitat

A third set of possible explanations of these policy extinctions is analogous to some of the 'loss of habitat' ideas of why the dinosaurs died out. This explanation relates public policy to sociotechnical structures. The basic idea is that particular social structures form the 'habitats' for corresponding types of public policy. So when social structure changes, policy habitats alter.

A simple example of such habitat change comes when economic development puts the problems of affluence on the policy agenda instead of the problems of poverty. For instance, after the Second World War in Singapore, social deprivation was widespread and intense. For most of the population, housing was cramped and insanitary. Basic food was in very short supply. Living standards were extremely low. These conditions formed the 'habitat' for well-meaning (but probably not very effective) measures by the then colonial government directed at the many Singaporean schoolchildren who did not have enough to eat.

By the 1980s, the spectacular economic prosperity of post-independence Singapore had produced exactly the opposite problem. Many children travelled by car rather than on foot. They had ready access to fast foods of both the Western and the Asian variety. More comfortably housed, they followed the sedentary pursuits of affluence (such as watching TV and computer games) rather than the street games of the slum children of the 1940s. In these circumstances, the incidence of child obesity rose dramatically, particularly among males. By 1985, 10 per cent of boys starting school were obese, double the figure of only four years before (see *The Sunday Times* (Singapore) 24 March 1985). Grossly overweight schoolboys became a common sight on the streets. So the 'habitat' of public policy had changed totally, and government programmes on the feeding of children started to develop exactly the opposite emphasis from that of the hungry 1940s, with efforts to promote exercise and check overeating by schoolchildren, by advising school principals to forbid the sale of fattening foods in school canteens (see *The Sunday Times* (Singapore) 16 January 1985).

Could something similar have happened to the social 'habitat' of the economic policy dinosaurs considered in this book? Could it be that those policies fitted a particular social 'ecosystem' which disappeared with growing affluence and changes in social structure? For example, was old-style public enterprise largely a product of poorly developed capital markets? Did old-style progressive income tax structures basically stem from an income distribution structure in which most voters were at the bottom of the heap? Was old-style full-employment policy a product of a structure of single-income families living at not much more than subsistence level? Was old-style public management a product of an industrial society in which demands were simple and relatively homogenous? (see Osborne and Gaebler 1992: 14–15). If so, social changes such as the de-velopment of capital markets, more pyramidal income distribution patterns and the disappearance of the traditional single-earner family may have helped to bring about the extinction of those policies.

To look at policy extinction in this way is to take what in the jargon of public policy analysis is called a 'society-centred' approach. That means relating policy changes to the background changes in technology and social structure. Perhaps the most popular current form of this type of analysis is that which relates policy changes to a general process in which 'post-industrial society' is said to be replacing earlier 'industrial society', in the context of the late twentieth-century Kondratiev cycle and its attendant leading technologies.

Such ideas began to be developed by Daniel Bell (1973) in the late 1950s. But they were taken up and developed in the 1970s by the 'regulationist' school of Marxism, which relates the way that the state is shaped to the rise and fall of particular historical 'accumulation regimes', and which claims that one historical 'accumulation regime', termed 'Fordism', was coming to be replaced by another, 'Post-Fordism'. For Marxists, an 'accumulation regime' is a relationship between production and consumption which allows capitalism to develop, sustaining profits and investment. The three basic ideas of this approach are: (a) that policy choices are related to the functional 'dictates' of particular accumulation regimes; (b) that accumulation regimes 'wear out' through time and come to be superseded by newer, more effective, ones; (c) that capitalism is currently moving from one historical accumulation regime, 'Fordism', to a 'post-Fordist' accumulation regime. If we look at policy change in this way, the dynamic involves a wearing out of institutional structures associated with fading accumulation regimes, allied with technological devel-opments and the ideas associated with them.

The term Fordism is taken from Henry Ford, the self-styled philosopher of 'Fordism', who pioneered modern assembly line production with his famous Model T, the first mass-market car, which first appeared in 1908. The distinctive characteristic of the Model T was that it was relatively cheap to buy because it was built by semi-skilled workers on an assembly line and was a totally standard product which could be had 'in any colour you like as long as it's black'. In modern Marxist parlance, the term 'Fordism' (resuscitated by Aglietta, 1976, from the writings of Gramsci) was used to denote an economic regime which came into existence in the early part of the twentieth century. 'Fordism' consists of machine-paced, assembly-line production of low-priced standard goods in large factories, linked to a system of standardized mass consumption based on a wage economy with a large element of semi-skilled workers. But, the argument goes, Fordism is now being replaced by Post-Fordism.

Both Marxist and liberal variants of theory about post-industrial society imply that we are seeing the dissolution of the social structure associated with traditional industrialism; that is, a pyramidal income distribution structure reflecting a mass working class based on mass production of standard goods. In its place comes a more diamond-shaped income distribution, with a less ho-mogeneous labour force, now sharply divided among a secure and well-paid, high-skilled group, a non-working underclass and a secondary labour force which is ill-paid, insecure and often part-time. Niche markets replace mass markets, and 'flexible specialization' replaces standardized mass production (see Aglietta 1976; Piore and Sabel 1984). The new production structures, together with the changes in the labour force and consumption patterns, can be claimed to feed public policy both through the supply side and through the demand side. That is, they create new ways of providing public services (for instance, in information technology linked services) and new patterns of demand for public services (for instance, in the emergence of new social problems such as 'part-time unemploy-ment'). The notion of a new policy 'habitat' has often been invoked to explain the decline of universalist high-spending public policies and of public enter-prise in the 1930s style, through the relative shrinking of the traditional mass working-class group.

'Loss of habitat' explanations of this type clearly need to be taken seriously. But they are not without their critics. Some claim that public policy change does not automatically or immediately follow on from technological change. After all, as Edward Katzenbach (1958) has shown, the horse cavalry was not abandoned as soon as the tank and the machine gun were developed, even after what might have been thought to be the decisive military lessons of the First World War. Indeed, paradoxically, it was the most technologically developed major country, the USA, which was the last to abandon a serious military commitment to horse cavalry, as late as the 1950s. Moreover, even when similar policies are adopted by different societies, it does not necessarily mean that they are responses to the same 'functional' problems. For example, Hans Mueller (1984) has argued that the introduction of merit selection for the civil service in Britain and Prussia in the eighteenth and nineteenth centuries was a case of a common policy pursued for different political reasons in each of those countries: an attempt to preserve the gentry's privileges in one case and to destroy those privileges in the other. And social change is not necessarily an independent factor from which everything else stems. It may itself be a product of other policies, designed to 'shape' preferences, for example by increasing the numbers of 'centre ground' voters (Dunleavy 1991: 119–25), or by slum clearance policies designed to break up homogeneous ethnic ghettoes. And, like earlier Marxist ideas of politics being driven by an inexorable socio-economic 'base', such explanations are often claimed by their critics to be too 'technocentric', leaving too little room for the autonomous dynamics of politics.

Policies and institutions as their own worst enemies

Finally, instead of postulating an external shock to the system, extinction might be explained by blaming the victims. Indeed, some have speculated that the dinosaurs' demise may have been partly self-inflicted. Their very evolutionary success may have sown the seeds of their own destruction, in that their own 'exhalations' could have triggered off the very climate change which was to destroy them as a species. In other words, extinction came not from 'autonomous' forces like meteorites but from 'internal' ones rooted in the basic acts of digestion and breathing.

Could some internal self-destructive dynamic have been responsible for the extinction of the economic policy dinosaurs? After all, institutions are often their own worst enemies. The tendency of solutions to turn into problems is, after all, a frequent human experience, and 'a problem for every solution' is a common jibe in public policy.

It is true that many contemporary 'institutional' analysts in political science stress the effect of established organizations in promoting stability over time through the effect of inertia and established policy legacies, as in the 'dead hand' effect of established bureaucracy (cf. Evans *et al.* 1985; Hall 1986; Steinmo 1989). But stability and 'mortmain' is only half of the story of how institutions work. Policies and institutions can often be their own undoing, in the same way that the dramatic fall of great societies of the past have often been attributed to internal processes of self-destruction as much as to external assault, as in the historian Arnold Toynbee's (1972: 141–210) analysis of the 'nemesis of creativity' in accounting for the breakdown of historic civilizations such as Athens and Venice. Policies and institutions are highly dynamic, often creating changes and surprises, which in turn feed back into their environment, with self-destructive effect. They can trip over their own feet and dig their own graves.

For example, Mancur Olson (1982), in Toynbee-like vein, argues that long settled periods in politics (without revolutions or military defeats) allow the power of 'rent-seeking' interest groups to accumulate in a way which is eventually (but unintentionally) self-destructive. 'Rent-seeking' in the language of institutional economics means the search for resources to be transferred from one group to another through the compulsory legal power of the state, rather than through market exchanges or voluntary transfers. According to Olson, the accumulation of rent-seeking interest groups during long settled periods produces an increasingly sclerotic economy, such that the basis on which the political structure rests will eventually be destroyed, if the state does not collapse through invasion or revolution.

Another very well-known argument in this vein is Aaron Wildavsky's (1980) analysis of 'policy as its own cause'. Wildavsky's claim is that policies tend to create unexpected and problematic side-effects, which in turn create conditions for the introduction of new policies to correct or modify the effects of the earlier ones. More specifically, what Wildavsky calls 'The Law of Large Solutions in Public Policy' implies that 'the greater the proportion of the population involved in a policy problem, and the greater the proportion of the policy space occupied by a supposed solution, the harder it is to find a solution that will not become its own worst problem' (ibid.: 63). The problem-creating effect comes about by the unanticipated effects policies in one sector have on policies in other sectors as well as in their own sectors.

Common examples of policy solutions turning into problems in this way, according to Wildavsky, include tax collection and business regulation. From this perspective, it is easy to see how policies such as public enterprise might generate awkward side-effects requiring other sorts of corrective policies. But it is not clear from Wildavsky's account that such a process must necessarily lead to policy reversal or extinction. Indeed, Wildavsky stresses the tendency for policies to generate their own supporting stage armies (in the sense of constituencies of beneficiaries) such that the in-built dynamic is to crowd on ever more policy canvas rather than to shorten sail or turn round.

Much the same goes for the dynamics of public policy as portrayed by Brian Hogwood and Guy Peters (1983). They argue that, at least for the wealthy western-type democracies, there is coming to be less room for policy innovation, which they define as government moving into a previously uninhabited area of policy. Over time, ever-more policy making becomes 'policy succession', that is, the replacement of existing policies by new ones in the same area. The growing importance of policy succession arises because the 'policy space' becomes more crowded, like an area in which real-estate developers have run out of empty sites and need to concentrate on redeveloping existing properties for their future projects. It also arises because of fiscal pressures and the unexpected 'policy as its own cause' effects discussed by Wildavsky. Like Wildavsky, Hogwood and Peters (ibid.: 111) see dissatisfaction with existing policies as the main dynamic for policy succession, and hence would expect policy extinction to be driven by reactions against current orthodoxies as much as by positive attachment to an alternative.

For Hogwood and Peters, client groups are likely to play a larger part in the political dynamics leading to policy succession than in those applying to policy innovation, because once established, policies programmes tend to mobilize client groups and indeed are often introduced precisely for that purpose. For the same reason, policy shifts involving reversal of thrust are likely to be hotly contended by the beneficiaries of the original policy. And policy reversals themselves are rare compared to cases in which policy moves 'sideways' into a new channel (Hogwood and Peters 1983: 64–5). Hence we would expect that, if the cases considered in this book are to count as policy extinctions, the new life forms which succeeded the policy dinosaurs would suit many of the same interests that had been benefited by the dinosaur era.

A better known 'dissatisfaction-driven' explanation of policy self-destruction comes from Albert Hirschman (1982, 1991), whose account combines intellectual change, institutional self-destruction and changing balances of interests. Hirschman claims there are 'long swings' between collectivist and individualist attitudes to economics and politics. When collectivism is in the ascendant, institutions such as public enterprise and big government projects will be favoured. Under the individualist orientation, the emphasis is laid on attendance to private affairs. 'Western societies appear to be condemned to long periods of privatization during which they live through an impoverishing "atrophy of public meanings", followed by spasmodic outbursts of "publicness" . . .' (Hirschman 1982: 132).

Why should the 'long swings' take place between these two orientations? For Hirschman, the answer is disappointment, or an inevitable cycle of euphoria and disillusion. Both the public and the private approaches contain the seeds of their own destruction, like the old maxim that opposition parties do not win elections so much as governments lose them. Once one of the two approaches has become dominant, dissatisfaction builds up over time. Unwanted side-effects of the policy will be ever more clearly perceived the longer the 'track record' it has to expose. At the same time, the shortcomings of the alternative orientation will be forgotten, because they have not been recently experienced, like the 'atrophy of vigilance' which tends to develop in safety policy between the last disaster and the next one (see Freudenberg 1992). Pressure will then start to build for the policy orientation to go over on to the other tack. But there is no disappointment-free state at which the system can settle down. As Hirschman puts it:

> . . . individuals create new . . . organizations which they believe will better achieve what they regard as desirable outcomes than existing arrangements. But anticipation turns out to be better than realization . . . When one set of institutions fails, disillusionment and disappointment take over, and the search begins for new arrangements and institutional innovation.
>
> (quoted by Veljanovski 1987: 53)

Other ways in which policies are often said to bring about their own downfall include the processes of 'ageing' and 'wearing out' through 'capture' and value-degradation. 'Capture' is a process in which organizations responsible for policy direction come to be 'owned' by organized groups which 'distort' the policy for their own interests, as in the traditional 'ownership' of European agriculture ministries by farmer groups. Capture has been much discussed in the regulation literature, as we will see in the next chapter. Clearly, it constitutes a mechanism in which policy can self-destruct through the build-up of opposition among those whose interests are damaged by the way that policy is distorted to benefit the group which has captured the institutional system.

More generally, Martin Painter (1990) argues that processes of capture often lead public institutions to destroy the values which they were originally set up to enshrine, guard and promote. From this viewpoint, far from making for stability in policy direction, institutions create a self-exciting or self-destroying system by steadily undermining the values which originally led to their creation, and in the process setting off a policy dynamic of reaction and reversal. Using the examples of the values of 'merit' and 'efficiency' in public services, Painter argues that these values came to be captured by particular interests and defined in ways that suited those interests, meaning that the values in a broader sense came to decay until challenged by those with a different sense of what 'merit' or 'efficiency' should mean. An example is the way that feminists in the 1970s argued that public service procedures ostensibly designed to protect 'merit' in appointment and promotion, in practice hampered 'merit' by effectively discriminating against women. So policy reversal is a hybrid of institutional self-destruction, habitat change and changing interest configurations.

Simple 'ageing' and 'wearing out' may also play a part in institutional self-destruct processes, particularly for control systems, which almost invariably tend to lose power over time. For example, from an analytic base in cybernetics, Andrew Dunsire (1990) has identified 'simple steering', 'homeostasis' and 'collibration' as the three basic forms of institutional control. Under *simple steering*, controllers alter direction whenever they want to change course. Traditional public management doctrines, with bureaucracies theoretically at the instant beck and call of politicians, embody this approach. In *homeostasis*, explicit targets are set and mechanisms developed for detecting movements away from the target and returning the system to its course, such as French *contrats du plan* for controlling state-owned enterprises, and current developments in performance-measured control of units in the public sector across many OECD countries. Under *collibration*, 'opposed maximizers' are set up so that the system is exposed to a series of 'double binds' (cf. Hennestad 1990) and controllers can 'steer the equilibrium' by selectively inhibiting some of the opposed maximizers, rather like the way that colonial governments practised political management by shifting their support among rival indigenous groups.

No human control system can ever be perfect (see Hood 1976). And control frameworks wear out over time. So we might expect control frameworks in public policy to be dynamic, shifting among the three basic modes and thus producing reversals or major transformations. For instance, shifts from public enterprise towards privatization or even from classical regulation to pro-competitive regulation might be interpreted as a reaction to worn-out control systems, in the same way that national independence coalitions such as the Indian Congress destroyed the 'balancing game' of colonial government.

From all of these viewpoints, there is an inevitable built-in instability to policies and institutions. Although 'institutionalists' often stress the effects of institutions in promoting policy stability and in sustaining distinctive 'national' patterns over time, there is nothing in the basic logic of institutional analysis to suggest that institutions cannot self-destruct, and plenty of reasons to suppose that such a process may quite commonly occur. Moreover, if we look at policy dynamics in this way, there is no once-for-all extinction process in public policy. The implication is that, despite Fukuyama's (1989) well-known thesis, history can never be over as far as economic policy ideas are concerned. The policy dinosaurs will be back in some form after a generation or two of negative experience with their successors, maybe less.

Summary and conclusion

Drawing a loose analogy between the extinction of the dinosaurs 60 million years ago and the apparent disappearance of a number of orthodox lines of economic policy in the 1980s, this chapter sketches out four broad ways in which such policy extinctions can be explained.

As can be seen, the different classes of answer are hard to keep separate. Even in the writings of the theorists, the boundary lines tend to blur. A few years ago, London Zoo had problems in its insect house, where exotic cockroaches were on display. For once, the problem was not that the exhibits were escaping. It was that other uninvited cockroaches had walked in off the street and joined the display, so that 'ordinary' and 'exotic' cockroaches were mixed up together. Obviously, the perplexed zookeepers could not use pesticide to get rid of the intruders, without also dispatching the legitimate tenants. This problem is similar to the difficulty of keeping different lines of explanation for policy extinction relatively distinct. Put 'ideas' in a glass case, and 'interests' start crawling in too. Put 'institutions' in the case, and sociotechnical changes start to intrude. Much the same no doubt applies to the problem of explaining the disappearance of the real dinosaurs. The different possible explanations – self-produced climate change, the development of new predators, loss of habitat and meteorite attack – run into one another, and much of the available evidence is consistent with more than one interpretation.

Accordingly, Fig. 1.2 depicts some of the ways in which the different approaches can interact and overlap. Even from the very simple distinction with which we began in Fig. 1.1, we can identify 13 possible types of policy reversal. And as is shown in Fig. 1.2, several of the specific ideas discussed earlier fit into the interstices between the basic elements [(e) to (m) in Fig. 1.2] rather than in the 'pure' areas (a) to (d). Examples are the ideas of policy entrepreneurship as the dynamic of changing policy (i), the idea of policy change as driven by 'post-Fordist' processes (j), the Hirschman idea of long swings in policy on collectivism and private finance (k), the 'value degradation' ideas of Martin Painter (l).

In the next six chapters, we look at a set of apparent policy dinosaurs against the backdrop of this analysis, asking:

• What sort of 'extinction' really took place and how much of a 'surprise' was it for received interpretations of policy development?

Figure 1.2   'Pure' and 'hybrid' types of policy reversal

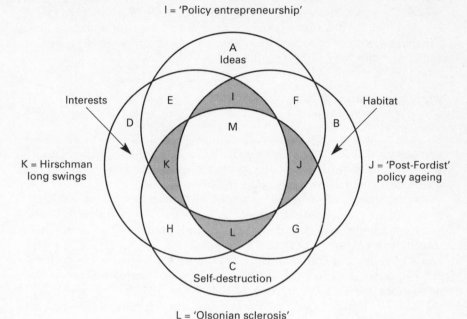

I = 'Policy entrepreneurship'

A
Ideas

Interests

E

I

F

Habitat

D

M

B

K = Hirschman
long swings

K

J

J = 'Post-Fordist'
policy ageing

H

L

G

C
Self-destruction

L = 'Olsonian sclerosis'

• What is the relative plausibility of different accounts of policy extinction in each area, from such evidence as is available, and how does it relate to the types of extinction sketched out above?

We will return briefly to these questions in Chapter Eight, after we have looked a little more closely at the six policy reversals seriatim, asking whether the same explanation is applicable to different groups of dinosaurs, or whether the policy dynamics involved might differ from case to case.

2

Regulation, deregulation and reregulation

... few regulatory policies have been pursued unless they proved acceptable to the regulated groups or served the interests of those groups.

(Edelman 1964: 24)

The main lesson of pro-competitive deregulation for a general theory of
policy-making ... is the necessity of taking the politics of ideas into
account.

(Quirk 1988: 40)

Introduction

This chapter looks at business regulation, the first of the apparent 'policy
extinctions' considered in this book. In many OECD countries, the 1980s saw
the transformation of traditional regulatory regimes in some important economic sectors such as the financial sector, aviation and telecommunications. In
order to understand this major shift, we look at the literature which purports
to explain why government regulation waxes and wanes.

In European usage, the word 'regulation' is sometimes taken as a synonym
for 'governance' in general (see Majone 1989b: 1–2). But the word is used here
in its narrower, traditionally American, usage – to mean a specific kind of
policy-making, designed to interfere with the way that markets would otherwise operate by making and enforcing standards or rules (see Noll 1987: 464).
But regulation in both senses ultimately comes from government's traditional
role in providing a basis for trading, by setting standards and rules for the
operation of markets.

Regulation in the narrower sense can take many different detailed forms, in
the way standards are set and compliance obtained. Although regulatory reform
in the 1980s went under the slogan of 'deregulation', regulation was massively
extended in some areas, notably safety and pollution (see Ayres and Braithwaite
1992: 7–12). And even in areas of regulatory reform, what happened was not
so much a complete withdrawal of government interest in areas such as telecommunications or aviation, but rather a change in the way that public authority

was used to shape these markets. Many have pointed out that 'reregulation' would be a more accurate term (Majone 1989b).

How can we explain changes in regulatory policy such as the reshaping of telecommunications markets in the 1980s in the USA, Japan and the UK? Are there general theories which can reliably tell us when to expect regulation, 'deregulation' or 'reregulation'?

This chapter briefly traces the development of the interest group theory of regulation up to the late 1970s. It then explores the 'problem' of regulatory reform for that approach. Does the deregulation story fit with the earlier understanding of regulation, or challenge it?

The development of the interest group theory of regulation

Although the study of economic regulation goes back at least as far as eighteenth-century 'police science', no single academic discipline came to 'own' the subject of regulation. Perhaps for that reason, a coherent body of middle-level theory in the area was fairly slow to develop in the modern period, and ideas about the subject tended to be either fragmented or eclectic.

Many early accounts of regulation were 'practico-descriptive' rather than analytic and often consisted of history as written by the victors. The story of regulation was told as a 'Whig tale' of the 'good guys' defeating the 'bad guys', particularly in the historiography of the progressive era in the USA, which produced a spate of independent regulatory commissions from the 1880s (see Olson 1979: 6–8). Virtue battled to overcome privilege and oppression, and good arguments vied with self-interested and specious defences of the *status quo*. Successful regulatory activists and regulatory agencies, naturally enough, tended to write about regulatory development in this heroic vein. Many still do, especially in newer regulatory areas such as environmental or equal opportunities policy. Equally naturally, much of the early writing about regulation came from this source.

More surprisingly, economics – traditionally the 'dismal science' of public policy – also took a fairly benevolent view of government regulation. Mainstream Anglo-American economics in the early twentieth century assumed that government's aim in regulation was to promote general economic efficiency. When markets failed, governments stepped in to check monopoly and to manage 'spillover' problems which could not easily be handled by conventional private ownership (such as management of common-pool resources like radio frequencies, sea, water, airspace and space itself: see Hardin 1968; Laver 1983). A set of standard 'welfare economics' justifications for regulation developed, identifying types of 'market failure' and 'welfarist' problems which government, as a rational and disinterested overseer, should seek to correct (see Breyer 1982: ch. 1).

This perspective was ironic, in several ways. First, to interpret regulation as a corrective to market failure implied a functional explanation of government behaviour; that is, a vision of government as a dispassionate 'super-capitalist', prompted solely by an interest in the long-run viability of the market system and better able to spot and correct weaknesses in the market than other actors. Such an explanation of public policy is the normal stock-in-trade of Marxist political economy – not a branch of social science with which mainstream economics traditionally had much affinity. A strain of Marxist 'state theory' explained policy as a *deus ex machina*, which popped out in the nick of time to put the crisis-prone capitalist system back on its feet and get capital accumulation going again. What exactly brought the *deus* out of the *machina* was obscure; the possibility of disastrous mistakes and miscalculations little considered; and the whole style of argument is deeply teleological.

Second, the functional interpretation of regulation sat ill with the tradition of Adam Smith, who had portrayed public regulation as typically error-prone, welfare-minimizing and reflecting the entrenched power of unrepresentative interests. Why, in a world of selfish, 'rent-seeking' private actors, should public officials – of all people – be able and willing to act in an altruistic, system-maintaining fashion? Was it not more plausible to see government regulation as a product of the self-interest of politicians and bureaucrats, allied with self-interested interest groups?

Indeed, it was liberal political scientists, to whom it was natural to see public policy as the outcome of a play of interests, who first developed a 'realist' view of regulation, putting the mobilization of political power at centre stage and rejecting any teleological or functional explanation of policy. An early and influential political science interpretation of regulation is Marver Bernstein's *Stigler?* *Regulating Business by Independent Commission* (1955). Bernstein, building on earlier work by Herring and Landis, argued that originally 'functional' activity by government could be 'corrupted' by a process of capture. 'Capture' meant effective control of regulatory agencies by the regulated interests which the agencies were originally set up to oversee. The mice ended up in charge of the cheese.

Some claim that 'capture' is a peculiarly American concept, presupposing a clear separation between the state and the private sector which is not found in other state traditions. Leigh Hancher and Michael Moran (1989) substitute the concept of 'regulatory space' within which a legitimate interplay of interest occurs. But, nevertheless, the idea of capture has spread far beyond the USA. In Bernstein's account, capture implied a view of regulation in terms of original purity – a process beginning with general benefit and ending in venality. There is a whiff of Wordsworth's poetic idea of human infants as born morally perfect, with vices only developing as a result of the corrupting influences of society rather than from original sin. Readers who are parents will have their own views about the realism of such romantic ideas.

Capture, for Bernstein, resulted from an 'ageing' process in which the original reforming thrust of the regulatory activity came to be lost. Bernstein saw regulatory agencies as originating in political campaigns to protect 'the public' from corporate misdemeanours. The issue might typically be thrust into the centre of the political agenda by some major disaster or system failure. Obvious examples are the carnage created by the early days of passenger aviation in the 1930s or the stock market crashes of the late 1920s, which generated calls for protecting the public from unscrupulous or incompetent financial services. Hence regulation typically began as a 'hot' issue, claiming the politicians' attention, and attracting political and bureaucratic 'zealots' to the regulatory cause.

The subsequent 'ageing' process happens in several ways, according to Bernstein. Administrators in regulatory agencies begin to suffer from 'tired blood'. Youthful committed firebrands, who joined the regulatory agency at the peak of the political campaign which set it up, start to leave the agency. They may go for opportunistic self-seeking reasons, as they perceive that the heat of the political 'action' has moved elsewhere, and they move with the new agenda to boost their careers. Or they may leave for 'principled' reasons, rejecting the inevitable compromises and constraints which start to appear as the fledgling regulatory agency struggles to live in the real political world. If they stay, they may turn into ageing, cynical, case-hardened bureaucrats. If they go, they may be replaced by 'go-anywhere' bureaucrats of lower calibre and with less commitment to the agency's original policy goals. Moreover, political commitment to the original regulatory goals starts to fade as the original reforming campaign or catastrophe which spurred the advent of regulation becomes more distant and the media caravan moves on to other ground (cf. Freudenberg 1992). The life-cycle terminates in capture by the regulated industries. At this point, the gamekeeper has turned into the mouth-piece and instrument of the poachers.

Bernstein's ideas of 'capture' attracted attention and influenced ideas about regulatory design, for example in the campaigns of 'Citizen Nader' (Ralph Nader, the best known consumer activist in the USA in the 1960s and 1970s) to reform the Federal Trade Commission and other US regulatory agencies. The 'life-cycle' model was compelling. Bernstein's underlying metaphor of original purity inexorably becoming corrupted was deeply rooted in 'reason and nature', as all successful institutional thought is said to be (Douglas 1987: 45). But the assumptions underlying the model came increasingly into question. Some political scientists pointed out that regulated industries were often less 'monolithic' than the 'capture' theory supposes, and that there was not therefore necessarily a 'public interest' clearly separate from the 'regulated interest' (see Williams 1976).

The development of the 'Chicago theory' approach to regulation

The 'capture' debate was not limited to political science. As so often happens, economists started to go one better. From the late 1960s, the 'Chicago theory of government' started to make the theoretical running in this area. Instead of Bernstein's idea of a decline from an original state of grace, a new breed of economists began to substitute a doctrine of original sin (Wilson 1984: 205). From a historical viewpoint, Gabriel Kolko (1977) put forward the controversial thesis that US regulation *originated* in self-interested demands by business groups for government action to stabilize market shares, prices and profits rather than in public-spirited campaigns to curb those interests. In other words, regulation was not diverted or captured from an original high purpose. It never served the interests of consumers or other vulnerable social groups in the first place, for one simple reason – it was *never intended to*.

Other instances were discussed in which regulatees ended up as beneficiaries rather than maleficiaries of regulation, even if there was no evidence that demand for regulatory control had actually come from business. An example is Gabriel Doron's (1979) account of US cigarette advertising regulation. Doron argued that banning cigarette advertising actually benefited tobacco firms, because the market was relatively stagnant and oligopolistic (that is, dominated by six large firms). Each of the big firms could only increase its market share by heavy advertising expenditure which increased costs. So, according to Doron, each of those firms was made better off by the advertising ban, since they could cut costs and prevent new unfamiliar brands from entering the market. Also, regulation promoting cigarettes with lower nicotine content conveniently meant that children were less likely to be put off by their first cigarette. Smokers would need to smoke more to get the same nicotine content, and so needed to spend more, on more cigarettes.

Leading institutional economists, notably George Stigler (1971) and Sam Peltzman (1981), started to develop models of regulation which were more extreme and more formal than those of political scientists like Bernstein. In the 'Chicago theory', *all* the actors in the process are self-interested. And there is (of course) no truck with Wordsworthian ideas of original purity. Politicians pursue self-interest by aiming to win votes for re-election to public office, since public office will give them power to reward themselves and their followers. In pursuit of votes, politicians 'sell' legislative protection to the interest groups most likely to benefit their electoral cause. In a regulatory context, this activity typically implies setting rates above costs for some (or all) users of a service, and using the 'rents' thus obtained to benefit other groups, such as producers or powerful users (see Keeler 1984: 107). Interest groups, too, are self-interested. They pursue 'rent-seeking' activities, aiming to bribe or threaten politicians into using legislative power to transfer wealth to themselves at the expense of other groups. In this stark world of calculating self-interest, politicians sell regulatory policy to the highest interest group bidder able to sway votes, either directly or through campaign contributions. Such a theory claims to offer a parsimonious but powerful explanation of why regulation develops and which interests it benefits (workers or employers, consumers or producers, truckers or railway companies).

Weaknesses of the 'Chicago theory' approach

Such models of the 'self-interested regulator', controlling the supply of legislation, were undeniably crude. Like other aspects of the Chicago theory of government, it can be attacked for lack of consideration of culture or ideology. But even in its own terms, some of the potentiality of the 'self-interest' approach itself was not fully developed, in at least three ways.

First, the assumption that self-interest leads politicians to value re-election above all else is questionable. Such an identity need not always hold. Incumbent politicians, thinking of 'number one' as the Chicago approach requires, might not in fact be rational to prefer re-election to all other career openings. They might be able to raise their lifetime earnings substantially by quitting politics at a strategic moment to sell their services to an outside bidder who can use their knowledge and contacts for profit in dealings with government. After all, such behaviour by politicians is hardly uncommon. So regulatory behaviour might well be shaped not by re-election considerations alone, but also by those of bettering the prospects for a future private sector career.

Second, even if politicians *do* value re-election above all else, they need to provide for the downside risk of *not* being re-elected. If they are even moderately risk-averse, it will make sense for them to take out some 'insurance' against defeat. Again, this consideration would imply a bias in regulatory policy in office conditioned by the aim of possible 'post-politics' employment in the regulated sector (see Shubik 1984: 657). Politicians who lose elections still need to eat. Only an economically 'irrational' politician (or one *not* wholly concerned with individual self-interest) would ignore the fact.

Third, self-interest might have other implications than the standard capture model implies. Even quite a narrow and 'economistic' idea of self-interest might lead regulators to pay attention to factors other than their bank balances, prospects for future employment or legislative power. Self-interest in preserving their own lives or way of life would presumably also play a part. Hence, for example, we might expect self-interested politicians to pay more attention to air safety than to safety on ships and buses, given that politicians nowadays tend to travel by air rather than by sea or bus (see Kingdon 1984: 56). For the same reason, politicians are likely to be more interested in controlling firearms than in curbing dangerous dogs, since in their circumstances they are more likely to be attacked with guns than with dogs.

There is, perhaps, more subtlety and mileage in the notion of regulatory self-interest than the orthodox 'economics of regulation' approach allows for. Nevertheless, such models lent a powerful intellectual force to the 'original sin' interpretation of regulation. Their implication was that 'capture' of a public regulatory agency was not an abnormal condition or the result of a fall from grace. Rather, capture was the *normal*, inevitable and permanent condition of such an agency.

The Chicago theory became intellectually dominant in this area, as in many other aspects of public policy. It was not systematically tested by empirical work. But it did lead to some conceptual refinement. Instead of the simple view that all regulation is both demanded and obtained by self-seeking firms in their own interests, a more interesting question concerned the *circumstances* in which 'rent-seeking' interest groups would be most and least likely to obtain

Table 2.1 Politics of regulation (Wilson)

Benefits of regulation	Costs of regulation	
	Concentrated	*Dispersed*
Concentrated	'Interest group politics' (1) *Example*: railway freight rate regulation	'Client politics' (2) *Example*: restrictions on imports
Dispersed	'Entrepreneurial politics' (3) *Example*: restriction on tobacco sales	'Majoritarian politics' (4) *Example*: public smoking bans

Source: Wilson (1980: 357–74).

favourable regulation. To answer that question, James Q. Wilson (1980) used the concept of 'client politics', applying to regulatory lobbying Mancur Olson's ideas about conditions for effective collective action in politics.

In a famous book, Olson (1965) argued that efforts towards collective action to benefit a particular group (for instance, labour union tactics for collective wage rises rather than individual employee attempts to gain a raise from the boss) would tend to fail because of 'free-riding' behaviour by potential beneficiaries. That is, a 'smart' if selfish strategy by those who stand to benefit is to let others pay the cost of collective action, while enjoying the benefits themselves. For example, rational selfish workers would not join trade unions. They would aim to let the other workers bear all the costs of paying union dues, loss of earnings, etc., in strike action, while themselves collecting any higher pay rates that their colleagues' collective actions secured. Olson argued that collective action would only be able to avoid such a fate if the group involved was small, able to use coercion or similar strong pressures to quash free-riding, or able to deploy 'selective benefits' (i.e. benefits which would accrue to members but not to non-members, such as professional liability insurance).

On this basis, Wilson argued that the conditions most likely to lead to the 'original sin' process of regulation as modelled by Stigler, were circumstances in which a concentrated group, with high per capita stakes, was able to transfer wealth to itself through regulation at the expense of a diffused group, with low per capita stakes. This outcome could be expected, because in such circumstances the beneficiaries have strong incentives to organize and lobby, while those who bear the cost have no such incentive. Hence the 'win window' for a rent-seeking interest group aiming for a favourable regulatory regime was cell (2) in Table 2.1 – the 'client politics' window. Conditions for interest group lobbying in favour of regulation were much less likely to be favourable (for overcoming the Olson 'free-rider' problem) when:

- *both* benefits and costs were concentrated, in which case anti-regulation interests would be as well equipped to mobilize as pro-regulation interests [cell (1), 'interest group politics'];
- *both* benefits and costs of public regulation were diffused, in which case neither pro- nor anti-regulation interests would be well placed to organize [cell (4), 'majoritarian politics'];
- benefits of public regulation were diffused, but costs concentrated [cell (3), 'entrepreneurial politics'].

From a Chicago theory perspective, other aspects of institutional design are often argued to make democratic government peculiarly vulnerable to exploitation by organized rent-seekers. One is representative rather than direct democracy (in the sense of legislation by referendum and initiative), which is often claimed to be more vulnerable to 'capture', particularly where key legislative committees can be dominated by a handful of members who are effectively in the pocket of organized interests (see Walker 1987). Another is the level of government at which regulation operates, with centralized regulation by organizations like the European Community (EC) or national-level monopoly bureaux more likely to be captured by well-funded lobby groups than competing bureaux or sub-national government jurisdictions (see Niskanen 1971). A third is the electoral system and the organization of the legislature. For example, Roger Noll (1987) claims that proportional representation systems are more likely to throw up counterweights to producer groups aiming to capture regulation than first-past-the-post systems (but the logic is obscure, and seems questionable) and that separation of legislature and executive, as in the USA, encourages particularistic politics in regulation.

Hence, by the late 1970s, a relatively coherent explanation of regulatory development had emerged. Early 'heroic' views of the regulatory process had been altogether discarded in the academic (if not the practitioner) literature. The new orthodoxy was even capable of some discrimination and refinement. Outcomes could be predicted by analysis of the nature of goods and of transactional circumstances. Self-interested public regulators controlled the supply side of regulation, selling legislative protection to the interest group capable of swaying the most votes, without concern for economic efficiency in the orthodox sense. Self-interested interest groups controlled the demand side of regulation, with transactional conditions systematically loading the dice in favour of concentrated groups with high stakes in wealth transfers.

The 'problem' of deregulation

Why deregulation was a problem

The philosopher Georg Hegel once said that Minerva's owl takes flight as the shades of night are falling. It is a flowery way of saying that we come to understand something only when it has started to disappear or to become obsolete – a concept which has become all too familiar with computers and software. Just as the final spit and polish was being put on the Chicago theory of regulation, the Hegelian nightfall came, dead on cue, in two forms. One was the extension of regulation in the field of pollution, health and safety, which was generally opposed by the regulatee industries, contrary to the theory (Noll 1987: 489). The other was the onset of 'deregulation' (cf. Keeler 1984: 104). Deregulation started to roll from the late 1970s in the USA and other countries, coming as a major surprise to 'Chicago theory' economists. As Sam Peltzman (1989: 3) put it: 'Not one economist in a hundred practicing in the early 1970s predicted the sweeping changes that were soon to happen . . .'. Developments such as the break-up of the US 'Bell system' (AT&T) in 1982, and moves towards deregulation in other fields (such as finance, railways, trucking and airlines), seemed to pose a major puzzle for conventional interest group explanations. If regulation was to be explained as a product of 'client politics', normally serving the interest of concentrated easy-to-organize producers at the expense of diffused hard-to-organize consumers, why were the laws of politics (apparently) being suspended in a reversal of the process?

At first, many accounts of deregulation were couched in the heroic style of 'functional' analysis, which had earlier lost favour as an explanation of regulatory development. The implication was that government had turned from regulator to deregulator in the disinterested pursuit of economic efficiency or overall social welfare, as a result of some sort of deathbed conversion to economic virtue.

Such explanations, of course, can be challenged on the same grounds as the original 'functional' explanations of regulatory development – namely, their teleological character and their failure to demonstrate precisely what are the political forces which might lead government to act in a 'welfare-beneficial' way (even if it could clearly be demonstrated that deregulation *is* welfare-beneficial). Moreover, the 'functionality' of deregulation is highly contestable. For instance, some have claimed that particular deregulatory changes were simply an 'accident', the product of a series of tactical mistakes and miscalculations by key actors in the process (see Coll 1986). Such an explanation, akin to the 'traffic accident' explanation of wars favoured by some international relations theorists (see Blainey 1973: 127ff.), has a certain appeal. It fits with recurring ideas about the role of chance in human affairs, for example in Tolstoy's great novel *War and Peace*, and perhaps it could be linked to current ideas of 'chaos theory'. After all (as I was once reminded by a colleague), every one of us is a historical accident.

The 'accident' theory, however, does not have a large following in this area. Most observers see regulatory reform as too widespread and not quickly enough reversed to be explainable as a set of chance blunders. Current political science accounts of deregulation can be divided into two main types, which are summed up in the epigraphs to this chapter. One type stresses the 'power of ideas' as producing deregulation. The other type seeks to explain deregulation in terms of interest group processes.

Power of ideas explanations

There are at least three ways in which deregulation could be attributed to the power of ideas. At the least critical and reflective level is the triumphal accounts of the victorious economic rationalists or their sympathizers (cf. Breyer 1982). Such accounts are another example of history as written by the victors – like some of the early accounts of regulation referred to earlier, and again much of the early literature came from this source. So it is not surprising that explanations of deregulation in this vein stress the special heroic qualities – such as moral courage, intellectual force of argument, or tactical brilliance – which led to the econocrats' triumph.

An alternative, but little-explored, way of explaining deregulation in terms of the power of ideas is to couch it in terms of the 'observer paradox'. The observer paradox refers to the tendency for scientific observation and explanation itself to change the object of observation. Karl Marx thought that it was more important to change the world than to explain or observe it. But it often happens that we change the world in the very process of observation or explanation. Indeed, such self-fulfilling or self-defeating processes are pervasive in social science, and most of all in economics. Here the argument would be that the 'Chicago' explanation of how regulation worked was (paradoxically) self-defeating because the theory was fed back into policy design. The claims of economics professors about 'welfare losses' caused by regulation and their ideas about regulatory redesign turned out to be more powerful than the supposedly 'iron laws' of self-interest in politics on which their theories were built.

The observer paradox could work in at least two ways. First, the development of the 'capture' idea (as amplified through publication and diffusion) might have helped to spark off the deregulatory movement. Second, observation of capture might have been fed back into regulatory design, in a conscious attempt to reshape regulatory agencies and programmes in order to reduce the risks of capture. One example of conscious anti-capture measures is the adoption of automatic enforcement rules in some US regulatory policies in the early 1970s, with the aim of preventing regulatory agencies from accommodating regulatee interests in their enforcement practices. Another is the development of regulatory programmes going beyond the confines of a single industry (for example, in health and safety or equal opportunity regulation), which made it harder for regulatee producer groups to 'capture' regulatory agencies in the classic style (cf. Weidenbaum 1981).

In short, the very *prescriptive* success of the Chicago theory of regulation might, ironically, have been what swiftly undermined its *descriptive* accuracy. That way, we could explain the irony of the extraordinary ease and speed with which the regulatory citadel fell into the hands of the 'enemy', contrary to the presuppositions of the Chicago theory.

A third, not necessarily independent, 'power of ideas' explanation attributes regulatory reform to the persuasive power of the New Right and doctrines of economic rationalism from the 1960s and 1970s. The success of those ideas

*This is a real ministrone soup - perhaps it was X ⁓ Y ⁓ Z etc..
Why can't there be different explanations for each case?*

Regulation, deregulation and reregulation 29

might be viewed through Gramscian spectacles as a new ideological hegemony developed by the ruling class. Or it might be seen, less grandiosely, as a rhetorical phenomenon characteristic of Kenneth Minogue's idea of a 'loquocentric society', as discussed in the last chapter.

Perhaps the leading 'power of ideas' approach in this vein is Martha Derthick and Paul Quirk's (1985) account of US deregulation, which was also mentioned in Chapter One. Derthick and Quirk argue that normal interest group processes were overcome by a new intellectually driven process of economic rationalism which, contrary to the theory of 'client politics', actually benefited scattered consumer groups at the expense of concentrated producer groups. This claim was built on apparent (but contestable) evidence that residential consumers benefited from the deregulation of airlines, trucking and railways.

Undoubtedly, a powerful attack was launched on traditional regulation in the 1960s and 1970s from a number of quarters – liberal economics, consumerism, law and political science – culminating in a devastating critique of progressive-era regulation. Regulation was attacked in terms such as 'producer capture', weak enforcement by agencies, self-defeating bureaucratization and juridification, failure to balance costs of compliance against regulatory benefits, and often ineffective programme design. It would be surprising if such ideas had failed to strike a chord.

However, one of the problems with the 'power of ideas' interpretation is that deregulation was quite selective and, as has been noted, was by no means a one-way street. The conventional interpretation of deregulation as reflecting the ideological hegemony of 'small government' New Right ideas, has to account for some notable counter-trends. Regulation has intensified, not fallen back in areas such as pollution, smoking, equal opportunities and finance in several countries (replacing an older tradition of a 'gentlemanly' system of self-regulation in the financial services community). Its extension has even been part of the New Right's agenda in some contexts, for example in the case of trade union regulation introduced by the UK Thatcher government in the 1980s to curb labour union power, modelled on the US style of labour regulation. Similarly, privatization of public utilities such as telecommunications has led to a substantial extension of regulation and 'juridification' as a substitute for government ownership. *Regulation of those areas where there is severe market failure Deregulate where it isn't so severe?*

Power of interests explanations

As with the earlier case of regulatory growth, not everyone interprets deregulation as a case of ideas triumphing over vested interests. Some explanations of deregulation are couched in much the same kinds of 'realist' interest-group terms as was the Chicago theory of regulatory development described earlier. As with the 'power of ideas' approach, there are several possible variants of a 'power of interests' explanation.

One variant can be taken from the schema drawn up by Wilson to depict different types of regulatory politics (described earlier, and summarized in

Table 2.1). From Wilson's perspective, the advent of deregulation could be not so much as a triumph of ideas over interests, as Derthick and Quirk claim, but as a classic case of 'entrepreneurial politics'. If we believe Derthick and Quirk's assertion that domestic customers as a group really stood to benefit from deregulation in a clear-cut way [an assertion which is contested by many other writers such as Hills (1986: 192) and Dempsey (1989)], the 'cost structure' of the political situation was essentially that of a 'small claims' issue or 'class action' suit – a lot of parties with a minor stake who might stand to benefit at the expense of a few parties who have a great deal at stake.

What is needed for 'class action' politics of this type is the presence of a 'political entrepreneur' of sufficient skill who, like the 'class action' attorney, can effectively mobilize the 'small claims' of the diffused beneficiaries of *de*-regulation and turn them into votes. The question that naturally then arises is why such a 'class action' structure of political entrepreneurship should have suddenly started to emerge in the 1970s, and failed to develop during the growth of regulation in the 'progressive' era. Was it the power of ideas or sociotechnical changes making class action politics less expensive (by cutting down on communication costs) and even new political technology, in the form of more intensive opinion polling allowing politicians to pinpoint rich and potentially extractable lodes of electoral ore?

A second type of 'power of interests' approach might relate it to major corporate *producer* interests. There might be reasons why regulatee producers might find it in their interests to go along with deregulation, or even to propose it. At least two variants of a producer-driven, interest-based explanation can be identified. One is the idea that producer interests backed deregulation as part of a 'lose to win' strategy, and the 1982 AT&T divestiture in the USA has been claimed to reflect such a strategy (MacAvoy and Robinson 1983). The argument is that AT&T opportunistically moved out of slow-growth (local) telephone markets to gain access to the high-growth and more profitable markets of computer and value-added services. But there are two problems with such a 'lose to win' account. First, it is debatable whether the explanation can be plausibly applied to areas of deregulation other than telecommunications. Second, it may not even be plausible for the AT&T case itself (given AT&T's subsequent financial losses in computer markets and poor corporate performance after divestiture).

The other possible variant of a corporate producer-driven, interest-based account of deregulation is to see it as a strategy by multinational corporations to break into national markets previously protected by regulation, or by major corporations to gain business at the expense of smaller players whose market share is sheltered by regulation. Paul Dempsey (1989) argues that the winners from domestic deregulation in the USA are the 'Fortune 500' companies, the largest carriers and shippers. Jill Hills (1986), in her account of telecoms deregulation in the USA, UK and Japan in the 1980s, stresses the role of multinational corporations in deregulation. She explains the developments as a self-interested strategy on the part of the two biggest US telecom multinationals (IBM and AT&T) to roll back the regulatory power of governments overseas and hence give themselves a clearer field for expansion. Deregulation, she declares, is 'part of the strategy of the rich to stay rich and of the large to grow larger' (Hills 1986: 20). Hills' account is somewhere between a domestic interest group approach and a 'realist' international politics account of deregulation, in that part of the deregulation process she portrays seems to come from élites trying to shape policies to give their countries a competitive edge *vis-à-vis* rival economies.

A third, closely related, variant sees deregulation as the outcome of pressures by corporate *consumers* as a countervailing force against regulated producer interests. The importance of business 'consumers' has long been recognized as a key factor in regulatory politics, and it is possible to cast such a group in a key 'client politics' role for deregulation. It would follow that altered conditions such as a change of the proportion of the output of a regulated industry bought by concentrated users, perhaps in conjunction with changes (such as a profits squeeze or technological development), could shift the balance of power from organized producers to organized consumers. A clear example is the growth of 'business users' of telecommunication services in the 1970s and 1980s. It is even possible that in some cases government itself might be the consumer, for example if its interest in selling bonds gives it a stake in financial deregulation.

Indeed, 'corporate consumer' pressure for deregulation features to some extent in Hills' own account. Given the role of advanced communications in giving financial market players a competitive edge, it is notable that the three countries vying for world financial leadership (USA, Japan, UK) were the first substantially to liberalize or deregulate their national telecommunications industries in order to accommodate financial trading. Hills shows that in these three countries, much of the impetus for deregulation came from influential financial services firms and other users of computerized communications.

A fourth class of interest-based theory comes from those working broadly within the 'Chicago' approach to account for the reversal of regulation. Two main mechanisms have been identified: a process of wealth dissipation and a process of counter-mobilization through political entrepreneurs. The wealth dissipation approach has been advanced by Peltzman (1989), one of the doyens of the Chicago theory. He claims that the Chicago approach can be readily modified so that deregulation becomes 'endogenous' rather than a surprise for that theory. His claim is that regulation tends to dissipate wealth by generating inefficiencies. When the wealth available for redistribution has gone, regulation will lose its political support base:

> Regulation occurs when there is a wide discrepancy between the political balance of pressures and the unregulated distribution of wealth. This regulation (of, say, price) then creates incentives for wealth dissipation (through, say, cost increases) which ultimately make restoration of the preregulation status quo more attractive than continuing regulation. In such a model deregulation is not the correction of some belatedly recognized policy error. It is the last stage in a process about which, in principle, all the actors could have had perfect foresight at the beginning . . .

Peltzman was not in fact the first to link deregulation to wealth dissipation. Noll (1987: 490) argues that regulation is 'a sloppy form of cartel; if it becomes one, the inefficiencies tend to dissipate the gains of cartel members', thus paving the way for a shift to deregulation. Theodore Keeler (1984) also argues that profits tend to fall in the profitable services which are intended to cross-subsidize the privileged high-cost users in the conventional support-maximizing versions of regulation, so that the rents available for redistribution tend to disappear. Evidence for the wealth dissipation theory is patchy, but it is an attempt to create a theory which can explain both regulation and deregulation (so that deregulation ceases to be a 'surprise') and which can explain the various 'rents' which remain in regulatory structures even after 'deregulation'.

The other main mechanism leading to deregulation which has been identified by those working broadly in the 'Chicago theory' framework is a 'backlash' process in which the diffuse 'losers' of regulation become counter-mobilized through political entrepreneurs. Keeler (1984: 130) argues that: 'The larger the cost of regulation becomes, the greater incentive the losers have to learn what they are losing, to organize and to do something about it.' Noll (1987: 488) argues that regulation set up to benefit compact groups at the expense of a large diffuse group of losers will tend to attract political entrepreneurs just as public safety issues attract 'class action' attorneys in the USA, so that 'regulation that becomes protectionist creates the conditions for its own reform; at some point, the redistributional effect of the inefficiencies becomes sufficient to cause a backlash'. The problem remains, however, how such policy entrepreneurs are to be rewarded, why it took policy entrepreneurs so long to get round to regulation [Noll (ibid.: 488) argues that such entrepreneurship will only take place outside wars or times of high international tension], why policy entrepreneurs seem to have been so much more effective in rolling back regulation in some settings (such as US airline regulation) than in others (such as airline regulation in Europe), and why the concentrated potential 'losers' from such entrepreneurship are unable to counter-mobilize to defend their privileges.

Indeed, Jonathan Bendor and Terry Moe (1985) show how concentrated 'losers' can counter-mobilize against regulation with diffuse 'winners' (such as consumer or environmental protection). In their model, regulation is a product of interaction among vote-seeking politicians, a slack-seeking bureaucracy (that is, a regulatory agency seeking a bigger budget and more free or uncommitted resources) and rent-seeking interest groups (in the form of one group which benefits from expanding a regulatory programme and another that is hurt by it). The vote-seeking politicians control the regulatory agency's budget and how closely it is overseen, on the basis of expected electoral support as interpreted by them from interest group activity. But these politicians are far from the perfectly informed rational calculators of conventional economic models. They are short-sighted and fallible, working through trial and error and responding to what they see as the electoral pressures of the moment. But their judgements will frequently turn out to be wrong.

In such conditions, regulation may change direction as it imposes greater costs on the losers. If regulatory policy encompasses a large and diffused 'consumer' group which benefits from more regulation and a small and concentrated producer group which pays the cost of extra regulation, the legislators may well start off on the 'entrepreneurial politics' foot. After all, consumers with their superiority in numbers only need to pay the relatively minor cost of casting a vote in order to secure increases in regulation. Their opponents need to pay much larger costs in order to swing politicians and public opinion the other way.

But at some point, the consumers' 'dream run' in obtaining extra regulation will be checked, as the concentrated group at whose expense the extra regulation is bought eventually comes to pay the cost of political lobbying, to sway votes and pay off politicians. At this point, the stage may be set for deregulation, since the small producer group is inherently better placed for collective action than the large consumer group, and their efforts may cause legislators to see electoral advantages in reversing regulatory growth. Such a process would, for instance, resemble the growth of consumerist 'Naderite' regulation in the 1960s and 1970s, followed by a backlash as producers got organized and built up an electoral war chest to sway voters and legislators in the opposite direction. Counter-mobilization can work against 'entrepreneurial politics' as well as against 'client politics'.

Auto-destruct of client politics?

Just as regulatory policy might self-destruct through wealth dissipation or counter-mobilization by the losers, 'client politics' might itself have inherent political tendencies to self-destruct. Some have likened regulatory 'producer coalitions' to 'Prisoner's Dilemma' games, in which the partners have an incentive to 'cheat' on other members (for example, in attempts to increase market shares relative to their competitors), creating a bias towards destruction of the coalition and a possible deregulatory 'snowball' (see Hammond and Knott 1988). Hence there can be a self-disequilibrating dynamic towards 'de-capture'.

There are several ways in which client politics could 'self-destruct'. For example, a regulatory policy might destroy its own electoral base by encouraging automation (for example, if it raises regulatees' profits to enable them to make investments which could not be financed from a lower profit base), since machines do not have votes. The unforeseen long-term result of such a programme may be a reduction in the regulatee labour force (and hence voting bloc) *vis-à-vis* the scattered consumers who pay for the regulatory programme. At some point, the direct electoral benefits to be obtained by the self-interested regulator in promoting the 'client politics' interests of the regulatees may be outweighed by the direct electoral benefits of pursuing the opposite course of 'entrepreneurial politics', and picking up the consumers' votes through deregulation. However, agriculture seems to have defied such a process up to now, with continuing heavy agricultural protection in OECD countries despite regulation and subsidy having automated much of its voter constituency out of existence.

A second possible auto-destruct route for 'client politics' regulation is through the creation of substitute products just outside the regulatory 'ring-fence', as often happens with orthodox regulation. That is, if regulation follows the classic 'client politics' pattern, with costs diffused among a scattered group of consumers and benefits concentrated on a small, well-organized producer group, there may be a point at which unregulated producers start to offer near-substitutes to the regulated product. Such a move could trigger a dynamic process which causes the whole regulatory structure to unwind, culminating in a situation in which the original 'client politics' group starts to lead the move to deregulation.

To illustrate, take a hypothetical case of bank deregulation. Imagine a country – call it Amnesia – which develops a structure of bank regulation following the orthodox client politics pattern. Banks are regulated by measures which were typical of many countries up to the 1980s, that is, interest rate ceilings, restrictions on freedom to lend, mandatory minimum liquidity levels, barriers to market entry (for example, through licensing) and barriers to capital export through exchange rate controls. We could interpret such a structure in orthodox Stiglerian terms as protecting banks from foreign and domestic competition.

But the next stage in the process is that the rationing of credit for Amnesian banks leads to the proliferation of institutions offering close substitutes, such as merchant 'banks', finance companies, building societies and credit unions. Such institutions can attract depositors and borrowers away from the regulated banks. Regulation has prohibited banks from offering interest on cheque accounts (providing a cheap source of credit from small unsophisticated customers to swell bank profits), so non-bank financial institutions are able to woo depositors away from banks by offering interest on ordinary accounts. The regulatory structure gives licensed banks a monopoly on offering cheque accounts (intended to protect them from competition in a lucrative market), but the non-bank financial institutions successfully market close substitutes to the banks' personal deposit accounts by means such as offering cheques written by the institution itself and increasing the number of accessible branches. Interest rates offered by banks are centrally controlled by regulation (to limit competition), but non-regulated institutions can attract more depositors with attractive interest rates on effectively the same product.

The result is that 'ordinary' customers increasingly desert the banks, to the point where the unregulated near-substitutes threaten to gain more customers than the original regulated product. The banks cannot compete on level terms with the unregulated non-bank financial institutions. If matters are allowed to get to this point, the original 'client politics' group of regulated banks starts to suffer major costs from the regulatory structure which that group had invoked for its own collective benefit. Hence the cost structure of regulation starts to alter. Instead of costs diffused on consumers and benefits concentrated on the banks [cell (2) on Wilson's matrix], the structure changes so that costs are concentrated on the banks (who cannot compete on level terms with unregulated non-bank institutions), plus the banks' captive customers who have chosen to stay with them. Benefits now accrue either to the mass of customers who had 'voted with their feet' for the unregulated structure, or to the non-bank financial institutions. In other words, the cost structure has shifted to cell (1) or cell (3) on Wilson's matrix, heralding a move towards 'interest group politics' or 'entrepreneurial politics'.

At this point, the banks face a dilemma. Essentially, they have two options. One is to press Amnesian politicians into new regulatory measures which will push their rivals out of their traditional markets, by tighter definition of 'banks', financial services, etc. But Amnesia's politicians, if they are the ordinary vote-seeking variety portrayed by the Chicago theorists, may be reluctant to adopt such a course. If there are more customers using substitute products, the direct electoral effect of tightening up the regulatory structure to put the banks back into their 'client politics' position may be negative. Only massive indirect electoral support – through campaign contributions and the like – is likely to persuade them. Yet if bank profits are falling, they may not be able to come up with the necessary cash.

The other option for Amnesia's banks, particularly if the first fails, is to lead moves to deregulation so that they can compete on 'a level playing field' with their enemies and win back market share. Banks could be winners from deregulation if they used their new-found freedom to hurt their rivals through predatory pricing and encourage customers to switch back from the substitute products to which they had shifted in the regulatory era.

The parable of Amnesian bank deregulation is potentially generalizable beyond this particular case – not only beyond the hypothetical case of Amnesia to real-life financial deregulation in several countries, but also outside financial deregulation to other types of deregulation, such as aspects of telecommunications. Just as in our parable, the regulatory structure itself may make it possible for less regulated producers to develop close substitutes for the regulated product, such that regulation starts to lose its original 'client politics' structure. Unless checked by 'reregulation', such a situation can lead the original client politics group to press for deregulation to compete on level terms with producers of close substitute products. Again, the seeds of auto-reversal can be built into the process from the start.

Conclusion

Though the development of new economic theories clearly played a part, we do not need to believe in a complete suspension of interest-group policy processes to explain why some of the traditional regulatory 'dinosaurs' became extinct in the 1980s. It is possible to derive plausible accounts of deregulation in the 1980s using the same sort of explanatory ideas which were used for the development of regulation up to the 1980s. And the weakness of relying wholly on the force of new ideas or ideology as the explanation of deregulation is that it does not account for the areas where deregulation did *not* occur or where regulation was extended.

Indeed, the power of ideas clearly overlapped with the power of interests in regulatory reform. The dichotomy is hard to sustain at the margin. For example, if think-tanks financed or encouraged by 'New Right' interests produce influential policy proposals, is such an outcome to be taken as signifying the power of ideas or the power of interests – or both? If some ideas are vigorously marketed while others are left to gather dust on the academic shelf, does this outcome testify to the power of interests or the power of ideas? As we saw in the last chapter, for economists to believe, with Keynes, that the world is 'ruled by little else' than economic ideas, may be a case of economic vanity triumphing over economic analysis.

It also seems plausible that strong elements of institutional self-destruction helped to bring about regulatory reform, since many of the eight or so variants of an 'interest' approach to deregulation which were discussed there – including the more reflective variants of the Chicago model – incorporate a self-destruct dynamic. What is not so clear is the role, if any, played by broader sociotechnical developments, since few accounts of deregulation put this element at centre stage and it seems at best to have been part of the background. It would seem from this exploration of the literature that the forces accounting for the demise of some of the old regulatory 'dinosaurs' belong in one of the hybrid areas portrayed in Fig. 1.2, and that the most likely area is that which is labelled (k) on Fig. 1.2, that is, the area where intellectual change, new interest coalitions and the process of institutional self-destruction overlap.

3

Public enterprise and privatization

The literature . . . tells us . . . about the way a tide once established maintains its direction but the literature on Thatcherism confines itself to establishing that it represents a change in the tide without providing any explanation of why the change took place.

(Douglas 1989: 423)

. . . the broad historical sweep of this movement [= privatization] is quite intriguing. Why so many countries and why now?

(Ikenberry 1990: 88)

Introduction

Econocrats invented many new jargon terms in the 1970s. Many of them had a mercifully short shelf-life. Who now remembers 'recesso-petroflation'? But one coinage at least proved more enduring and turned into one of the international watchwords of the 1980s. The word was 'privatization'. Privatization, like all successful slogans, means different things to different people. Here, it means introducing private ownership into trading enterprises previously owned by governments. Privatization in that sense seemed to herald the demise of another set of economic policy 'dinosaurs' – state-owned trading enterprises.

Such forms of organization have a long history. They include: fiscal monopolies, such as the Japanese cigarette and salt monopolies, created in 1904–1905 to pay for war with Russia (Sato 1985: 121); state mail services, often originally set up as public monopolies so that governments could more conveniently spy on their subjects' correspondence; and the production of armaments. Perhaps the most famous historical example of the latter was the Venetian arsenal, copied from a Byzantine model in 1104 and operating for nearly 700 years (Lane 1966: 269–70). So there is nothing new about public enterprise. Indeed, it 'has been around as long as civilisation and organised government', according to Roger Wettenhall (1988: 44).

Public enterprise was a prominent part of the policy furniture in many states in the era of industrialization and the mass franchise. The late nineteenth and early twentieth centuries saw a worldwide development of state enterprises,

picking up the mantle of Self

particularly for transport, energy and telecommunications utilities. Many were organized as part of the ordinary public service, like the famous Prussian railways, nationalized in 1878 and run by the civil service. But a major new organizational form came in the form of the statutory state trading corporation, said by Wettenhall (1963) to have been introduced into the English-speaking world by the Australian state of Victoria when it reorganized its railways in 1883, though Christopher Foster (1992: 76) sees its origins in eighteenth- and nineteenth-century UK turnpike and port trusts. Whatever its origins, the statutory state trading corporation began to be widely replicated, and spread to Japan under the occupation regime after the Second World War.

Of course, there was no uniform pattern. Some countries, like France, developed large public enterprise sectors, while others, like Sweden and the Netherlands, had fairly small ones (see Vickers and Wright 1988: 9–11). The USA set up regulated private utilities in many areas where other countries adopted public enterprise. Italy developed a structure of state-owned, company-law companies in areas where other countries used statutory corporations. Some countries favoured public enterprise monopolies, whereas others, like Australia and Canada, adopted 'metaphytic competition'. Metaphytic competition means competition between public enterprise and the private sector, for example in airways, banking or broadcasting (see Corbett 1965).

Little more than a generation ago, public enterprise was widely seen as the wave of the future. By the late 1940s, public enterprises had rapidly grown as a proportion of the industrial structure in countries like France and the UK (see Robson 1948). Indeed, James Burnham (1942), the prophet of the 'Managerial Revolution', predicted that most industrial enterprises in the developed countries would be state-owned by the mid-1960s. Up to the 1970s, public enterprise was a standard ingredient in recipes for modernizing developing countries, notably the strategy developed by Jawaharlal Nehru for post-independence India. The recipe was endorsed by the same international organizations that backed privatization in the 1980s. Indeed, as with privatization today, academic commentators of many different stripes assumed there was a long-run international trend to public enterprise, which would inevitably grow in a modern industrial economy.

Like deregulation, the onset of privatization came as a surprise to this once-conventional way of thinking. Paul Starr (1990: 22) declares: 'Whether or not the current turn toward privatization discloses a general failure of government, it certainly discloses a general failure of social theory.' This chapter aims to explore that proposition. Was privatization indeed inexplicable from the standpoint of earlier interpretations of public enterprise growth? If there was a failure of theory, did it lie in faulty predictions, or in the lack of development of a coherent explanatory theory of public enterprise?

Explanations of public enterprise

As with regulation, most writing on public enterprise is 'practico-descriptive'. Much of it is narrative history or 'politics-blind' statements written for public consumption by or for international bodies (Cook and Minogue 1990: 400). But, unlike the regulation story discussed in the last chapter, no well-developed body of theory appeared to explain how public enterprise emerges, how it behaves, and why it grows up in some areas (and countries) more strongly than in others. Orthodox explanations are often implicit rather than explicit.

At severe risk of over-simplification, we can perhaps group the main received explanations under three headings. That is, public enterprise is often explained as:

- a 'functional' state response to market failure;
- a product of international competition, nationalism and the development of the modern sovereign state; and
- a product of domestic politics.

Public enterprise as a functional response to market failure

One received explanation of public enterprise growth resembles the 'Whig tale' of regulation considered in the last chapter. Public enterprise is explained as a functional policy response to the inherent shortcomings of capital or product markets. The assumption is that private markets are the normal social allocation mechanism and that public enterprise appears in response to 'market failure' of some kind.

Like its analytic cousin in regulation, this explanation either leaves much unexplained or is simply tautologous – wherever there is public enterprise, the market must have 'failed' in some sense. Yet public enterprise frequently appears in cases – like steel, shipbuilding and banking – where it is perfectly feasible for markets to operate. To understand why governments set up public enterprise in such cases – to gain revenue, fulfil an ideological programme, win or retain votes – takes us well beyond technical market failure. Even when there *is* technical market failure, we still need to understand why governments choose *public enterprise* rather than other policy instruments, such as regulation or subsidy, to deal with it (see Noll 1987: 464–5).

Take the case of 'network' services, which were central to nineteenth- and early twentieth-century technological development, with the advent of railways and the 'pipe and cable' technologies (electricity, telegraphs, telephones, gas). Such technologies are problematic for ordinary commercial development. Negotiations over routes for the lines may produce bargaining deadlocks as stubborn landowners 'hold out' for the best price. Such markets may be in principle 'contestable', but the chances of rival firms running competing networks for any length of time will be slim. But why should governments choose to use public enterprise rather than regulatory power to tackle such issues? After all, the UK ran its railways for over a century through regulated private companies when other European countries used public enterprise (see Parris 1965). Many countries used regulated private companies rather than public enterprise for telephone services (see Hood and Schuppert 1988: 42).

To be convincing, an explanation of public enterprise as functional policy

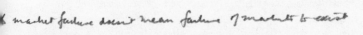

market failure doesn't mean failure of markets to exist

response to market failure must explain the circumstances in which *only* public ownership can overcome market limitations, or where the costs and benefits of the various policy alternatives clearly favour government ownership and operation. Such an explanation was scarcely offered by the traditional literature on public enterprise.

It might perhaps be possible to 'reconstruct' a functional explanation for public enterprise which would not suffer from this defect, using ideas from the 'property rights' school in economics (see Hart 1989). Property rights analysis aims to identify ways in which owning an enterprise does make a difference from dealing with it at 'arm's length' through contractual arrangements. It claims that ownership makes a difference where contracts cannot cover all possible contingencies or for actions which are hard to perform through contract.

For instance, owners (but not contractors or regulators) can appoint or dismiss an enterprise's top managers *selectively*. Regulators can close down an enterprise, but only owners can decide to keep it going. Indeed, the only way to ensure continuous operation, and prevent 'here today and gone tomorrow', is physical ownership of bricks and mortar, files and information systems. Hence where institutional stability is of the political essence, for instance with central banks, ownership *does* matter.

Ownership also matters where *honest* observance of contract or regulatory law is in doubt. For example, in broadcasting, public ownership may be the only effective way of stopping crooks or fanatics from buying up all the news reporting facilities. And where public contracting is dominated by organized crime, public enterprise (even if ordinarily inefficient) may still cut costs and limit criminal dominance. Such considerations have often been important, for example in the development of state lotteries and casinos. They link to 'progressive era' ideas of public management, to be discussed in Chapter Seven.

But, granted that ownership sometimes allows actions which are not possible through contracts or regulation, what exactly might motivate governments to act 'functionally'? Could it perhaps be a product of the pressures of international economic competition, just as business rivalry is held to motivate firms to increase efficiency? Indeed, it is often claimed that international competition produces a tendency towards policy homogeneity among states (see Ikenberry 1990: 101; North 1990; OECD 1990: 9).

In fact, it seems doubtful if the rise of public enterprise could be plausibly explained in those terms, given the degree of policy variation. For instance, after the Second World War some states with high exposure to the world market (like the UK) developed large public enterprise sectors, while others (like Japan, the Netherlands, Sweden) operated with small ones. Similar variation developed in states with relatively low exposure to the world market at that time (for instance, a large public enterprise sector in France and a small one in the USA). If the conclusion is that the same institution may produce different outcomes in different contexts or that there is no single functional response to market failures (see March and Olsen 1989: 54–6), what explanatory power does the functional market failure approach have? For all its popularity, it seems to raise more questions than it answers.

State enterprise as a product of nationalism and international state competition

A different explanation of the rise of public enterprise sees it as a product of nationalism and aspirations for economic 'sovereignty'. From this viewpoint, public enterprise is seen as a way of warding off foreign capital or as a strategy for international competitive advantage. Hence the 'flag-carrier' airlines, the 'strategic' oil companies, the corporate 'national champions', the enterprises launched to counter the power of foreign multinationals or 'buy back the farm'.

Indeed, the first Western European state to nationalize its railways was Belgium in 1834, a move usually attributed to fears of Dutch domination (see Wettenhall 1970: 10). Japan's creation of state enterprises after the 1868 Meiji restoration to counter the threat of Western colonization illustrates a recurring strategy of modernization by states facing competition from more technologically advanced societies (Sato 1985: 119). Fascist regimes often fostered public enterprise too, as in the case of Mussolini's creation of the Italian IRI in 1933 and Franco's creation of the Spanish INI in 1941 (Vickers and Wright 1988: 12).

If public enterprise reflects nationalism and international politics, the incidence of public enterprise might vary considerably, whereas assuming a general drive for functional efficiency might lead us to expect policy homogeneity. For instance, countries like Sweden or the USA which have not been historically threatened by a 'dominant neighbour' would not be prompted to develop a large public enterprise sector, while countries like Canada, Mexico or France might be expected to develop public enterprise in many 'strategic' sectors.

Such a perspective also helps us to understand the use of public enterprise by countries whose key industries are exposed to foreign takeover, even under right-wing governments ordinarily opposed to state expansion. A classic example is the takeover of abandoned German-owned firms by the conservative-dominated provisional Austrian government in 1945, to get the plants going again and stop them from being confiscated by the occupying powers after the Second World War (see Bös 1986: 30). Another well-known case is the nationalization of the UK aero-engine manufacturer Rolls-Royce by a Conservative government in 1971, to safeguard the UK's presence in a key international market.

If the rise of public enterprise stems from nationalism and international politics, we still need to explain why national economic 'sovereignty' needs to be pursued through public ownership rather than other measures (such as 'soft contracts', subsidies or regulations aimed to support domestic firms). Perhaps in a crisis a quick transfer of ownership can often work faster than other policy instruments to prevent foreign takeover. Perhaps, too, public ownership may be considered more reliable than other instruments in the face of uncertain court decisions and smart lawyers. State support of public enterprise may also conveniently be less transparent than public subsidies in the face of free-trade regimes like the EC (in which the position of public enterprise is ambiguous).

Even so, it seems hard to interpret all state enterprise as attempts to assert state sovereignty and beat off foreign rivals. Fiscal monopolies do not easily fit that picture, and domestic politics often seems to intrude. For example, when the UK Conservatives nationalized telegraph companies in 1869, considerations of national security may well have been *invoked*. But it is also notable that the event took place just before a general election and was used to pick up rural votes by cross-subsidizing less profitable rural telegraph services from the proceeds of profitable urban areas (Hood and Schuppert 1988: 41). Domestic politics matters too.

Power-of-interests explanations

Indeed, the rise of public enterprise is often seen as a product of domestic political forces. Conceivably, it might simply be a response to popular demand from the mass voters or consumers, but there is little evidence that public enterprise (or privatization, if it comes to that) typically springs from such demand. But producerist interest groups, such as business lobbies and trade unions, are often seen as key elements in the rise of public enterprise.

Marxists often interpret public enterprise as a product of 'state capitalism', in which states subsidize and underpin development by taking over capitalism's 'basket cases' – the unprofitable or high-risk industries (see Dunleavy and O'Leary 1987: 238ff.). Success in business means privatizing profits and socializing losses, so if the state takes the losses, private capital is left to 'cream' the easy and profitable areas of industry. Conversely, any public enterprises which become financially successful are likely to be privatized.

At first sight, the simple logic of such an analysis is appealing. But there is much that it fails to explain. Why should state *ownership* rather than subsidy or guarantee be used to bail out sick industries? If a firm ails, why should state ownership be more beneficial to capitalism than its bankruptcy and closure? Why do labour unions often seem to be more powerful advocates of state enterprise than business lobbies? And why should 'the capitalist state' have taken so long to get round to privatizing its financially successful enterprises, such as telecommunication companies?

More liberal variants of political science acknowledge a similar logic in the interest group process, in that efforts by business lobbies to offload losses or subsidize development costs may well help to explain the development of public enterprise, but other lobbies, notably trade unions, are expected to be influential too. Economics-of-politics analysis also tends to stress the role of 'producers' in building up public enterprise. Indeed, William Niskanen, in his path-breaking *Bureaucracy and Representative Government* (1971), treated public enterprise as a variant of orthodox public bureaucracy.

Economics-of-politics theory of public enterprise as a specific organizational form remains fragmentary, by comparison with equivalent work on regulation. Economics-of-politics theory typically takes the role of top bureaucrats to be crucial in shaping the general public service, so it might be expected that self-regarding senior managers might be equally crucial in shaping the structure and extent of state enterprise. Typically, top managers are assumed to aim at maximum wealth and power, but also to foster organizational 'slack' – resources in the organization which are controlled at their discretion – and to make their own jobs as pleasant as possible.

Public ownership may be attractive to top managers with such preferences if it limits the competition that they face (removing the risk of hostile takeover and dismissal for managers and workers); if it means less stringent oversight than they would face under private ownership, and gives them more opportunities to divert blame for failures on to others; and if they can reduce their personal risks (by avoiding the situation, common in private business, where top managers must tie up personal wealth in the corporation through shares, stock options or pension plans). Such factors are often invoked in explaining why managers might prefer a 'soft life' under public enterprise. Christopher Foster (1992: 72) notes in the UK that most owners and operators of the firms concerned supported nationalization in the 1940s, though there was tactical opposition designed to raise compensation levels and affect the shape of industries under public ownership.

But why should managers press for state ownership rather than public support of industry in general? And are politicians just passive respondents to outside pressures, or do their *own* personal and vote-winning interests affect their choice of policy instruments? There are at least five ways – albeit 'unmentionable' ones – in which public enterprise might enable politicians to gain benefits that cannot be achieved by the 'sale' of regulatory power (*à la* Stigler and Peltzman) or distribution of cash from the public purse.

First, public enterprise offers *'waiting rooms and exits'* for politicians themselves (see Derivery 1975: 222). Core public service bureaucracies, even in modern 'business look-alike' style, do not always offer such possibilities because of merit appointment rules and career service structures, to be discussed in Chapter Seven. But like the EC Commission or UK House of Lords, public enterprises can be used as a source of jobs for retired (or just tired) politicians. Unlike the House of Lords, attractive salaries and perks can be attached to the jobs.

Second, public enterprise can be a source of *hands-on political patronage* in jobs and contracts. Sometimes, public enterprise profits may also offer politicians a more convenient source of funds than other tax-gathering methods. For instance, Gareth Austin (1992: 13–14) notes that government marketing boards in tropical Africa (with monopoly power over crop exports) were ways of taxing export producers to pay for government growth in the late colonial–early independence era. And public enterprise can be a fruitful source of clientelist or 'patrimonial' power; that is, power to reward supporters individually, win over waverers and placate enemies (see Sandbrook 1988; Cook and Minogue 1990: 396)). Whether such power is used mainly for top boardroom appointments (as in the UK), or extends to more run-of-the-mill jobs down the line, it gives politicians a major resource.

Third, public enterprise offers a resource for use in *territorial politics*. Like US military bases, public enterprise offers politicians the chance of directly steering attractive developments towards politically favoured areas. Key plants and desirable investment projects can be placed in marginal constituencies, while unwanted or 'bile barrel' operations go elsewhere, such as the borderlands with rival states. For example, in Japan, the nationalized railway company was for many years used as part of electoral strategy, by targeting expensive new rail developments on marginal constituencies (Sato 1985: 120–21).

Fourth, public enterprise offers hands-on opportunities for *timing business decisions to fit in with the political cycle* (to which we return in the next chapter). Incumbent politicians can synchronize what public enterprises do with the vote-winning cycle of machine politics. For instance, in the run-up to elections, it may be convenient to hold public enterprises' prices down, give pay rises to their workers (but hold back directors' salary rises), announce attractive new investment projects in key areas and run 'lifestyle' advertising to help make the voters feel good. The corresponding job cuts, price rises, wage restraint (coupled with directorial salary rises) and cancellation of investment projects can be conveniently timed for the 'bad news' period after elections.

Fifth, public enterprise in the public corporation mode *combines the possibility of maximal hands-on influence with minimal political accountability*, and in that sense could be seen as the answer to a harassed politician's prayer. When politicians are directly accountable for public enterprise, they face a dilemma. There may be potential political advantages from 'hands on' control via ownership, for example in avoiding plant closures in marginal constituencies or price rises before elections. On the other hand, there are advantages in *not* having responsibility, to avoid blame for risks, mistakes and failures.

In principle, the political invention of the 'independent board' gives unscrupulous politicians a chance to have it both ways. They can shape public enterprise policy by backdoor arm-twisting, while maintaining the convenient façade of an independent board working at 'arms length' from the regular executive. It would thus be no surprise if governments often prefer to escape accountability by using behind-the-scenes influence over public enterprises instead of intervening openly in their affairs, despite 'rational' management regimes designed to make political intervention transparent, for example publicly issued directives or public subsidies for unprofitable, politically favoured activities (the so-called 'recoup concept': see Wettenhall 1966). Much was written in the 1970s about the growth of public bodies outside the 'core' of government and not subject to the full rigour of the public accountability regimes applied to that core (see, for example, Hood 1978; Sharkansky 1979; Barker 1982).

Such 'unmentionable' political advantages of public enterprise can explain more satisfactorily why politicians might *not* be indifferent between general support of industry, regulatory control or public enterprise as alternative policy instruments. Indeed (as the 'property rights' school discussed earlier would imply), such political advantages can *only* be gained from public ownership, not from other policy measures. To suggest that public enterprise was adopted from the start for such purposes would be, perhaps, to attribute extraordinary powers of rational calculation to politicians. Yet, once the ball started rolling, politicians might well have come increasingly to appreciate such advantages in a mass-franchise era. But if public enterprise really suited those interests so well, why should privatization come along?

Privatization

Privatization was not unknown before the 1970s. For example, the Italian IRI disposed of state holdings as well as acquiring them; the German federal government sold stock in several enterprises in the 1950s and 1960s; and UK Conservative governments engaged in some modest privatizations in the 1950s and early 1970s. But the international privatization wave that began in the late 1970s caught much more attention. Ironically echoing the opening words of the 1848 Communist Manifesto, Richard Rose (1989: 248) declared: 'A spectre is haunting socialism, the spectre of privatisation.'

But, like public enterprise, privatization did not happen everywhere in the same way or to the same extent. Harvey Feigenbaum and Jeffrey Henig (1993: 439–40) distinguish 'pragmatic', 'tactical' and 'systemic' privatizations. 'Pragmatic' privatizations are those introduced by bureaucrats or managers as technical solutions, while 'tactical' privatizations are introduced by politicians to alter the balance of power and votes, and 'systemic' privatizations are intended to transform an entire society (as in former Communist states). Over the 1980s, most OECD countries carried out some 'pragmatic' or 'tactical' privatization, but the most radical changes seem to have been the 'tactical' privatizations carried out by the UK Thatcher government and the Chirac government in France (Vickers and Wright 1988). Though the literature on privatization is massive, there is no convenient cross-national scorecard of privatization, partly because of differences in national accounting conventions on what counts as public enterprise and partly because, as noted earlier, privatization is a word with several possible meanings. Table 3.1 (based largely on Vickers and Wright 1988: 10–11) indicates some very broad-brush differences among selected OECD countries.

Privatization was much discussed by international institutions like the World Bank, Asian Development Bank, IMF and OECD, which helped to spread the ideas (Ikenberry 1990: 100), though in many of the less developed countries it seems to have been more talked about than actually carried out (see Adam *et al.* 1992: 39). But in the 1990s privatization had a massive second wind with the disposal of state assets in the ex-Communist countries on a scale which dwarfed even the radical OECD privatizations of the earlier decade.

Privatization took many different forms. In the 1990s some ex-Communist countries engaging in 'systemic' privatization (such as Russia and the former Czechoslovakia) adopted Milton Friedman's (1977) idea of giving away state enterprises through 'voucher' schemes, but in the 1980s privatization meant sales in one form or other. Detailed methods varied. In some cases government sold only part of the stock in public enterprises, whereas in others all the stock was sold. Some sales took place through stock market share flotations, others through trade sale or by management or employee buyouts (see Bradley and Nejad 1989; Foster 1992: 116–34).

Table 3.1   Variations in public enterprise base and privatization: selected cases

Public enterprise base in 1980[b]	Degree of PE privatization to 1989[a]		
	High (over $10bn receipts)	Medium (between $1 and £10bn)	Low (less than $1bn receipts)
High (score 7.5 or more out of 11)	UK, France	Italy	Austria
Medium (score between 5.25 and 6.5 out of 11)		Former Federal Republic of Germany	Sweden, Netherlands, Australia, Switzerland
Low (score less than 4)	Japan	Canada, USA	

Source: Largely based on Vickers and Wright (1988: 10–11).

[a] Degree of privatization of public enterprise to 1988: states making more than $10bn sales from privatization score high, those making less than $1bn score low, and the remainder score medium.
[b] Size of public enterprise base in 1980: out of eleven industrial sectors in 1980, states score 1 for over 75 per cent public ownership in each sector, 0.75 for 75 per cent, 0.5 for 50 per cent and 0.25 for 25 per cent, making a maximum score of 11.

Though privatization went furthest in the OECD world in the 1980s under fully-paid-up right-wing governments, not all right-wing governments were high privatizers, and privatization was also pursued by 'centrist' governments. An example is the early steps taken by the Social Credit government in British Columbia, Canada, in the mid-1970s, which seem to have been the first major OECD move to privatization in the 1970s. Indeed, some avowedly socialist governments, such as the Spanish Socialists, adopted privatization – in that case, as a reaction against the corporate fascist state of the Franco era. Even the French Socialists engaged in *privatisations silencieuses* in the mid-1980s, letting public enterprises sell their subsidiaries to the private sector and raise funds on the stock exchange (Bauer 1988: 50–51).

Privatization as an international 'policy boom' (Dunleavy 1986) attracted many explanations, both 'instant' and 'academic', of why it should be the wave of the future (cf. Letwin 1988; Pirie 1988). Political science explanations of the move to privatization (such as Vickers and Wright 1988; Henig *et al.* 1988) often invoke a bewildering multiplicity of causes for the policy shift. But, as the epigraph from James Douglas reminds us, it is easy to identify turning-points in retrospect, but harder to explain exactly why they took place when they did or what caused the reversal.

Although often couched in terms which imply a radical break with the past, it is interesting to note that many explanations of the shift to privatization can be grouped under much the same heads as those used a generation earlier to explain the growth of public enterprise – namely, explanations of policy as a functional response to government failure, international-politics explanations and explanations focusing on domestic interest group processes.

Privatization as a functional policy response

Like public enterprise in an earlier era, privatization is sometimes presented as a functional policy of 'economic rationalism'. The claim is that privatization increases economic efficiency, typically as a response to 'government failure' rather than 'market failure'. Such a functional explanation raises similar questions to those raised earlier for equivalent functional explanations of the rise of public enterprise. The interesting question, however, is how it relates to such interpretations. Does it show up a 'failure of social theory' in that those earlier understandings of the rise of public enterprise were based on faulty arguments? Or does it simply mean that circumstances have changed, such that what might have been efficient a generation ago is no longer efficient today? If it is the latter, the earlier 'market failure' interpretation of the rise of public enterprise might actually *help* us to explain the rise of privatization. After all, policy might shift from public enterprise to privatization if technology or other developments reduced the market failures that originally prompted public enterprise. If such a shift occurred when the policy habitat changed, it would show the theory to be successful, rather than expose a failure of theory.

The standard 'New Right' critique naturally implies that the basic premises of the efficiency case for public enterprise were always faulty. On the other hand, several commentators on privatization have argued that technology and other changes helped to weaken 'market failures' in some important areas, and so reduced the 'functionality' of public enterprise (see Vickers and Wright 1988: 2). For example, public enterprise is often said to have developed in areas where only the state could raise funds for large capital projects. But the growth of sophisticated financial services industries and global money markets, may reduce constraints which could have deadlocked private-enterprise project development in an earlier era. If government capacity to provide investment finance is simultaneously reduced through growing fiscal stress (as occurred after the 1970s oil shocks for most OECD countries), 'market failure' could start to go into reverse.

A related example is the development of technology making competition more feasible in telecommunications (the shift from telephone-specific electromagnetic switching systems to electronic processing, microwave, satellites), and similar technology making banking and finance more competitive. Foster (1992: 73) suggests that information technology has created a more 'privatization-friendly' climate for electricity in the UK:

> . . . the building up of a publicly owned electricity grid after 1926 to be used competitively by both private and municipal distributors was then beyond the competence of the regulators to coordinate and this was a

fundamental reason for the eventual nationalization of the whole industry . . . Public ownership seemed the only way of managing such a system – the computers and computer-based mathematics did not exist which would have made it possible for there to be a truly commercial electricity market buying and selling through the grid.

Perhaps sociotechnical changes associated with a shift from 'industrial' to 'post-industrial' society might weaken the 'market failure' basis for public enterprise in several areas. If such habitat changes did indeed help to tip policy from public enterprise to privatization, it would not necessarily invalidate the functional explanation of the rise of public enterprise.

International politics and competition

As with public enterprise, privatization has often been attributed to international politics. John Ikenberry (1990) sees it as a worldwide 'policy bandwagoning' process adopted by trading rivals trying to lower their 'overhead costs' and modernize their economies. An international-politics perspective can explain why the policy turning-point seems to have come at the same time in several states (Ikenberry's 'why so many countries and why now?' question).

An international-politics interpretation of privatization would not necessarily mean a 'failure' of orthodox international-politics accounts of the rise of public enterprise. If public policy in this area is shaped by international politics, there is no more surprise about governments adopting privatization policies at odds with their domestic ideological bent than there is about the nationalization 'anomalies' referred to earlier. What needs to be shown is how international politics should have changed to cause governments to reverse policy. Again, it may simply be that the 'policy habitat' changed. So if the international politics regime favoured public enterprise from the 1940s to the 1960s, what changed the nature of the international game by the 1980s?

There are several possible answers. First, technological competition may have changed the kind of assets which counted as 'strategic' for state sovereignty. For example, nationalization of railways in Japan in 1906 was heavily motivated by military considerations (see Sato 1985: 120), and the same went for telecommunications in many states. In 1911, Weber wrote that 'the modern Occidental state can be administered the way it actually is only because the state controls the telegraph network and has the mails and railroads at its disposal' (Gerth and Mills 1948: 213). But as transport and communication technology moved on after the Second World War, railways or telephone systems may have become increasingly irrelevant to defence and security.

Second, as noted in the last section, globalization of markets may have transformed some traditional public enterprise sectors, notably banking and airlines. Global competition makes it harder for governments to oversee public enterprises or limit financial risk, and if nervous oversight ministries make public enterprises forgo profitable international expansion, their managers may demand privatization.

Market globalization might induce moves to privatization from two opposite directions. At some point, privatization may be the only way to salvage anything from the older 'nationalist' agenda – as the only feasible means of recapitalizing formerly public enterprises to make them competitive in global markets. At the same time, multinational corporations may be better placed to push for the removal of the barriers to their expansion which public enterprise represents. As we saw in the last chapter, Jill Hills (1986) sees telecommunications de-regulation in these terms, and the same logic can be applied to privatization, particularly in areas where technological development makes public enterprises less 'insulable' from the private sector.

Interest group explanations

Some, like Kenneth Wiltshire (1988), see privatization as inspired by ideology. But, like the growth of public enterprise, it can be seen in more mundane terms as the product of interest group politics. Again, such explanations do not necessarily imply that understanding of the growth of public enterprise in terms of interests is necessarily erroneous, merely that interests may alter as conditions change or new options open up. Rational vote-seeking politicians will repeatedly review the privatization option for the political advantages which it may bring as against the political advantages of public enterprise, as discussed earlier. If, at some point, privatization becomes more attractive than the option of continuing with public enterprise, that does not necessarily mean that the political attractions of public enterprise never existed, any more than a decision to deregulate means that regulation was never politically attractive.

Mariusz Dobek (1993: 24) argues that privatization reflects politicians' desire to acquire power, rejecting the implicit assumption in much of the economic literature on privatization that 'politicians running the government behave as public policy maximizers, devising and pursuing primarily those policies which promote the greatest benefit to the general public'. He argues (ibid.: 32) that political goals will always trump 'economic' goals wherever there is a conflict, claiming that the Thatcher government's privatization policy in the UK was *politically* quite coherent, contrary to the argument of economists who interpreted it as 'a policy in search of a rationale' (Kay and Thompson 1986). Dobek's claim is that UK privatization was in effect a product of activity by policy entrepreneurs who had hit upon a new instrument for expanding the Conservative Party's electoral base and weakening that of its opponents. If economists failed to see the 'rationale', it was because the policy objectives were essentially political and electoral, and hence were mostly unstated or 'unmentionable'.

At least four 'unmentionable' advantages are available to politicians from privatization, comparable to the unmentionable advantages of public enterprise, as discussed earlier. First, privatized firms (or companies operating as brokers for privatization) may offer even *more* lucrative possibilities than public enterprise for 'in-between' or 'post-politics' jobs for politicians. Consultancy fees and top pay may be less politically constrained than in public enterprises, since it can be claimed that salaries are commercially confidential and/or that they spring from 'market forces'. So privatization may create a more lucrative post-politics career path for politicians than public enterprise. Of course, there is a risk, particularly if capital market pressures limit the security of such jobs and the market value of ex-politicians of a particular stripe falls as a result of electoral defeat. But a shift in parties in power is also likely to threaten patronage jobs in the public enterprise sector, so the 'downside' risk is perhaps little different.

Second, privatization, like public enterprise, offers politicians a means of buying votes and rewarding friends. A fire sale of public assets below market value will offer potential campaign contributors or marginal voters with spare cash the kind of no-lose investment opportunity that is all too rare in the perilous world of stocks and shares. Such a strategy was a marked feature of the UK Thatcher privatizations of the 1980s. And the cash realized from the fire sales can be used to fund benefits or tax cuts targeted at key groups of voters (cf. Rose 1989: 262–3; Dobek 1993: 27). Of course, such a strategy is likely to be a once-only move, since assets suitable for fire sales will inevitably run out and political gratitude is short. But, after all, it is often claimed that politicians have a short time-horizon, focused mainly on the next election. So a rational politician would need continually to weigh the expected short-term marginal votes purchasable from asset sales against votes purchasable from patronage over public enterprises. When the former exceeds the latter, policy shifts from public enterprise to privatization.

Third, privatization may be a means of gaining electoral campaign funds, and thus buying votes indirectly. Normally, public enterprises cannot contribute directly to political parties. Of course, they may legally be able to fund lobby groups or provide campaign funds illegally, as has been claimed for India (see Cook and Minogue 1990: 392). But privatized companies, or the beneficiaries of privatization, *can* be used as a direct source of campaign contributions. And if government keeps regulatory power over privatized companies, it can reap more than a one-off windfall from 'selling the family silver'. Regulatory power can provide further income, in that further donations to campaign funds (or employment of ex-politicians) may be needed to preserve a sympathetic regulatory regime. From this perspective, exchanging public enterprise for regulation need not necessarily be as pointless in *political* terms as some commentators have suggested.

Fourth, privatization may be a further step towards minimizing public ac-countability. In that sense, it can reflect exactly the *same* political logic that underpins a move from the mainstream public service to independent public enterprises, rather than a shift to a different logic. Cross-subsidization of one group of politically favoured customers over another can still easily be achieved through regulation, so powers to interfere are not sacrificed.

Why should politicians' preferences shift from valuing the advantages of public enterprise discussed earlier to valuing the advantages of privatization discussed above? For two of them (jobs for politicians and minimization of

Table 3.2 The unmentionable politics of public enterprise and privatization

Dimension	(1) Public enterprise	(2) Privatization	(3) Conditions for switch
Politicians' own welfare	Creates 'waiting rooms' and 'exits'	Creates more lucrative (but risky) waiting rooms and exits	Pre-existence of public enterprise
Patronage and vote-buying	Hands-on patronage, territorial management, manage electoral cycle	Buy votes by sale of assets below market value, gain electoral campaign funds	Changing structure of marginal voters, rising cost of politics, silting up of patronage
Avoidance of accountability	Independent board provides 'screen', avoids blame	Privatization enables avoidance of blame	Evidence of backdoor interference in public enterprise makes 'screen' unconvincing

accountability), all that it would take for one choice to succeed the other is the passage of time and the prior existence of public enterprises available for privatization. For the other two – the patronage and vote-buying considerations – background conditions would need to change, creating a different 'habitat' for policy choice.

Such a habitat change might come from a shift to a 'services' economy, weakening the power of manufacturing interests and trade unions (the political support base for many traditional public enterprises), and increasing that of financial and professional business interests (cf. Vickers and Wright 1988: 17). A sociotechnical structure which stresses information-handling and financial services may be a much less favourable political 'climate' for public enterprise than a manufacturing-heavy structure with poorly developed financial services. Table 3.2 summarizes the possibilities.

We saw in the last section that the rise of public enterprise might be linked to managers' interests. But privatization, too, potentially offers benefits to managers, and managers may be as important in pushing policy towards privatization as towards nationalization. Though privatization rhetoric tends to harp on 'market discipline' and consumer benefits, reality need not conform to stereotype. Whether slack-seeking managers opt for privatization or continued public enterprise may depend on their assessment of the oversight regime to which they will be subject under each system.

Managers are likely to want privatization: if they can keep monopoly or market power and avoid the break-up of their enterprises; if privatization reduces the effective scrutiny of their operations by outsiders (for example, prohibition on foreign shareholdings, as in the case of the NTT privatization in Japan); or if it is accompanied by other measures (such as debt write-offs or privatization 'dowries') which produce more organizational slack.

In such circumstances, privatization can be attractive to slack-seeking managers. It means that top managerial salaries can soar after privatization, as has typically occurred in the UK, since there will neither be market checks on their pay (in the form of threat of bankruptcy or takeover) nor the restraints imposed by public opinion on top public sector salaries. At the same time, managerial accountability can be reduced, with sensitive decisions being shielded from scrutiny as 'commercially confidential' information. Indeed, if the stocks of privatized enterprises can be distributed to ordinary voters in the name of 'popular capitalism', managers have even more protection, since unsophisticated and poorly informed 'donkey' shareholders will be less likely to produce effective pressure for greater managerial efficiency than even relatively incompetent oversight ministries. It is interesting that Michel Bauer (1988: 60), commenting on the Chirac government's privatizations in France between 1986 and 1988, claims that 'the heads of privatised firms benefit today from numerous safeguards which shelter them from political changes [i.e. the spoils system] but also ultimately from economic sanctions'.

Auto-destruction explanations

As can be seen, for every orthodox explanation of the rise of public enterprise, there is a parallel explanation for privatization. Far from demonstrating the failure of orthodox explanations of the rise of public enterprise, this parallelism may demonstrate the relative success and durability of the raw materials used by political scientists to explain policy development. But it may be that what tipped the policy balance from public enterprise to privatization is self-destruction rather than an exogenous change in habitat. Public enterprise might have dug its own grave and become its own worst enemy. It could have happened in at least three ways: policy degradation, the wearing out of control systems and self-destroying 'success'.

Policy degradation

First, public enterprise might destroy its original rationale by policy degradation. If public enterprises are run solely on the stark 'political' logic sketched out above (for patronage, jobs for ex-politicians, etc.) their growing inefficiency over time will drag down national economic performance. Once such macroeconomic failure leads to voter discontent or negative reactions among international lending and aid bodies, vote-seeking politicians do have an incentive to raise overall economic efficiency, which might prompt them to look more closely at privatization.

Even the *political* efficiency of public enterprises might weaken over time. Patronage systems can 'silt up' and become an embarrassment to the patrons. For example, once marginal voters have been 'squared' by public enterprise patronage, they may cease to be marginal. At that point, political logic would suggest relocation of public enterprise to new marginal areas, but such logic may be frustrated by institutional inertia and resistance. Moreover, demand for patronage may come to exceed the realistic supply (as it often does) and the the cost of buying off marginal constituencies through public enterprise investment might come to cripple the enterprises.

Moreover, the political attractions of 'depoliticized' arm's-length public enterprise may become corrupted through abuse. Politicians' attempts to slough off public accountability for public enterprise policy may become ever-less convincing as more allegations of backdoor 'interference' build up, as seems to have happened in the UK (Foster 1992: 95). And the dream may go sour for public enterprise managers, too, particularly if their salaries become politicized and visible (ibid.: 88). They will need to lobby hard to justify salaries and perks much higher than those of their supervising ministers or top bureaucrats. Once their pay has become intertwined with general government policy on public sector pay (as is so apt to happen to politicians' own salaries), escape from the public sector may become much more attractive to managers.

Auto-destruction of control systems

A second possible route to privatization is the autonomous 'wearing out' of policy control frameworks for public enterprise. If control shifts among the three basic types identified by Dunsire and discussed in Chapter One (the 'simple steering', 'homeostasis' and 'collibration' modes), as each form 'wears out' in use, privatization might be interpreted as a product of control-system dynamics. The UK case might be interpreted in these terms, with privatization and regulation claimed by some to be the 'logical conclusion' of control systems pushing state-owned industries to increasingly commercial operating regimes (cf. Abromeit 1986: 173–4). And the UK public utilities case might even be seen as a shift from 'collibration' through 'simple steering' and 'homeostasis', and back to 'collibration' within a generation.

The pre-1940s structure consisted of a statutory regulation framework governing multiple local authorities and other agencies (such as railway companies). Many accounts of the move to public enterprise in the inter-war years and the 1940s saw nationalization as a response to the perceived failures of the previous regulatory framework, for example in providing stable, user-friendly and integrated urban public transport (see Foster 1992: 73). After the 1940s bout of nationalizations, the original method of controlling public enterprise consisted of attempting to bring an industry under a single command, putting trusted individuals at the helm (often people who had had a 'good war' and a military background) and relying on these 'Platonic guardians', as Rose (1989: 256–7) calls them, to get results. Dissatisfaction with the Platonic guardian system led to attempts to develop a more 'homeostatic' style in the 1960s and 1970s, with successive Treasury-inspired efforts to develop financial targeting and performance indicators. In practice, public enterprises seem to have quickly learned to live with the targets and investment criteria with little basic change in their behaviour, while ministers paid little attention to the target-setting process (Foster 1992: 86). With the failure of that approach, it was perhaps predictable that the balance would start to shift back to 'collibration' from the 1970s, with independent regulation pulling against profit-seeking providers. With the Thatcher privatizations, utility policy was set, not simply by a homeostatic target-setting process (though there were elements of that in price control), but more broadly by the push and pull of independent 'profit-seeking' public utilities, vote-seeking politicians and 'welfare-seeking' independent regulatory bodies.

For those 'of the faith', of course, the current control system is seen as a way of solving the problem at last. But if the historical pattern is interpreted as successive shifts prompted by the inherent limitations and degradation of the preceding control system, the current regulatory system can itself be expected to wear out in time. Such a view of the shift to privatization would give us an endogenous explanation of the policy dynamic, that is, an explanation which springs as much from the inherent institutional dynamics as from external shocks or technological development. But it has been as yet little applied even to the UK case, and its application to other contexts remains undeveloped.

Victim of its own success?

A common explanation of 1980s privatization is that public enterprise had simply 'failed' as a social experiment. On this view – naturally much trumpeted by privatization advocates – the public enterprise experience over a generation in the international 'laboratory' had shown that privatization had to be a better way. Of course, this view is contested in academic debate (see Henig *et al.* 1988: 442). It is hard to identify any 'crucial experiments' which heralded the policy shift. The literature comparing costs and performance of public and private enterprises tends to be ambiguous and methodologically problematic (see, for example, Borcherding *et al.* 1982; Parker 1985). And it is commonly argued that competition makes more difference to efficiency than ownership *per se*. If so, governments concerned with enterprise performance should have concentrated on competition rather than privatizing ownership – yet in many cases it was exactly the other way round (see Abromeit 1986: 161–2).

Nevertheless, a 'failed experiment' interpretation would fit Hirschman's (1982) ideas, discussed in Chapter One, in which both statism and individualism ultimately fail by generating sufficient disappointment about their results to bring the opposite ideas back into favour. And if the current wave of disappointment is tipping the cultural scales towards a more pervasive individualism, as Mary Douglas (1990: 12) has suggested, such a shift would necessarily weaken the social bases of public enterprise.

From this viewpoint, 1940s enthusiasm for public enterprise is to be attributed to fresh memories of the world slump of the 1930s and disillusion with private ownership (as associated with under-investment, unstable cycles of boom and collapse and, particularly in France, collaboration with foreign invaders during the Second World War). But forty years of public enterprise in the long peace after the Second World War in turn exposed the shortcomings of the alternative model, while the grim memories of the earlier era faded.

At that point, public enterprise becomes more vulnerable. Instead of a promising institution with no history, it has a lengthening track-record available for its critics to attack. Its enemies – those who have to pay the costs of the 'rents' extracted by the beneficiaries – have had time to regroup and counter-mobilize. So after a generation or so, the system goes on to the opposite tack of privatization.

As noted in Chapter One, on this view of the process there can be no cumulativeness, no once-for-all change to an 'end-of-history' equilibrium. Sooner or later public enterprise dinosaurs will be back as dissatisfaction grows with experience of the alternative. Perhaps the scene is already being set with the collapse of many of the 1980s high-flying business entrepreneurs and the worst world slump since the 1930s. The news in 1991 that New York was setting up new public enterprises in areas where the 'free market' for public construction materials was dominated by organized crime interests might even be interpreted as an early sign of public enterprise dinosaurs returning in an unexpected habitat.

But this elegant theory does not really help us to answer Ikenberry's question: Why so many countries and why *now*? Why did the reaction against public enterprise come in the 1970s and 1980s, rather than in the 1960s or the 2020s? And could we not construct an account of privatization in at least some areas in exactly the *opposite* terms – that public enterprise becomes vulnerable to privatization when it has been so successful that it has worked itself out of a job and destroyed its political habitat?

For example, if public enterprise is a cement for holding together a fissiparous political system by 'clientelist' patronage (as has commonly been argued for less developed countries), its very success in helping to produce a less 'baronial' political structure can undermine its political foundations. Or if public enterprise is a 'hospital' for sick or premature capitalist companies, as in the Marxist stereotype, successful nursing or incubation will in time destroy its political rationale. Again, if public enterprise is part of a state's competitive strategy for economic modernization, the rationale for such enterprises may disappear at the point where they have become large or experienced enough to be effective players relative to the international competition, and need to go beyond domestic state boundaries for large-scale capital mobilization. Public enterprise can be too *successful* for its own good.

Conclusion

Paul Starr seems correct to see 1980s privatization as a failure of social theory. It was not predicted from such explanations of public enterprise as had developed by the 1970s, and clearly showed up the lack of a coherent explanatory theory of public enterprise. Despite all the writing about public enterprise, a clear predictive theory of the conditions in which public enterprise appears and grows never really developed. But with the 20/20 hindsight of history, it is not so clear that privatization ran completely at odds with the ideas conventionally used to explain the growth of public enterprise. As we have seen, explanations of privatization have often invoked ideas similar to those which were offered earlier to explain public enterprise. They differ in the habitat conditions rather than in basic theoretical elements.

In this sense, it seems doubtful if privatization is best understood as a sudden ideological bolt-from-the-blue analogous to the meteorite which some believe to have destroyed the dinosaurs' world. Hence it seems difficult to place this case in the 'intellectual' sector of the approaches discussed in Chapter One [sector (a) in Fig. 1.2]. And if, as some economists have argued, privatization is a case of a policy which tended to precede its rationale (at least in publicly mentionable form), it seems to differ from the case of deregulation considered in the last chapter, where rationale developed in advance of the policy shift. On the other hand, habitat change, including the globalization of markets (massively increasing financial risks for governments running enterprises trading across frontiers), the development of financial markets and the erosion of technological insulation of some sectors, are stressed by many commentators as part of the explanation for the shift to privatization. Hence such habitat changes are hard to separate from the changing patterns of interests, particularly the rise of a 'privatization complex' and the role of policy entrepreneurship in using privatization to extract new lodes of vote-bearing ore, as stressed by Dobek (1993) and others. And policy self-destruction is stressed by commentators such as Foster (1992). Hence, once more, a 'cocktail' of processes may have been at work, incorporating some combination of habitat change, self-induced destruction and the development of new predators (including vote-seeking policy entrepreneurs) hunting these life forms to extinction. That suggests that this case may belong in sector (l) of Fig. 1.2.

However, it is not clear that the dinosaur analogy is entirely appropriate here. Despite well-publicized privatizations, public enterprise is far from extinct. New public enterprises keep appearing even in countries where privatization has been taken furthest, like the UK. The need for an 'extinction science' in this area may therefore be premature. What we do need is more attention to relatively parsimonious *explanatory* accounts of why public enterprise waxes and wanes, even if it comes at the expense of the endless polishing of efficiency arguments for or against public enterprise and privatization.

4

Macroeconomic policy: from Keynesianism to monetarism

In view of the history of economic policy-making in the post-war years, a strong case can be made for the proposition that changing fashions in economic theory probably have more influence on outcomes than any political factors.

(Whiteley 1986: 82)

Introduction

Regulation and public enterprise are policies which are usually aimed at specific markets or particular issues. In economists' jargon, they are 'microeconomic' policies, that is, policies for particular industries, markets, areas, sectors or firms. But macroeconomic policy denotes policies intended to affect total output and incomes by managing overall levels of unemployment and inflation. Conventionally, a government's main macroeconomic policy instruments are the power to vary public spending and employment levels, tax levels, public borrowing and interest rates.

As with regulation and public enterprise, another set of policy 'dinosaurs' seems to have disappeared – at least temporarily – in macroeconomic policy in the 1980s. The dinosaurs which faded from the scene were the 'Keynesian' policies, which were seen as the highest form of macroeconomic evolution after the Second World War. The life forms replacing them were the 'monetarist' and 'new classical' policies often linked to the rise of the 'New Right' (cf. Hall 1990).

The term 'Keynesian' is used here loosely to mean a style of macroeconomic management in which full employment is the central goal of public policy. Controlling inflation is of secondary political concern (and the associated economic theory claims there is a trade-off between inflation and unemployment, so that governments can choose which mix of the two they wish to have). Governments with these political aims vary public spending and borrowing to keep aggregate demand at full-employment level. In the 'monetarist' and 'new classical' style of macroeconomic management, low inflation is government's central political goal. It is full employment which is secondary (and indeed dependent on control of inflation, in the associated economic theory). Governments following this policy style vary public spending and interest rates to keep inflation rates low.

Figures 4.1 to 4.3 give an indication of macroeconomic changes in five OECD countries and the OECD as a whole over two (in one case, three) decades. Apart from Sweden and Japan, *de facto* political tolerance of unemployment seems to have increased sharply from the late 1970s, to the point where mass unemployment had become the norm in many countries by the mid-1980s – something which would have been considered 'unthinkable' in the 1950s and 1960s. At the same time, political tolerance of inflation (Fig. 4.2) seems to have decreased, with CPI rises trending downwards for most of the 1980s. And real short-term interest rates (that is, the interest rate that depositors get for their money after accounting for its loss of value through inflation) – having been negative in many cases for much of the 1970s – rose sharply, as Fig. 4.3 shows. We consider public spending in the next chapter.

Is the apparent demise of 'Keynesian' macroeconomic policies related to the extinctions considered in the last two chapters? Did it amount to a 'surprise' for earlier understandings of the politics of macroeconomic policy in the same way that deregulation and privatization are claimed to have done? If so, how can it be explained? To explore these questions, this chapter looks first at three conventional political science explanations of the determinants of macroeconomic policy to assess how much 'surprise' the demise of Keynesianism produced for those explanations, and whether we need to look for other kinds of explanations.

Three conventional accounts of the determinants of macroeconomic policy in political science

In what political circumstances might government be expected to play a 'Keynesian' macroeconomic policy game, with unemployment as the primary evil to be avoided, and under what conditions will it play a 'monetarist' game, with inflation chosen as the chief enemy? Political scientists in the liberal (non-Marxist) tradition have conventionally offered three main answers to that question. One says that macroeconomic policy choices mainly depend on whether political parties of the right or the left control the government. Another says that such policy choices depend on whether an election is approaching or not, and whether incumbent political parties need to pump up the economy to be sure of gaining re-election. A third explains macroeconomic policy by the effect of entrenched institutional structures. Can these explanations shed any light on the apparent extinction of Keynesianism?

Explaining macroeconomic policy by political incumbency

As noted above, one conventional explanation of whether governments choose a 'Keynesian' or 'monetarist' macroeconomic strategy relates to the nature of

Figure 4.1 Unemployment as % of total labour force 1960–90

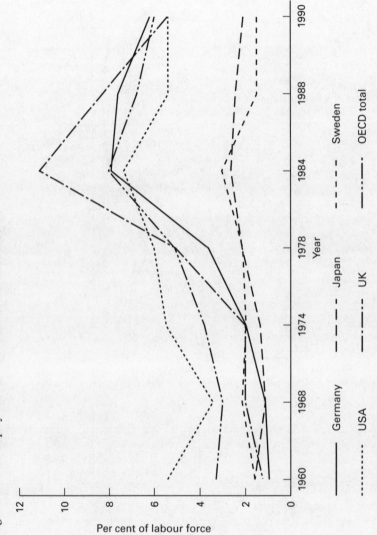

Source: OECD Hist Stats 1960–90, table 2.15.

Figure 4.2 Consumer price indices (CPI): year-on-year percentage changes 1973–90

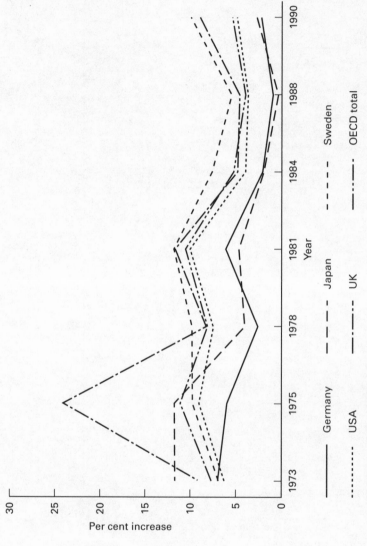

Source: OECD Hist Stats 1960–90, table 8.11.

Figure 4.3 Real short-term interest rates 1973–90

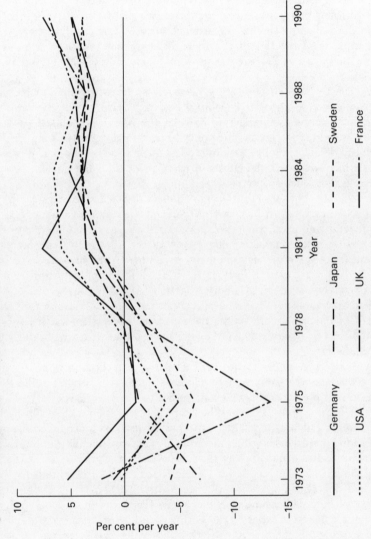

Source: OECD Hist Stats 1960–90, table 10.8.

political parties in office. Left-wing parties tend to draw support from social classes or groups which are different from those which represent the support base of right-wing parties. So left-wing parties in government are expected to differ sharply from right-wing parties in their choice of a 'Keynesian' or a 'monetarist' approach.

Such an explanation deserves some attention. It has a commonsense appeal. And politicians themselves stress the difference that party stripe can make to inflation and unemployment. For instance, before Margaret Thatcher became prime minister of the UK in 1979, she declared that her access to power in place of the previous Labour regime would change 'everything' (von Beyme 1984: 5).

What exactly party stripe changes, however, is surprisingly hard to determine with confidence. Comparative political scientists have now spent close to a quarter of a century investigating how far the nature of political parties in office is linked to macroeconomic policy. The difficulty in returning clear-cut answers to what seems like a simple question lies in the number of possible factors which may mask the effects of party stripe on policy and the problem of turning those factors into countable units.

For instance, how are coalition governments (which rule many of the EC states) to be categorized in terms of 'party stripe'? What about federal and quasi-federal countries, where no single party or party grouping controls all the levers for macroeconomic policy? How do we allow for varying weight of different factions within the same party over time? After all, a labourist party controlled by a right-wing faction will have different propensities from the same party controlled by a left-wing faction. And how do we compare the 'leftness' or 'rightness' of parties across countries? How do we allow for varying strength of interest groups or the nature of the opposition? Such issues are easy to raise, but typically take us beyond the realm of what we can easily turn into numbers.

The pioneering empirical work on the relationship between party stripe and macroeconomic policy was done by Douglas Hibbs (1977, 1982) in the 1970s. Hibbs set out on a path of systematic cross-national analysis of OECD data that later became well-trodden. The analysis began from a class approach to party support. Hibbs assumed that left-wing parties drew much of their support (in votes and campaign contributions) from lower socioeconomic groups, whereas right-wing parties drew much of their support from higher social classes. He also assumed that those of lower social classes (who by definition have few assets and investments) are most concerned with employment as the key to their well-being, while those of higher social classes are more concerned with inflation. He therefore expected right-wing parties to prefer to control inflation at the expense of unemployment, while left-wing parties prefer to protect employment at the expense of inflation.

This reasoning may seem robust enough at first sight. But it is not unchallengeable. Why should office-seeking political parties – of left or right – concentrate on policies which will reward their core supporters, who will presumably vote for them anyway? Would it not be more logical for vote-seeking parties to tune their macroeconomic policies to fit the demands of the middle-ground marginal voter? That is the expected result of party competition according to a theory first developed by Anthony Downs (1957), using an analogy with the spatial location of rival businesses. If party competition is indeed conducted in that way, we would expect the macroeconomic policies of different parties in office to *converge*, not diverge. And whether they converged on 'Keynesianism' or 'monetarism' would depend on where the marginal voters were and what their circumstances were. Hence it would be changes in location and/or economic circumstances of marginal voters which would account for a shift in macroeconomic policy, not changes in party incumbency alone.

However, Hibbs ignored this alternative line of reasoning and argued that the facts supported his hypotheses about the effects of party incumbency on macroeconomic policy. In cross-national comparisons, he claimed to find the expected link between party stripe and economic outcomes. In a study of twelve OECD countries, using data from the 1960s, he found that higher inflation and lower unemployment rates were indeed associated with countries regularly governed by 'left' parties, while countries regularly governed by 'right' parties revealed the expected pattern of higher unemployment and lower inflation rates (Hibbs 1977). But Hibbs' results were not replicated in later studies.

If we follow Hibbs, we would expect a shift from Keynesianism to monetarism to stem from a move from left-of-centre to right-of-centre political parties in government (which itself would merit some explanation). There are certainly some cases which fit such an expectation. But as a general explanation, it does not seem very plausible. The shift from Keynesianism to monetarism happened under 'left' as well as 'right' parties – for example, under Jimmy Carter's Democratic presidency in the USA and under James Callaghan's Labour premiership in the UK as well as under Reagan and Thatcher (Alt and Chrystal 1983: 116). Indeed, the link between party incumbency and the trade-off between unemployment and inflation which Hibbs had found using data from the 1960s could not be demonstrated from equivalent data from the 1970s.

Of course, even those who champion the 'party matters' explanation of macroeconomic policy will accept that the approach has its limitations. It will not account for periods when 'normal' party competition is suspended, notably during wars or major economic shocks. Could the 1970s and 1980s have been such a time? Some would certainly make that claim. It is often suggested that the 1970s were a time of exceptional volatility for OECD countries, with global economic disruption caused by a sudden twelve-fold increase in oil prices in that decade. And Hibbs' 'party matters' logic (even if it is accepted) may not apply to countries where economic policy settings are determined less by *domestic* party competition than the dictates of the world economy. So small open economies may virtually have to follow trends determined by powerful trading partners or competitors, irrespective of the party colour of their governments. Hibbs did not fit such 'coerced choices' into his analysis (Alt and Chrystal 1983: 117). But if such choices are allowed for, the theory would need to be modified to give extra weight to party competition within the 'pacemaker' countries in the world trading scene, and less weight to the 'follower' countries. Hence the consequences of political movement to the right in two of the three world locomotive economies (USA and Germany) in the early 1980s might be expected to shape the choices available to politicians governing smaller and weaker economies.

The political business cycle as a determinant of macroeconomic policy

A second conventional political science explanation of macroeconomic policy focuses on 'political business cycles' (PBCs). From this viewpoint, the crucial information needed to predict a democratic government's macroeconomic policy is not the name of the political parties in office, but the probable date of the next election and the standing of the incumbent party in the opinion polls. This approach follows popular folklore about the way that politicians are said to cunningly 'massage' the economy to improve their re-election chances. It suggests that governments choose a 'monetarist' game early in their term of office (when voters cannot punish government for inflicting economic pain), then switch to a 'Keynesian' game to deliver more jobs and fuller pay packets at election time, banking up the inflationary costs for the post-election period when voters have once again lost their power over politicians.

The term 'political business cycle' was originally coined by a Marxist economist, Michael Kalecki (1943). For Kalecki, it meant a tendency for the upswing of the 'normal' trade cycle to be damped by governments before the point of full employment is reached. Contrary to what Keynes had implied, Kalecki argued that it was not in the interests of big business to have permanent full employment. Such a pattern would push up general wage levels and squeeze pay differentials, threatening labour indiscipline and making management more difficult. Hence, while business interests would welcome pump-priming public spending in the depths of a recession, they would press for expenditure cuts well before the economy reached full employment.

However, Kalecki's ideas were left aside with the onset of the Keynesian era. Instead, the term 'political business cycle' came to be used in a quite different sense, building on Downs' seminal work, which was mentioned earlier. The aim was to predict how 'rational' politicians could be expected to manage macroeconomic policy to maximize their chances of winning elections. This approach involves four basic ideas, some of which relate to 'Chicago theory' economics-of-politics assumptions which have been discussed in previous chapters:

- Politicians are rational vote-seekers. They aim to win the next election so that they can continue to enjoy the fruits of office.
- Politicians choose economic policies during their incumbency to maximize their chances of victory at the next election.
- Politicians believe voters are selfish and preoccupied with the state of their own bank balances. Voters are assumed to make their decisions on election day mainly on 'pocket-book' considerations. That is, they reward or punish

incumbent parties depending on what is happening to their real disposable income.

• Politicians believe voters have short memories and no expectations. Voters are expected to make their choice at the ballot box on the basis of what has happened to them over the last few months before the election. Voters are not expected to decide on the basis of what has happened to their economic well-being over the *whole period* since the last election or even according to what they expect to happen *after* election day. Their expectations about the future are expected to be governed simply by what has happened to them in the very recent past. As Edward Tufte (1978: 10) puts it: 'The politicians' economic theory of election outcomes gives great weight to economic events in the months before the election; thus the politicians' strategy is to turn on the spigot surely and swiftly and fill the trough so that it counts with the electorate.'

This explanation of macroeconomic policy choices flowered in the 1970s, beginning with the work of William Nordhaus (1975). Nordhaus argued that immediately after an election the victorious party will raise unemployment to fight inflation. But as the next election approaches, unemployment will be reduced. Before long, falling unemployment will produce accelerating inflation. But there is assumed to be a 'window' or time-lag before this inevitable effect occurs.

The analogy is with the 'free credit' period available with most credit cards. Most readers will be familiar with that beguiling interest-free interval which comes between obtaining the goods and the time when the credit card company demands either that the debt be settled in full or that the cardholder borrows the money at the company's exorbitant interest rates. In pre-election periods, politicians are like cardholders going on a shopping spree and enjoying the goods they have taken home from the store during the free credit period. Immediately after the election, they choose to settle the bill in full – writing the cheque from the voters' taxes. Nordhaus tested this proposition by looking at the time pattern of unemployment rates in nine OECD countries from 1947 to 1972, but found little clear evidence of the expected effect. Only the data for Germany and the USA seemed to fit the expected pattern. The data for the remaining seven countries did not.

Edward Tufte (1978) developed a similar idea, with a study of electoral-economic cycles in twenty-seven democracies. He argued that incumbent politicians who believe that a booming pre-election economy will help to get them re-elected will reach for 'quick-acting' policy instruments to yield clear and immediate benefits to the mass electorate. A 'free credit' period, after all, is of little benefit if goods cannot be delivered until after the credit card company's bill comes in. Tufte claimed that the instruments which act most quickly on voters' disposable income are transfer payments, tax cuts and post-ponements of tax increases. In particular, 'The quickest way to produce an acceleration in real disposable income is for the government to mail more people larger checks – that is, for transfer payments to increase' (ibid.: 29).

Tufte claimed to find evidence of PBCs in nineteen (70 per cent) of the countries studied, in that short-run rises in real disposable income were more likely to occur in pre-election years than in other years. For the USA, he claimed to find a two-year 'Congressional' cycle in the growth of real disposable income and a four-year 'Presidential' cycle in the unemployment rate.

As with Hibbs' party-incumbency studies, the findings of Nordhaus and Tufte have been challenged by later writers and attempts to replicate their studies have failed to reach the same conclusions (see Alt and Chrystal 1983: 125; Whiteley 1986: 82). By 1991, in another careful review of PBC studies, Leif Lewin (1991: 63) argued that: 'research of the 1970s and 1980s gives only very weak support to the theory of political business cycles if, indeed, one can speak of support at all . . .'.

Moreover, as with Hibbs' ideas, the basic logic is highly questionable. It is ironical that an approach derived from the 'rational' approach to politics should assume voters to be so gullible and naive. Voters live only in the immediate present like newborn babes. Unlike even very young children, they have no capacity for dread and do not learn from experience. Such a picture hardly fits conventional assumptions about the behaviour of rational egoists (cf. Nordhaus 1989: 4). And if incumbent politicians are really the rational vote-seekers that the theory implies, would it not be more logical for them to target the marginal voters only for the key handouts, rather than a blunderbuss strategy of measures directed at all voters – confirmed supporters and implacable enemies as well as the waverers? After all, why waste hard-won resources on the people who will never vote for you or on those who will always vote for you, no matter what? The answer, presumably, must be two-fold. First, incumbent politicians do not *know* exactly who are the loyalists and who are the waverers (and rational voters will aim to keep politicians in the dark on that subject, for example by lying about their voting intentions in opinion polls). Second, politicians lack 'directional' policy instruments which will concentrate all the goodies on the former without squandering them on the latter. But neither of those conditions is cut into stone. Information resources can change. New policy instruments can be developed.

Both the Tufte and (early) Nordhaus approaches embodied the conventional economics of politics assumption that rational self-interested politicians are wholly concerned with re-election. As we saw in Chapter Two, that assumption can be challenged even from within the 'self-interest' framework. However, later approaches modified the assumption of pragmatic vote-seeking by introducing an 'ideological' element into politicians' preferences. Moreover, 'popularity' as well as election dates came to be introduced into the analysis.

Introducing 'ideology' means that politicians are treated as more than amoral vote-gathering machines. They have real preferences about public policy which are not just a by-product of the search for votes. Inside every pragmatic vote-seeker, it seems, is a 'conviction politician' struggling to get out. But, like child smokers who only light up when the expected risk of punishment is low, politicians can follow their ideological preferences only when the electoral coast is clear. When the electoral pressure is on, they have to put their conviction politics away and tailor policies to the preferences of marginal middle-ground voters.

In developing this idea, Bruno Frey and Friedrich Schneider (1982) suggest that political parties aim to pursue ideologically oriented policies, but can 'afford' to do so only when when their poll popularity is high enough to make them feel comfortable about their chances of re-election. Popularity is in turn, they suggest, mainly related to economic conditions in terms of inflation and unemployment.

When poll popularity drops below some critical figure, re-election panic bells sound and government switches from its preferred 'ideological politics' mode into 'pragmatic politics' mode. It will aim to improve economic conditions for the middle-ground voters, mainly by raising public spending, to get popularity back up to an acceptable level. Frey and Schneider developed their ideas using US data from 1953 to 1975, and later, jointly and severally, they applied the ideas in modified form to other countries (see, for example, Pommerehne and Schneider, 1983, for an Australian application).

Unlike the Hibbs party-incumbency explanation, the PBC approach can explain why 'left' governments as well as 'right' ones should sometimes adopt 'monetarist' macroeconomic policies. But it is open to the same objections as the party-incumbency approach. In particular, the dominance of one economy over others (for example, the effects of booms and busts in the big economies such as the USA, Germany and Japan) may completely cut across attempts at political 'massage' of the smaller ones whose economic fortunes depend on the larger world economic system.

Moreover, the 'popularity' factor introduced into the PBC model may drastically change expected behaviour. Presumably, under those conditions, rational voters could prevent governments from inflicting high economic pain after election victories (to pay the political credit card bill, as explained above). All that voters need to do in post-election opinion polls is register very low approval for the government they have just voted for. Popularity panic would then drive victorious politicians away from their preferred post-election 'settlement in full' strategy and into a strategy of spreading out the cost, which may in turn threaten their re-election. The simple logic of the PBC then starts to unravel.

Indeed, the whole PBC approach could be seen as an inherently 'self-destruct' phenomenon. Once the 'game' became known, both voters and other economic actors (notably international capital markets) would take compensatory action to counter the expected 'cycling' behaviour of politicians and reflect the expected post-electoral pain. The crucial 'free credit' period – the politically precious 'window' between action to reduce unemployment and the consequent inflation – would then disappear. And rational politicians in turn, anticipating such a response, would not attempt to produce a PBC. [Such behaviour would be consistent with economic ideas of 'rational expectations', and forms the basis of a strong critique of the PBC (Nordhaus 1989: 4).] If so, the PBC would either destroy itself as soon as it became established, never develop at all, or occasionally appear in the policy firmament like a comet, only to rapidly disappear again.

Once such modifications are introduced into the conventional PBC approach, the apparent extinction of Keynesian politics during the 1970s and 1980s might seem somewhat less surprising. The failure of incumbent parties to follow the traditional script of switching between Keynesian and monetarist strategies for electoral advantage at different points in the electoral cycle would simply reflect the fact that a PBC strategy, if not a 'one-shot' strategy, is one that could not be expected to operate repeatedly without breaking down. Apparently stable preferences for monetarist politics (even by 'left-of-centre' governments such as the Australian and New Zealand Labour parties) would then start to seem less politically inexplicable.

Moreover, apart from the 'self-destruct' elements which seem to lie at the heart of the model, the apparent extinction of Keynesian politics would not be a surprise for the PBC approach if it could be shown that conditions had changed in such a way that politicians' behaviour would be expected to be different even within the terms of that model. Three possible changes of circumstances might be candidates for this purpose. First, if incumbent governments could increase their electoral security (for instance, by developing more intensive and accurate polling techniques), it would be less necessary for them to pump up the whole economy in the run-up to elections. Second, and relatedly, if incumbents developed more efficient campaign technology, they might be able to win re-election through measures targeted only at marginal voters identified by polling techniques. Third, if socioeconomic or other changes took away the necessary macroeconomic management tools from national governments (in particular with the move towards more open economies and international constraints on government behaviour, notably by the EC), the *opportunity* to create PBCs would decrease even if the *motivation* remained strong. Even if the first two changes remain speculative, the third is commonly asserted to be a general trend. If so, the extinction of Keynesian politics may not so much indicate that the theory is wrong as that the conditions which it requires no longer exist.

The effect of entrenched institutional arrangements on economic policy

A third conventional political science approach focuses on the way that entrenched institutional structures and decision-making styles shape macroeconomic policy. Harold Wilensky and Lowell Turner (1987: 50) assert that, 'If the postwar history of . . . economic and social policies and their implementation tells us anything, it tells us that structures count.' But what exactly are 'structures'? How do they 'count'? And can 'structural' aspects help us to understand long-term shifts, or are they better fitted for explaining persistence of initial form and variations around a trend?

There are several variants of structure-oriented policy analysis in political science, and for macroeconomic policy two in particular have been developed. One is the 'state structures' approach, in which states are seen as autonomous actors with particular 'genetic codes' resulting from the long-term historical process which shaped their development. Policy choices are explained by a combination of accumulated 'policy legacies' from earlier eras and of the structure and capacity of the state. Those two factors in turn shape intellectual innovation in public policy, interest groups' and politicians' activity (cf. Hall 1990, 1992). Margaret Weir and Theda Skocpol (1985) have used this approach to explain different macroeconomic policy responses to the 1930s depression in Sweden, the USA and Britain. Their argument goes that it is not merely party political incumbency or electoral timing which shapes macroeconomic policy, but an underlying institutional structure which has developed some capacities but not others and hence has built-in biases for and against particular kinds of action. They say that the UK state structure at that time was closed against effective policy input from professional economists in a way that the Swedish state was not, meaning that Keynes had to work his ideas into an academic treatise, while his Swedish equivalents had ready access to the policy process.

Such an explanation has its attractions for explaining the details of difference or patterns of evolution in macroeconomic policy. But, even if its (contestable) historical accuracy was to be accepted, it is not easy to see how this approach can help us to explain the broad shift *away* from Keynesian politics in the 1970s and 1980s. We need an approach which can help us with broad reversals of trend, not the fine grain of policy differences among states. This approach tells us about why different types of dinosaurs developed, but not why the dinosaurs died out.

The other main 'structure matters' approach to macroeconomic policy is less concerned with the relative autonomy of state institutions than with the effects of different decision-making styles in terms of degrees of corporatism. 'Corporatism' is a word with many meanings. Loosely, it means the extent to which there are 'tripartite' institutional arrangements linking the state with peak associations of capital and labour. In the 1970s and 1980s, many political scientists argued that corporatism makes a key difference to macroeconomic policy, often in terms of superior macroeconomic performance as against non-corporatist rivals (see, for example, Schmidt 1982; Katzenstein 1985; Wilensky and Turner 1987). Specifically, states with a tradition of making economic policy in concertation with organized economic interests are claimed to be more capable of playing a 'Keynesian' game successfully than governments with a tradition of 'arm's-length' relationships with major economic interests.

Why does corporatism make a difference? There are several possible answers. Peter Katzenstein (1985: 32) claims that corporatism is a form of 'low-voltage politics', avoiding disruption from confrontational high-conflict politics. Low-voltage politics provides a stable, calm environment, which is particularly favourable for economic development. For Wilensky and Turner (1987), the causes are more specific. Corporatist democracies, they claim, show more policy continuity and policy linkage. Policy continuity means smooth progression of policy over time, without abrupt braking or crashing of gears. Policy linkage means that policies complement and relate to one another, rather than contradicting one another or developing in isolation. And policy continuity and linkage, they claim, are the crucial ingredients for success in a specific set of public policies – namely, incomes restraint policy, active labour market policy (training and job creation), industrial policy and social policies more generally. Manfred Schmidt (1982: 252–3) also suggests that corporatism is more likely to succeed in delivering effective wage restraint policies, thus creating favourable conditions for capital accumulation, as well as affecting policy through the 'demand' side, in that unemployment becomes more sensitive as a political issue in corporatist than in liberal states.

The corporatist approach to explaining macroeconomic policy outcomes boomed in political science during the later 1970s and early 1980s, attracting many followers (e.g. Shonfield 1984). But it has been heavily criticized, especially from the economics-of-politics school. Critics claim that the corporatist approach is inherently vague, that its basic elements are not specified clearly, and that categorization of states as corporatist or otherwise tends to be arbitrary. Moreover, it is not clear why corporatism should be a necessary condition for international economic competitiveness. Why can't a non-corporatist state with a permanent right-wing government (like Japan up to 1993) be able to achieve the same policy continuity as its corporatist rivals, and yet outpoint them because it is unencumbered by the constant need to 'square' labour union interests? Could not policy continuity be achieved by means other than corporatism – for instance, by institutional and constitutional arrangements making for coalition government (as in Switzerland) or by the effects of transnational institutions like the EC? And how can corporatist states avoid long-term processes of institutional sclerosis which threaten economic dynamism where interest groups are entrenched – according to Olson's (1982) argument, as discussed in Chapter One?

Nor are there just theoretical objections to the corporatist approach. During the 1980s, the macroeconomic facts started to rebel against the corporatist theories. By the early 1980s, even the 'flagship' corporatist countries had joined the general shift away from Keynesianism. Some of the star OECD macroeconomic performers, like Japan and Switzerland, were not corporatist in the ordinary sense, that is, they were not dominated by left-wing parties and organized labour was weak and fragmented. Some 'model' corporatist macroeconomic performers of the 1970s, like Sweden, got into trouble in the 1980s, and Goran Therborn (1987) found little evidence that corporatism 'made a difference' to macroeconomic outcomes in OECD countries over the period 1973–85. Indeed, New Zealand, counted by some of the corporatist writers (such as Schmidt 1982) as a corporatist state, performed so dismally in macroeconomic terms that the corporatist structure collapsed.

Like the state-centric model, the corporatist model is better geared to explaining detailed variations in policy style than across-the-board change. To be relevant in explaining that shift, it needs to be developed in some way which shows why corporatism seemed not to 'matter' in the 1980s in the same way as it had done in the 1970s.

Table 4.1 Three conventional accounts of macroeconomic policy choices: expectations, surprises and possible surprise-free modifications

Explanation	Conditions in which Keynesianism dies	Surprise	Possible alternative surprise-free formulation
Hibbs-type 'party matters'	Widespread shift from left-wing to right-wing parties in office	Shift occurred under left-wing as well as right-wing parties	Party competition centring on middle-ground voters
Nordhaus/ Tufte political business cycle	After elections or when incumbents are secure of re-election	Seemingly permanent extinction	Re-election strategies built on benefits targeted at key marginal groups
Katzenstein-type 'corporatism matters'	Not specified	Shift occurred under corporatist as well as non-corporatist states	Short-term and long-term dynamic of corporatism may have different effects

Keynesian policy extinction as a theoretical 'surprise'

Like deregulation, it could be claimed that the extinction of Keynesian macroeconomic politics posed a major surprise to each of these three conventional political science approaches. Those surprises are summarized in Table 4.1.

For the Hibbs-type 'party matters' approach, the major surprise is the fact that the policy shift is not clearly associated with a general move to right-wing incumbency in government, and that several left-of-centre governments took up the new approach just as vigorously as right-of-centre ones. For the Nordhaus-type political business cycle approach, the major surprise is the fact that the shift to monetarism was more than an ephemeral post-election phase, and that some governments have held onto office with unemployment levels that would have rendered them 'un-re-electable' in the 1950s and 1960s. For the 'structure counts' approach, the major surprise is that corporatist states have adopted the shift to monetarism as well as 'arm's-length' liberal states, and that state structures and policy legacies seem to have affected details rather than the broad direction of policy.

But was the 'surprise' caused by changed underlying circumstances or by inherent defects in the theories? Would alternative or 'reconstructed' versions of the theories face equal 'surprise' at the extinction of Keynesianism?

As has been suggested above, fairly minor modifications of each of the three approaches might remove much of that 'surprise'. For instance, once we introduce into corporatist theory the idea that corporatism, like any other institutional arrangement, can reach a 'sell-by' date, and that arrangements which produce stability in one era can produce sclerosis in another, the fact that corporatism did not seem to be a clear 'win window' for macroeconomic policy in the 1980s becomes easier to understand. Likewise, if we modify Hibbs' model by introducing internationally 'coerced' choices and a process of party competition targeted at the marginal middle-ground voter, convergence on different policies will no longer be a major surprise if a few key international players shift strategy or conditions change for domestic middle-ground voters.

Again, if we introduce rational voters into the political business cycle model, it will not be a surprise if there is no clear alternation between Keynesian and monetarist macroeconomic politics. Or if, in a rather more radical reconstruction, we revert to Kalecki's ideas about the political business cycle, the ending of the short-lived era of Keynesian politics in the 1970s might appear as a case of capitalism reverting to type after the long disturbance of the Second World War. By 'reverting to type' is meant dominance of public policy by big business interests, without effective power in the hands of other groups and specifically of trade union interests.

However, it could also be suggested that underlying circumstances changed, meaning that the change in behaviour can at least be retrospectively explained from each of these approaches. Hibbs' 'party matters' theory is built on two implicit assumptions. First, governments have a high degree of 'economic sovereignty', controlling the whole range of macroeconomic policy instruments mentioned at the outset of this chapter, from tariff policy to interest rate adjustments. Second, governments make political choices against a relatively 'benign' international macroeconomic backdrop (expanding world trade, cheap raw materials and energy). If governments start to lose effective control over some of the key macroeconomic levers (for example, with global trade liberalization removing the tariff weapon and global financial deregulation setting capital free to emigrate from high tax, high labour cost economies), very different outcomes can be expected. Similarly, if the global macroeconomic environment becomes 'malign', with more intense economic competition among states, the range of 'satisfactory' macroeconomic choices available to politicians will narrow. If both circumstances change at once, it would hardly be surprising if domestic party competition comes to be overshadowed by global economic pressures.

The same shift in circumstances also makes changed behaviour less surprising from the viewpoint of the other two approaches. If the traditional macroeconomic controls on which the corporatist low-voltage accord rests start to disappear or decline in efficacy, it is not surprising to find the results of corporatism altering. And if the same circumstances produce an environment in which a quick pre-election blow-out in public spending immediately triggers currency collapse and higher interest rates in anticipation of rising inflation, the incumbent politicians' 'credit card' has in effect been withdrawn. Once all pre-election goods have to be paid for on delivery, it is not surprising if politicians stop operating a conventional PBC.

Fritz Scharpf's 'concertation game' approach

It may be, then, that we do not really need to depart from the traditional lines of explanation to explain the Keynesian extinction, if the elements of those explanations can be modified or synthesized a little. Fritz Scharpf (1987) has indeed recombined parts of the familiar trio – party incumbency, PBC and institutions – to develop a more dynamic explanation of macroeconomic policy. He argues that it would be implausible to expect a single set of institutional arrangements to deliver favourable results for macroeconomic performance for ever. Life is not like that. As the macroeconomic problems faced by industrialized countries alter, so do the institutional and policy preconditions for success. Hence, he claims, we can explain why party incumbency seemed to make a difference to macroeconomic policy in the 1960s but not in the 1970s and why corporatism seemed to make a difference in the 1970s but not in the 1980s, by reference to the changing 'fundamentals' of the macroeconomic policy problem.

The argument goes that the global economic environment for OECD countries in the 1960s was generally 'benign' (as noted earlier). So politicians could choose among a range of positions on the unemployment–inflation spectrum, all of which were still 'satisfactory' in terms of macroeconomic performance. In these circumstances, it is not surprising that left-wing governments would tend to choose a different trade-off from right-wing governments, and hence Hibbs' 'party matters' conclusions drawn from 1960s data are plausible, even if hard to replicate.

But, as was also noted earlier, the 1970s macroeconomic policy environment suddenly became less benign. The oil price 'shocks' of that decade pushed up inflation (by cost pressures) and increased unemployment (because of the demand gap caused by OPEC oil-exporting countries not immediately spending their new wealth) *simultaneously*. Hence traditional approaches to macroeconomic policy built on the assumption that inflation varied inversely with unemployment did not work well any more.

The OECD countries could only get out of this mess, according to Sharpf, by adding a new policy instrument to their standard repertoire. To succeed, they had to go beyond the use of fiscal and monetary policy measures alone to influence wage settlements directly. Only by wage restraint could inflation caused by cost pressures be lessened without causing massive unemployment. Since countries with corporatist bargaining arrangements were best placed to deliver such wage restraint, it is not surprising that their performance in terms of unemployment rates and economic growth tended to be superior in the 1970s. If so, it would both explain why Hibbs-type 'party matters' approaches did not seem to work so well in the 1970s as in the 1960s *and* why corporatism became important during the 1970s.

However, by the 1980s, the conditions changed again. Once OECD governments had generally shifted to monetarism, wage restraint no longer depended on centralized collective bargaining. Decentralized and fragmented trade union movements were just as likely to moderate wage claims in such circumstances as centralized ones, simply because it is in their interest to do so. Hence we would expect the corporatist model to lose its explanatory lustre in such conditions.

Scharpf's explanation of how the Keynesian game comes to turn into a monetarist game is based on a nested game-theory model. He argues that macroeconomic policy can be interpreted as a 'concertation game', in which the main players are labour unions and elected governments. It is a 'concertation' game, because the joint outcome depends on the strategic choices made by each of the main participants. The game is portrayed in Table 4.2. Labour unions choose between moderate and aggressive wage strategies, while governments choose between Keynesian or monetarist politics. Each cell of the game therefore represents a different macroeconomic position in terms of inflation and unemployment.

The argument goes that if government follows a 'Keynesian' game of making full employment the top priority, labour unions are better off selecting an 'aggressive' rather than a 'moderate' wage strategy. But if government adopts a 'monetarist' game, labour unions are better off selecting a 'moderate' rather than an 'aggressive' strategy.

The question then is, what makes government choose a 'Keynesian' or a 'monetarist' strategy? The answer lies partly in the process of party political competition within this overall 'game'. Here Scharpf views party competition in class terms, which are broadly similar to Hibbs' approach described earlier. He assumes that party competition takes place between a left-of-centre party and a right-of-centre party. He divides the voters into three groups. The top segment consists of self-employed professionals, managers, entrepreneurs and *rentiers* whose fortunes are not directly affected by general movements in the labour market, but depend mainly on business profits and rates of return on capital assets. This group, Sharpf assumes, have much to fear from Keynesian macroeconomic policies, for the reasons Kalecki gave, and will always support monetarist politics. At the other extreme is a propertyless group which depends on relatively insecure jobs and government welfare benefits. This group will always support Keynesian politics.

So the group which swings the balance, according to Scharpf, is a middle stratum of voters who depend on earnings from skilled blue- and white-collar jobs but who also own property, especially in owner-occupied housing. This group does *not* have a *general* preference for either Keynesian or monetarist policy. It feels threatened by high inflation (although as a group it may profit from house price inflation) but also by high unemployment. Scharpf assumes that this group's jobs are more secure than those of the bottom stratum of voters, but these people have further to fall on losing them and hence have greater dread of unemployment.

Scharpf argues that this group will support incumbent parties at the ballot box in the economic circumstances of cell (1) of Table 4.2 irrespective of whether a 'left' party or a 'right' party holds office. He also argues that this group will vote against incumbents in the conditions of cell (4) whichever type of government is in power. Hence cell (1) is a 'win' window for a government of either stripe and cell (4) is a no-win window for either type of party.

Table 4.2 Scharpf's politics/coordination game

Government game	Union game		
	Moderate		Aggressive

Keynesian

(1)

Economic outcome
Inflation: moderate
Unemployment: low

Political reaction

Voter group			Govt party
top	middle	lower	
−	+	+	left
(+)	+	−	right

(2)

Economic outcome
Inflation: very high
Unemployment: low

Political reaction

Voter group			Govt party
top	middle	lower	
−	+	+	left
(+)	?	−	right

Monetarist

(3)

Economic outcome
Inflation: low
Unemployment: high

Political reaction

Voter group			Govt party
top	middle	lower	
−	?/+	(+)	left
+	−/+	−	right

(4)

Economic outcome
Inflation: high
Unemployment: very high

Political reaction

Voter group			Govt party
top	middle	lower	
−	−	(+)	left
+	−	−	right

Source: Scharpf (1987: 244).

Key: +, positive voting reaction to party in government; −, negative; (+), reluctant *faute de mieux* support for party in government; ?, indeterminate or doubtful support; ?/+, positive voting reaction to party in government if cell (3) entered from cell (4), but indeterminate or doubtful if entered from cell (1); −/+, positive voting reaction to party in government if cell (3) entered from cell (4), but negative if entered from cell (1).

Scharpf argues that the middle group of voters have asymmetrical preferences in terms of party choice in cells (2) and (3) of Table 4.2. In cell (2), characterized by low unemployment and high inflation, the centre group is more likely to move from a left government to a right opposition than vice-versa, because those voters would assume that inflation would worsen with a switch from right government to left opposition. A right party will thus have more 'inflation credibility' than a left party in those circumstances. Hence this cell is a no-win window for a left government but not for a right government.

On the face of it, we might expect the opposite type of asymmetry from the middle group of voters in the circumstances of cell (3), that is, a preference for a shift from a right government to a left opposition but not the reverse, since a left party will have more credibility on employment creation than a right party. However, Scharpf argues that such an effect will only occur when high unemployment is a relatively new phenomenon, as it was for most Western economies in the mid-1970s. He argues that after high unemployment has persisted for some time, its political implications change. The argument goes that the reality of mass unemployment does not affect the overwhelming majority of the middle group of voters, because their jobs turn out to be fairly secure. Once that security becomes apparent, self-interest will lead middle-level voters to support right-wing governments as well as left-wing governments in conditions of low inflation and high unemployment. So mass unemployment becomes politically invisible.

This model shows a political dynamic which will tend to transform Keynesian macroeconomic policy into monetarism. That is, if government is firmly committed to a Keynesian strategy, unions will be better off adopting an aggressive wage policy, pushing the game into cell (2). A right-wing government might achieve re-election in those circumstances, so it might be reluctant to take the risky step of switching from Keynesianism to monetarism, which will take the game into the no-win circumstances of cell (4). But a left-wing government which gets pushed into cell (2) is almost certain to lose office, on Scharpf's argument. So its choice is either to sit tight and wait to lose the election or – more boldly – to switch from a Keynesian to a monetarist game. Taking the latter course involves going into the dangerous no-win territory of cell (4). But whereas the former course is certain electoral suicide, the other strategy offers the hope that unions will have moderated their wage strategy in response to the government's strategy shift in order to move the game into cell (3) – electorally viable for a left-wing government – by the time the election comes.

Hence we might expect left-wing governments to be just as likely as right-wing ones to switch from Keynesianism to monetarism for reasons of electoral survival and not just of following the economic fashions. And once cell (3) has been reached, with middle-ground voters tolerant of high unemployment, there are major risks for a government of either political stripe in moving back to a Keynesian strategy [cell (1)], because of the danger of a switch in union strategy pushing the game back into cell (2).

Conclusion

Among economists, the story of the move from Keynesianism to monetarism is conventionally seen as a case of intellectual developments which changed the world. Milton Friedman, the high priest of monetarism, is popularly cast in the role of 'meteorite'. From this viewpoint, the extinction of Keynesianism is understandable in terms of the cumulative development of economic theory, with new ideas winning the argument and displacing their discredited rivals in the race for publications, research grants, preferment and prestige in the policy shops.

Certainly, intellectual developments were dramatic in this area, and (in contrast to privatization) it could not be said that policy developed before its rationale had been worked out. The implication of stressing the role of generic ideas in the extinction of Keynesian policy is to put relatively little weight on the long-run role of 'politics', in the sense of which political parties are dominant, how electoral strategies and institutional arrangements shape policy development. Rather, it is the technical quality of reasoning and evidence underlying rival approaches to macroeconomic management that determines which approach gets the ascendancy, not the packaging or the social context (for a lucid introduction to the economic theories of Keynesianism and monetarism, see Alt and Chrystal 1983: 54–69). Some political scientists also share this view, as shown in the epigraph to this chapter, where Paul Whiteley argues that the shift from Keynesianism to monetarism is most convincingly explained in terms of changing styles of economic thought.

But it seems doubtful if ideas alone carried the day in the 'extinction' of Keynesianism. Should we rule out more conventional political science accounts of the determination of macroeconomic policy quite so easily? As was suggested earlier, once we clarify the operating assumptions of those accounts a little, the change from Keynesianism to monetarism becomes much less puzzling. It looks much more like a case of 'habitat loss' arising from altered global conditions. The Keynesian politics option depended on a habitat of benign world macroeconomic conditions and hands-on control of a range of policy instruments by national governments. Once that habitat started to disappear, the Keynesian dinosaur went into extinction.

Moreover, a 'self-destruct' interpretation of the change also has to be seriously considered against the 'intellectual meteorite' view. The story could well be told in terms of policy 'ageing' or 'wearing out', as discussion in earlier sections has suggested. Such an interpretation is central to Scharpf's interpretation, as we have seen. He shows how Keynesian policies adopted by left-of-centre incumbents in Hibbs' approach can self-destruct if labour unions rack up progressively higher wage demands (knowing that members' jobs cannot be threatened by an aggressive wage strategy as long as governments follow the Keynesian script).

However, apart from the generalized rise of the 'New Right', it seems harder to identify specific interest coalition changes which helped to bring about extinction in a sense analogous to the 'privatization complex' in hunting old-style public enterprise to extinction or corporate users in pushing for deregulation. Hence in this area, the extinction factors would seem to be some combination of intellectual developments, contextual change and wearing out processes – perhaps taking us into sector (j) of the possible combinations depicted in Fig. 1.2.

The importance of Scharpf's work is that it provides a reconstructed explanation of a major policy shift by incorporating elements of each of the three conventional political science approaches, as discussed earlier. That is, it includes assumptions about the economic policy predilections of different political parties, the economic conditions needed for an incumbent party to gain re-election, and the effects of particular decision-making styles on macroeconomic policy. It sets a new standard for liberal political science explanations of macroeconomic policy. Its fairly precise specification contrasts with 'thick theory' institutionalism, in which almost any outcome can be 'explained' *ex post* by something vaguely described as institutional forces.

However, the Scharpf model still leaves some questions unanswered. It does not tell us why the relative fall in world oil prices in the 1980s did not lead industrial countries back into the partisan politics associated with the 'benign' conditions of the 1960s (unless the downturn in unemployment rates shown in Fig. 4.1 for the later 1980s reflects a more 'benign' environment). Why was there not a return to the familiar 'Phillips curve' trade-off of unemployment and inflation in which a Hibbs-type 'party matters' explanation would come back into its own, with 'left' party governments able to choose in relative comfort a different point on the inflation–unemployment curve than right party governments?

Moreover, even in its own terms, could the Scharpf model already be showing its age? It seems that unemployment became more 'democratized' in the early 1990s, with middle-class jobs more vulnerable than in the previous decade. In those conditions, Scharpf's assumptions about the asymmetry of the party preferences of the middle stratum of voters when the coordination game is in the high unemployment/low inflation cell [cell (3) in Table 4.2] may no longer hold. Indeed, in these circumstances, a left opposition might well be able to take substantial numbers of middle-stratum votes away from an incumbent right government. A shift from a right government to a left opposition would then be entirely plausible in that cell. The failure of Republican President George Bush to gain re-election in the 1992 US Presidential election, and his defeat at the hands of the Democrat contender Bill Clinton, would be consistent with such a change. If such a trend develops, the Keynesian dinosaur may be on the way back.

What Scharpf has shown, however, is that we do not need to invoke economic meteorites to explain the extinction of Keynesianism. We can understand the process in more conventional political-science terms, if we pay closer attention to changes in policy habitat and to self-destruct policy dynamics than the pioneers of those conventional approaches chose to do.

5

Government spending and employment: must what goes up come down?

> It [= the apparatus of the state] grows everywhere, whatever the political method a nation may adopt. Its expansion is the one certain thing about our future.
>
> Schumpeter (1952: 294)

> There is nothing inevitable or inexorable about the growth of government.
>
> Peltzman (1980: 287)

Introduction: flattening government growth curves and explanations of long-term government growth

Joseph Schumpeter's confident assertion (that continued growth of public bureaucracy is the one certain thing about our future) commanded ready assent when his epoch-making book *Capitalism, Socialism and Democracy* first appeared in 1944. Indeed, as early as the 1870s, Adolph Wagner (1883) had developed 'Wagner's Law' of public spending, which stated that government expenditure would grow in relative terms with economic development. So, in a world of industrialization and economic growth, government growth was as inevitable as death and taxes.

This idea challenged the views of nineteenth-century writers like Auguste Comte who thought social change would make government *smaller*, not larger. Even Karl Marx expected the state to wither away when capitalism collapsed, because without a ruling class and a ruled class, there would be no need for the state's coercive apparatus. But Wagner proved a more accurate prophet than Comte or Marx. And the Schumpeterian/Wagnerian view of the <u>inevitability</u> of long-term government growth became the orthodox position in the social sciences. But the logic underlying these ideas is far from unassailable. Aaron Wildavksy (1985: 232) claims that every argument for government growth as inexorable can be matched with an equally plausible counter-argument.

Today, we cannot even be sure that long-term government growth is continuing. The collapse of Communist regimes in Europe and the former USSR seems like an attempt to move radically in the opposite direction. Even in the more comfortable OECD world, it is doubtful whether public bureaucracy, in terms of government *employment*, 'grows everywhere whatever the political method a nation may adopt'. Figures 5.1–5.4 show data for five OECD countries and the OECD as a whole for 1960–90. A lot seems to depend on what cases are selected, what precise definition of 'government growth' is chosen and over what time period.

The clearest evidence of long-term growth comes in the growth of tax revenue (tax policy is discussed in the next chapter) and social security transfers as a proportion of gross domestic product (GDP). But for the countries in Figs 5.1–5.4, the relative growth of government *employment* tends to flatten out, and, with the important exception of Sweden (which peaks later), there is little evidence of substantial growth between the late 1970s and 1990. Something similar can be seen for government final consumption expenditure relative to GDP, though here again Sweden is exceptional. 'Wagner's Law' does not seem to apply within the OECD world today, and some even claim that it is going into reverse (see Gould 1983).

What do these flattening growth curves mean? Interpretations vary. To some, those curves might indicate another policy dinosaur on its way out – that is, the era of apparently inexorable government growth. Perhaps the flattening curves herald a shift to the kind of 'smaller government' that the New Right would like to see (see Naisbitt 1982; Macrae 1984; Flora 1986: xxii–xxiii). Against that, it must be said that the move as yet is, at most, from growth to stabilization. Up to now, there has been no general, sustained and substantial decline in the aggregate size measures shown in Figs 5.1–5.4. One famous interpretation of long-term public spending growth in the UK sees the process as a staircase – a series of sharp rises from one tread to the next, followed by a plateau at which public spending settles down for a while before climbing to the next tread (Peacock and Wiseman 1961). From that perspective, the 1980s stabilization might be interpreted as just another 'normal' plateau between peaks and nothing more.

But to the extent that the slowing of government growth *does* suggest a move towards extinction of earlier trends, would such an extinction undermine established ideas about what makes government grow? As we have seen, in other policy areas, the 1980s changes were claimed by some to represent a radical 'surprise' for orthodox explanations of policy trends, showing that those ideas were misconceived and out-of-date. Does that apply in this case? Do we need new ways of explaining the move from government growth to stabilization and cutback? Or can the established ideas explain why growth should occur in some conditions but not in others?

As we will see, there is no single accepted explanation of long-term government growth. Indeed, as noted earlier, Wildavsky claims that most received explanations rest on a shaky *ad hoc* logic. Even if that claim is rejected, the variety of available explanations is such that a move from growth to stabilization (if that is what we are really seeing) would be far more surprising for some approaches than for others. And for yet others that slowdown of growth represents no surprise at all, but exactly what would be predicted.

Figure 5.1 Government employment as % of total employment 1960–90

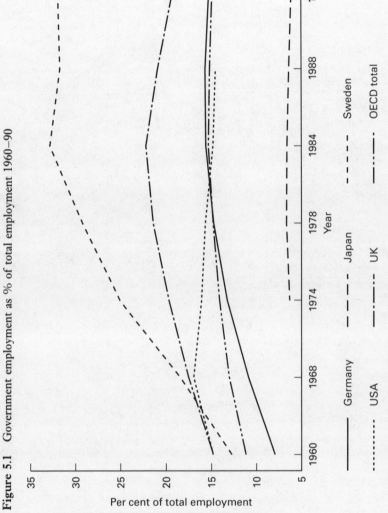

Germany —————— Japan – – – – Sweden – – – – –

USA .... UK –·–·–·– OECD total –··–··–··–

Source: OECD Hist Stats 1960–90, table 2.13.

Figure 5.2 Government final consumption expenditure as % of GDP 1960–90

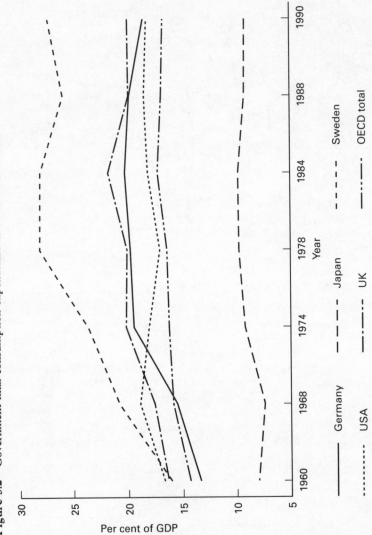

Source: OECD Hist Stats 1960–90, table 6.2.

Figure 5.3 Social security transfers as % of GDP 1960–90

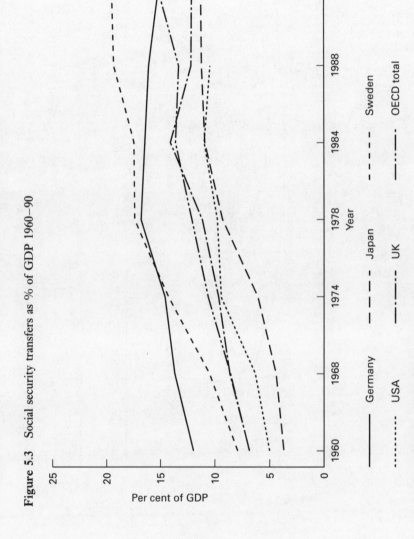

Germany ————————

USA ·················

Japan – – – –

UK —·—·—·—

Sweden – – – –

OECD total —··—··—

Source: OECD Hist Stats 1960–90, table 6.3.

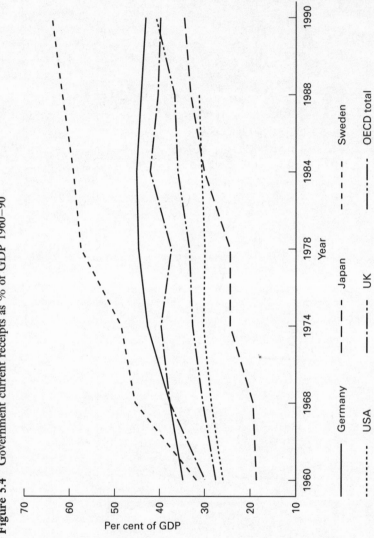

Figure 5.4 Government current receipts as % of GDP 1960–90

Germany ——— Japan – – – Sweden - - - -

USA ········· UK –·–·– OECD total –··–··–

Source: OECD Hist Stats 1960–90, table 6.6.

Accordingly, this chapter reviews some of the major conventional explanations of government growth to see what they can say about 1980s stabilization and cutbacks. We look at thirteen classes of received explanations of government growth, which are summarized in Table 5.1. The reader will need to refer to this table to keep track of the discussion below. We look at each of the thirteen types in turn, exploring what conditions are held to prompt government growth, and what if any are the extinction conditions – the circumstances in which government spending and employment could be expected to stabilize or fall.

Explanations of growth which preclude extinction

Any extinction of the pattern of long-term government growth in spending and employment would indeed be a major surprise for the first group of theories shown in Table 5.1. For them, government growth is irreversible. There can be pauses, plateaux but not real reductions. Of course, at some point, there must logically be built-in limits, in that government growth must tail-off when bureaucracy reaches some maximum size – though where exactly that maximum lies is obviously debatable (see Meyer *et al.* 1985). But absolute or relative shrinkage is 'unthinkable' from these viewpoints.

There are at least three variants of 'irreversible growth' theory. One is the idea that government grows because legal and bureaucratic regulation simply feeds upon itself. Bureaucracy is its own cause, we might say, paraphrasing Wildavsky (1980). Oliver MacDonagh's classic *A Pattern of Government Growth* (1961) depicts a process of self-fulfilling regulatory expansion, and accounts of an ever-developing 'juridification' (substitution of legal formalism for informal regulation) from authors such as Niklas Luhmann (1985) seem to suggest the same. At first sight, any check on government growth might seem to fly in the face of such ideas. But it is not very clear why a relentless drive to juridified regulation should necessarily translate into corresponding relative increases in public spending and employment. In many circumstances, it might generate less extra employment in the public sector than in the private sector, creating more work for lawyers and those who offer compliance services. Indeed, regulation can often be *substituted* for public spending and employment, as in the case of privatization of utilities considered in Chapter Three, by funding the process through 'compliance costs' on regulatees, or by using private actors for enforcement (for example, in planning law).

A second approach sees government spending as a ratchet turning only in one direction. In its modern form, this idea begins with Alan Peacock and Jack Wiseman's (1961) classic explanation of UK government spending growth, as mentioned earlier. Peacock and Wiseman argued that sudden social crises (mainly wars) make the public accept higher taxes, but once accepted, higher tax levels become permanent. Later, James Buchanan and Richard Wagner (1977) coined the term 'asymmetrical stabilization policy behaviour' to suggest that governments raise spending to bring down unemployment in a slump, but

Table 5.1   Thirteen types of explanation of government growth

No.	Type of explanation	Feature	Focus	Conditions for government growth	Conditions for government contraction
1	Bureaucracy as its own cause	non-reversible	S/D	response to self-generated problems	none
2	Government growth as a ratchet	non-reversible	S/D	social crises/ bidding for votes	none
3	New industrial state	non-reversible	S/D	longer investment lead-times/business concentration	none
4	Social mobilization	contingent on climate/habitat	D	long peace/ better communications/ industrialization/ wider franchise	social disruption; invasion/defeat
5	Inertia commitments	contingent on climate/habitat	D	growth of entitled groups	contraction/change in entitled groups
6	Public–private productivity gap	contingent on climate/habitat	S	economic growth/type of technology	economic decline/ type of technology
7	Linear growth-linked explanations	contingent on climate/habitat	D	economic growth	reversal of economc growth
8	Curvilinear growth-linked explanations	auto-destructible	S/D	economic growth	continuing economic growth
9	Electoral winning coalition	auto-destructible	D	median voter has less than mean income	median voter has mean (or higher) income
10	Client politics	auto-destructible	D	rent-seeking groups press key legislators for more public funds	lobby group develops for contracting out of public services

Table 5.1 (Cont.)

No.	Type of explanation	Feature	Focus	Conditions for government growth	Conditions for government contraction
11	Fiscal extractive capacity	auto-destructible	S	growth of large firms within the national unit	growth of selfemployment, MNCs and small firms
12	Cultural change	catalyst for other growth or contraction factors	S/D	hierarchist or egalitarian culture sets Nos 4–11 to growth	individualist culture sets Nos 4–11 to reverse growth
13	Change in sociotechnical system	catalyst for other growth or contraction factors	S/D	'industrialism' triggers growth conditions in Nos 4, 6, 7/8, 9, 11	post-industrialism sets Nos 6, 9, 11, possibly 4 and 8, to reverse growth

Key: S, focus on supply side of government growth; D, focus on demand side of government growth; S/D, focus includes both demand and supply factors.

do not make corresponding cuts to reduce inflation in a boom (see also Rose and Peters 1978: 135). But it is not clear why only one-way movement is possible, or whether the idea is an empirical generalization or a deductive theory, or something in between. In fact, Peacock and Wiseman (1961: 28) did consider briefly the possibility that the ratchet might operate in reverse, with spending being pushed down instead of up. But they did not develop the idea. No doubt it seemed far-fetched in the early 1960s.

A third variant is the view that government growth is an inexorable product of concentration of market power into fewer and bigger mega-corporations – a process which is itself seen as an irreversible aspect of capitalist development. The best-known version of this explanation is John Kenneth Galbraith's (1967) account of 'the new industrial state'. For Galbraith, relative government growth stems from the institutional instability of an economy controlled by a smaller number of giant firms which itself is the product of changes in the economics of production and distribution.

From such viewpoints, the stabilization of government spending and employment in many OECD countries in the 1980s would not necessarily be a surprise. After all, as noted earlier, government growth has to reach a limit somewhere. Actual downturns, however, are much more of a surprise. And even stabilization is not very satisfactorily explained by these approaches. For instance, why did stabilization cut in at such very different relative sizes of government in different OECD countries (as shown in Figs 5.1–5.4)? Why should the spending ratchet stop turning at close to 30 per cent of GDP for some countries and at less than 10 per cent for others? Are the limits temporary or permanent? What exactly defines them, and how do we know when they have been reached?

Environmentally contingent explanations of government growth

The second set of explanations in Table 5.1 have more application to the last question. This quartet of ideas are explanations of government growth which can turn into extinction if the social climate changes. Government growth depends on a favourable social habitat. So extinction of growth is no major surprise; it simply reflects changing environmental conditions.

Social mobilization and government size

One well-known explanation of this type relates government growth to 'social mobilization'. The most common argument is that social development (through urbanization and improved communication facilities) creates ever-more 'rent-seeking' interest groups able to press on government's electoral windpipe, as in Deutsch's (1961: 498–9) account. A simple example is the way that the advent of cheap Japanese bicycles in pre-Second World War Malaya helped Chinese rubber plantation workers to bring more effective political pressure on the colonial government of those days. Such a process must be to some extent logically self-limiting. The limits come in at the point where effective cross-pressures start to cancel one another out, so that government growth flattens. Such an effect is expected in the ideas which developed in the 1970s about the onset of government 'overload' and 'pluralist stagnation' (see Rose and Peters 1978).

However, a social mobilization explanation of government growth is not simply self-limiting, like the accounts considered in the last section. If there were to be social *de*mobilization, we could expect government growth to reverse. But is social demobilization itself possible, or is that another inexorable one-way process? Not according to Mancur Olson (1982), whose ideas were discussed in Chapter One. Olson argues that social mobilization can be destroyed by social upheaval or invasion destroying collective-action organizations. And though no developed theory of social demobilization yet exists, such a process might also possibly stem from less cataclysmic 'post-industrial' social trends like suburbanization, the professionalization (and 'mass mediaization') of politics or the supersession of broadcasting by 'narrowcasting'.

Inertia commitments

A second set of 'habitat' explanations links public spending growth to the way demography affects entitlements established by law, such as age pensions or family benefits. 'You don't miss what you've never had', says the proverb. And the converse is that taking away established entitlements will rarely be success-ful because it provokes massive political resistance. So government grows as entitlements build up and demography changes their impact.

For example, when public retirement pensions were introduced in the UK in 1908, life-expectancy was well below the age of pension entitlement. So only a lucky minority could expect to live to collect their winnings (such as they were) from the state. But now mean expectation of life at birth is five to ten years *above* the age of pension entitlement, causing the pension budget to blow out and presaging crisis early in the next century when the post-Second World War baby boomers start to line up for retirement pensions. Several researchers have found demography to be important in explaining public spending growth (see, for example, Borcherding 1977; Rose and Peters 1978: 54, 114; Delorme and André 1983: 106–107).

But if demographic and other changes can explain public spending growth, they also imply conditions for stabilization and contraction. Inertia commitments could shrink government in at least two ways. One is a *reduction* in the size of key entitlement groups resulting from demographic changes or economic growth. For instance, economic growth may remove some people from entitlement to income-tested benefits. However, some demographic changes may push the pressures for spending growth into reverse. For example, falling birth rates may cut demand for maternity and child-related services and benefits.

Even the assumption that established entitlements are sacrosanct can be challenged. Democratically elected governments have been known to cut entitlement benefits (and gained re-election subsequently, contrary to the folk-lore). Examples include the introduction of asset testing for age pensions in Australia and New Zealand in the mid-1980s and the substitution of health care charges for service free at the point of delivery by Japan in 1984. Inertia commitments can self-destruct as a result of the very spending blowouts which they create.

Government size and technological development

Third, government spending growth is often explained as a result of techno-logical development. Technological change is usually claimed to shape govern-ment spending and employment either through its effects on private sector productivity relative to that of the public sector, or through its effects on creating or destroying market imperfections.

The idea of a gap in productivity growth between the public and private sectors is one of the best-known explanations by economists of government spending growth, and is usually associated with William Baumol (1967). The basic idea is that government work tends to be more labour-intensive than work in agriculture and industry. So, as the economy grows, the public sector stays just as labour-intensive as ever per unit of output, while productivity grows in the other sectors. The conventional analogy is with a Beethoven symphony, which needs as many musicians to play it today as when it was first written. On these assumptions, it follows that a rising proportion of society's resources must flow into the public sector to keep public services constant per unit of output in the economy as a whole. The process reaches its ceiling when practically everyone works for government and economic growth stops.

But the argument depends on technology shaping productivity in a particular way, which is more redolent of the age of steam than that of microchips. And it is not difficult to turn the argument around by imagining technological change which could *extinguish* government growth, not fuel it. Relative government shrinkage would result from a slowing or downturn in private sector productivity growth. Such a downturn could itself stem from a switch to a labour-intensive services economy with lower scope for productivity increases than in a manufacturing economy going through robotization. Similarly, technological change might destroy the 'productivity gap' which is at the heart of public spending growth in Baumol's famous explanation. A possible example is development of information technology creating scope for major productivity gains in government work, reducing or even reversing the alleged gap in productivity growth between government services and the private sector. After all, in an important sense, the 'productivity' of the producers of Beethoven symphonies *did* rise sharply once recording and broadcasting methods developed.

The other conventional link between technological change and government spending growth is the claim that technological change can upset competitive market conditions. Accounts of government spending growth in this vein typically link market failure to changes in technology, economic growth or urbanization. Such factors figured in Wagner's own explanation for government growth (see Alt and Chrystal 1983: 179–82; Berry and Lowery 1987: 407).

The argument is that urbanization and technological change make economies more monopolistic, create demands for investment on a scale which overstretches the capacity of private capital markets, and produce more 'spillovers' – goods and bads which are not marketable or consumable in a strictly individual way. The growth in spillovers associated with dense urban settlement and new technology (air travel, broadcasting, atomic power, cable services, new lethal technologies) causes ever more problems to be 'dumped in government's lap', as Peter Self (1985: 30) puts it, using the spread of motoring as an example.

Such developments are often portrayed as a one-way street in government growth. But they could reduce public spending and employment, in at least three circumstances. First, as noted in Chapter Three, technological change can *reduce* rather than increase the transactional difficulties for private capital markets in operating on a very large scale, and thus reduce 'technical' pressure for public funding for major investments. Second, technology can destroy as well as create monopolistic niches in the economy (as with the development of microwaves or satellites rivalling cables for longline telecommunications), creating more competition rather than less. Third, technological change might reduce spillovers and produce more goods and services capable of 'possessive individualism' and therefore open to market rather than public allocation (as with the advent of video, cable TV and value-added telecommunications services in areas once dominated by broadcasting).

Government growth and economic development

The last explanation of spending growth in the second 'family' shown in Table 5.1 builds on Wagner by seeing government growth as a product of economic development. There are three main variants of this explanation. One is the idea that fiscal buoyancy makes government spending grow during economic prosperity. 'Fiscal buoyancy' refers to the way that economic growth swells tax revenue without the need to raise tax rates (see Rose and Peters 1978; Alt and Chrystal 1983: 190–91; Rose 1984). From this viewpoint, understanding government *expenditure* growth needs no elaborate treatise: it might simply follow Northcote Parkinson's (1965) famous Second Law, that spending tends to rise to meet income. It is *tax* revenue growth which must be explained, and the main source of such growth, it is claimed, is economic growth creating fiscal buoyancy. Fiscal buoyancy makes increased government spending 'costless' in the special political sense that such spending does not cut absolutely into citizens' take-home pay. A related approach is the view that government growth may stem from 'fiscal drag', the process in which real tax revenue rises because tax brackets are not indexed to inflation and inflation forces taxpayers into higher income tax brackets even if their income is doing no more than rise with inflation (see Saunders 1986: 23). Fiscal drag is discussed further in the next chapter.

Both fiscal buoyancy and fiscal drag, however, will go into reverse during a slump or prolonged deflation, or both. For instance, if the economy shrinks, fiscal buoyancy turns into fiscal shipwreck, weakening government's revenue base. Richard Rose and Guy Peters (1978) argue that politicians in such circumstances will normally reduce public spending rather than raise taxes and therefore cut voters' take-home pay. To raise taxes in those conditions, they say, is a recipe for 'political bankruptcy', a vaguely defined state of popular alienation and disaffection from government which stops short of revolution (see Tufte 1980).

A second common variant of the idea that economic growth causes government spending growth is the view that many government services are 'luxuries' – that is, things that we spend relatively more of our income on as we get richer, like yachts or champagne (goods with high income elasticity of demand, in conventional economics jargon). Some dismiss this idea as speculative (see Delorme and André 1983: 106–107); and indeed the stereotype of most public services is more one of bread and potatoes than yachts and champagne. But many argue that areas like health care, security, education and insurance – where most of the growth in public spending comes – are indeed 'luxuries', in that relative demand grows with absolute increases in living standards. Such an interpretation fits with 'responsive' explanations of government growth – those which explain government growth as a response to widespread popular demand rather than, as in Marxist or 'Chicago theory' explanations, a response to the needs of the ruling class or of unrepresentative minorities (see Berry and Lowery 1987: 406–409). Wagner himself saw government services as a 'luxury' in this sense.

In an economy close to subsistence level, the argument runs, people spend most of their income on things which are privately possessible and marketable. But as income begins to rise, demand for collectively consumed services, like other luxuries, will grow disproportionately. Clearly, such a process is reversible. If public spending grows relatively in the good times, it may fall back in the bad times. Indeed, a version of such reasoning is Peter Self's argument (in Wright 1980: 126) that social pressure for public spending will tend to fall in a developed democracy during prolonged economic stringency because expectations decline and economic stagnation reduces demand for further growth in areas of public spending which are related to economic growth (such as the rate of household formation).

The third variant of the idea that government spending growth is linked to economic growth is the view that economic prosperity leads to government growth because of the need to check underconsumption. Underconsumption means chronic weakness in aggregate demand, caused either by excessive downward pressure on workers' real wage levels (as in Marxist ideas of underconsumption: see Dunleavy and O'Leary 1987: 262) or by excessive saving (as in Keynes', 1936, ideas), or both.

Keynes argued that economic growth would mean that government spending had to grow. Spending growth would not be needed to counter falling business profits (as in orthodox Marxist theory), but because increased wealth would lead to a greater proportion of income being saved, with proportionately less spent on consumption. Left unchecked, this shift would produce economic and political crisis through mass unemployment. To stabilize the economy, rising government spending financed by borrowing would be needed to counter the recessionary effects of too much saving and too little consumption.

What is not clear from this approach is exactly what *political* mechanisms make government grow in such conditions. Is it just *noblesse oblige*, the Fabian social consciences of influential Brahmins like Keynes himself? What if the mass unemployed remain an electoral minority (such that politicians can win re-election without them) or sufficiently quiescent that they do *not* seriously inconvenience those who do not suffer the effects of underconsumption? Might not many of the gainers be quite content to leave matters like that, for exactly the reasons suggested by Kalecki and discussed in the last chapter? Even if not, might not governments tackle unemployment by measures which did *not* necessarily drive up their own spending and employment levels, for example by regulations to cut wage levels so that labour was cheaper for hard-pressed employers to hire?

However, if it is really true that underconsumption produces political pressures for correction, government's relative spending size could still go down sometimes. As long as economic growth is the long-term trend, government spending would rise in relative terms over time, but dip back when growth falters. On this view, government spending growth is not, like the dinosaurs, likely to become extinct for ever. It will merely stage temporary disappearances from time to time.

'Self-destruct' explanations of government growth

The ideas considered in the previous section predict that government will shrink if environmental conditions *opposite* to those prompting growth come into existence. But the third set of explanations in Table 5.1 suggest that the very *same* forces which drive government growth will *also* check and reverse the process at some point. They are akin to the idea of extinction being brought upon a species as a result of its own earlier success, because they see government growth as something which ultimately destroys itself. Four 'self-destruct' explanations of government growth are considered briefly here.

Government growth as curvilinearly related to economic growth

First, some see public spending growth to be linked with economic development in a *curvilinear* rather than a straight-line relationship. This explanation modifies the linear growth-linked explanation (number 7 in Table 5.1) in that it sees the relationship between economic development and government growth as variable. It may be positive at one point and negative at another. This explanation comes in two main variants.

One variant is a modification of the idea, discussed in the last section, of government services as a 'luxury'. But from this perspective, government is the kind of 'luxury' for which relative demand first rises and later falls as income rises. Such a change in relative demand can come about either because wants become more complex or because wants become satiated (see Herber 1967: 148). So the *relative* (not absolute) size of government *falls* with continuing economic growth, rather than sinking only when economic growth stops (as in the more conventional fiscal buoyancy approach).

Bernard Herber (1967) claims that, in a subsistence economy, demand is mainly for goods which can be marketed in the private sector without institutional failure, like basic food and clothing. When aggregate income rises above subsistence, he says, demand rises sharply for services which cannot be fully individualized for consumption and for which government involvement is therefore needed to avoid institutional failure (such as mass transportation, communications, education). But when economic growth lifts affluence to a higher level, there will again be an increase in demand for privately marketed goods relative to government-produced ones, since at this point it is assumed that government has already provided those services for which it has a comparative advantage as a producer.

This idea perhaps relates to Fred Hirsch's (1977) well-known argument, that as affluence grows, demand shifts away from items in which satisfaction can be obtained by some absolute level of provision and towards a focus on 'positional goods'. Positional goods are things that we value precisely because *not* everyone else can have them, like the fabled key to the executive washroom.

Desmond King (1989: 41–4) argues that relative demand for state-welfare spending will eventually fall back, because as income rises, welfare items such as education and health come to be seen as 'positional goods'. Government can regulate positional goods, but cannot – by definition – provide such goods for everyone.

The other variant of this 'curvilinearity thesis' is the idea that economic growth shapes government growth through the way that income changes affect attitudes to risk. Kenneth Greene (1973) argues that many government-provided services are forms of 'insurance' against risk (police, defence, fire, welfare, health care, etc.). You pay with your life or your possessions if worst-case outcomes occur and you have no insurance. Demand for insurance itself, he claims, depends on attitudes to risk, which themselves change as overall income level changes.

In a mainly subsistence economy, ways of insuring against crime, invasion, sickness and want may be devoutly wished for. But such insurance cannot be afforded. But in more affluent conditions, demand grows for insurance-type services which can only be provided by government, by compulsory pooling of risk. As affluence develops even further (the argument goes), attitudes to risk change again. People are ready to gamble with some of the surplus for a chance of the good life. So relative demand for insurance-type services falls, and government shrinks. In short, the demand for the safety net and other insurance-type activities of government grows strongly at just above subsistence level, and falls relative to income at a higher level of affluence (perhaps rising again relative to income at a still higher level of wealth).

Both variants of the 'curvilinearity' explanation of government growth rest on very casual evidence. The assumption of the 'insurance' variant that attitudes to risk depend on income levels fits to some extent with commonly accepted ideas about a putative hierarchy of human needs ranging from the 'basics' of food, clothing and shelter to pyschological self-actualization (see Maslow 1954), even though these ideas about risk have been strongly challenged by Mary Douglas and Aaron Wildavsky (1983: 11–14).

Government growth as reflecting redistributive politics

A second self-destruct explanation of government spending growth sees growth as caused by the spread of the mass franchise. Government growth reflects the political dominance of a winning voting coalition favouring high government spending to redistribute resources from the more to the less affluent. Over a century ago, Alexis de Tocqueville (1946: 149–56) linked public spending with the mass franchise and social structure. More recently, Tocqueville's ideas have been rediscovered by institutional economists (see Peacock 1979) and recast into modern terminology by models which combine unequal income distribution, equal voting rights, and the equilibrium position of a political system in which equal per capita transfer payments are financed by taxes proportional to income (see Meltzer and Richard 1981). Many accounts of government spending growth link it to the position of the 'median voter' in the income scale: that is, the middle-of-the-road voters whose preferences sway the balance in committees and elections (see Pommerehne and Kirchgässner 1988: 214–26).

Tocqueville's argument is that where the median voter has less than the mean income (and specifically where median voters have such low incomes that they cannot be effectively taxed), an electoral niche opens for a minimum winning coalition advocating high public spending to benefit the majority, financed by taxes on those with average or higher income. It follows that when the franchise is extended to those with less than the mean income, there will be a marked shift – perhaps after a learning interval – to higher government spending and taxing. As Tocqueville (1946: 150) put it:

> In countries in which the poor should be exclusively invested with the power of making the laws no great economy of public expenditure ought to be expected: that expenditure will always be considerable . . . In other words, the government of the democracy is the only one under which the power which lays on taxes escapes the payment of them.

Empirically, the major flaw in a franchise-driven explanation of government growth is that such growth is not confined to democratic countries, but also occurs under authoritarian regimes. And logically, there is no reason why government growth should go on for ever under such an explanation. Public spending growth will reverse if the 'habitat' changes into a different income distribution pattern. Tocqueville (1946: 152) himself noted that democratic pressure to increase tax-financed spending would be weakened if the most numerous 'lower class' *themselves* had a substantial stake in property ownership. Moreover, spending growth driven by electoral pressures can also *self-destruct*, and that is why it is placed in the third family of explanations in Table 5.1.

The self-destruction might come about through counter-mobilization by the group 'exploited' by the ascendant voting coalition, along the same lines as the models of regulatory reversal discussed in Chapter Two. Alternatively, public spending growth may itself change the income position of the median voter, such that the ascendant voting coalition comes to be automatically destroyed as a result of its own political success. Assuming that the tax and transfer system is moderately effective (i.e. not completely undermined by administrative failure), over time the median voter's income comes to approximate or exceed the mean income in society. The society's pattern of income distribution will become more diamond-shaped than pyramid-shaped (cf. Pommerehne and Kirchgässner 1988: 219). As that happens, the median voter comes to derive *negative*, not positive, personal benefit from increases in collective spending paid for by taxes on average or above-average incomes. So the original redistributive coalition will collapse and be replaced with a new dominant conservative coalition more resistant to tax increases. We might expect such a turnaround to take place most dramatically in countries which have traditionally relied on nominally progressive income taxes for a large part of their tax revenue (such as the USA, Germany, the Scandinavian countries, Australia and the UK).

Auto-destruction of 'client politics'

Growth of government spending and employment is also explained by some as the product of 'client politics' interest-group pressures, of the kind which were discussed for regulation in Chapter Two. It will be recalled that client politics means a situation in which concentrated 'rent-seeking' groups use their comparative advantage in collective action to gain advantages for themselves from government, spreading the cost among a wider group who have lower stakes in the issue and who face higher transactions costs in collective action.

Some economics-of-politics theorists expect direct democracy (through initiative and referendum) to check such 'distortions', and the case of Switzerland, where government spending did not blow out during the 1960s to the same extent as in other advanced democracies, is sometimes used as an example of the difference that direct democracy can make (see Walker 1987: 202). Some also expect that spending growth will be less marked where public services are funded by specific user charges or by special visible taxes which make costs transparent and relate 'pain' to benefits.

But if public services are financed by 'invisible' taxes feeding a general fund budget, there may be more scope for successful 'client politics'. Under those circumstances, rent-seeking groups may find it easier to play on 'fiscal illusion' – that is, an 'invisible' tax structure coupled to an opaque benefit structure, making it difficult for ordinary voters and taxpayers to work out exactly who benefits and who pays. Under such circumstances, politicians have plenty of scope for offering what looks like a 'free lunch' to each of their constituencies, paid for at someone else's expense (as, for example, in the budgetary politics of the EC). Such a process, it is argued, will cumulatively cause government budgets to expand (see Wilensky 1981; Baumol and Oates 1985; Saunders 1986).

Can this process ever go into reverse? In Chapter Two, we saw how client politics in regulation can auto-destruct (through the development of close substitutes outside the regulatory ring-fence). Similarly for public spending and employment, it seems hardly plausible that 'fiscal illusion' can last for ever, or that rational losers are incapable of learning and publicizing who benefits and who pays. Likewise, the effects of any distortion of true cost functions by bureaucrats aiming for higher budgets seems unlikely to remain invisible for ever to the 'rational politicians' posited by the Chicago theory of government. Given no more than moderate ingenuity, those politicians will at some point rediscover traditional ways of changing the bureaucrats' incentives – such as pay on performance, competitions for fixed funding, a greater element of financing from specific fees, charges and special-fund taxes. As we will see in Chapter Seven, changes along these lines were indeed introduced in public management in several OECD countries in the 1980s.

Moreover, it is easy to see how client politics pressures could develop for contracting out services previously provided directly by public bureaucracies in areas where traditionally there was no concentrated private sector. Market concentration over time in services like cleaning, security or even general office work (areas where large firms did not traditionally operate) can produce the basis for a pro-contracting lobby with transactional advantages greater than public service unions aiming to develop and maintain public bureaucracy employment, because such a lobby constitutes a smaller and more compact group with a clear interest in pushing for *less* government employment in specific sectors. There is a clear parallel with the nineteenth-century move away from traditional state arsenals and dockyards towards a contract sector for provision of military matériel.

Extractive capacity explanations

The final set of explanations of government spending growth in the third 'family' in Table 5.1 link growth to 'extractive capacity', that is, government's ability to raise taxes. As with the fiscal buoyancy explanation, it is held that public spending increases are easy to explain: it is the growth or decline of *tax* capacity which needs to be explained. But in this case, tax capacity is linked to the administrative capacity to control and exploit the society.

We look more closely at explanations of what shapes tax structure in the next chapter. But it needs to be noted here that public spending increases might be related to changes in social structure making it easier for government to enforce more productive tax laws. Specifically, a family-firm and small-farm, mainly agrarian, economy is an economic structure which is notoriously difficult to tax in a sophisticated way, even if it is quite prosperous. This is because of the ease of concealing cash takings, of doing business by barter and taking income in kind. Income is easier to tax in an economy of medium-sized firms than in a small-family-firm economy, because large businesses must resort to elaborate, often automated, internal security processes to prevent fraud by their own employees. By installation of such systems, it becomes harder for them to cheat the tax authorities, who can then 'piggy-back' an 'invisible' tax structure on top of the internal corporate controls (for a further discussion, see Chapter Six, pp. 102–24).

Hence a shift from the former type of economy to the latter will increase government's tax-extractive capacity and thereby allow its expenditure to grow (see Hinrichs 1966). In turn, the development of a more easily taxable economic structure may be self-sustaining if it makes possible a shift to a more productive and 'development-friendly' tax mix (for example, away from export taxes), which may provide the conditions for further government growth.

Such a process, however, is quite capable of auto-destruction. That is, when large and medium-sized firms become effective tax-gatherers for government, the structure on which the tax system is built automatically starts to collapse. A search for 'tax efficiency' reshapes the economic structure into a form which is less fiscally tractable. On the one hand, large multinational corporations develop effective (and legal) measures of tax avoidance which are not open to medium-sized firms because of their smaller scale and resources. On the other hand, tax efficiency encourages the growth of small firms, self-employment, sub-contracting, boutique-style operations. An example is the growth of 'boutique wineries' and 'boutique breweries', in response to the current fad for 'real ale'. In short, the tax rules change the economic structure in such a way as to put the earlier process into reverse, steadily nibbling at the readily enforceable tax base and perhaps forcing governments to shift back to cruder, more readily enforceable, tax structures. We return to this issue in examining tax structure change in the next chapter.

Cultural theory explanations of government size

As mentioned earlier, Wildavsky (1985) argues that most conventional explanations of government growth are unconvincing because each can be opposed by a counter-hypothesis of at least equal plausibility. He offers instead a cultural explanation for government growth, drawing on Mary Douglas' (1982) cultural theory. Douglas argues that cultural biases can be categorized into four basic alternative ways of life. The types come from combining two basic dimensions of organization, namely 'grid' (the degree to which social interactions are governed by generalized rules) and 'group' (the degree to which groups are insulated from the rest of society). Hence the four basic cultural types are 'fatalist' (high grid, high group), 'hierarchist' (high grid, low group), 'individualist' (low grid, low group) and 'sectarian' or 'egalitarian' (low grid, high group). Wildavsky claims that the rise of 'hierarchist' and 'sectarian' political cultures explains government spending growth. 'Hierarchist' regimes tend towards growth because they are characterized by beliefs in a 'caring' society, in which individual sacrifices are needed for the overall good and in which those at the top care about those they rule. Hence hierarchist societies are likely to produce public policy which involves an element of redistribution in society.

It is 'sectarianism', however, which is the biggest force for public spending growth, because sectarians are committed to equality of results. Hence sectarian regimes will aim to eliminate all social differences. Because sectarians abhor coercion or authority, 'sectarian regimes find it difficult to control envy or collect taxes or deal with conflicts of views. Equality of result makes their internal life easier by decreasing envy' (Wildavsky 1985: 264). Hence societies dominated by sectarian culture (as Wildavsky claims European social democracies to be) will produce stronger pressures towards spending growth than societies dominated by competitive individualism (such as the USA) or societies with more hierarchist traditions (such as the former Soviet Union).

Wildavsky claims that his cultural interpretation implies a causal sequence different from that implied by Wagner's Law. Instead of economic growth driving government growth, a change in inequality of result would reflect the ascendancy of hierarchist and sectarian political cultures, which would in time produce institutions leading to government spending growth. Hence 'cultural change precedes and dominates budgetary change; the size of the state today is a function of its political culture yesterday' (Wildavsky 1985: 267).

The cultural explanation suggests that none of the theories reviewed earlier can offer a convincing explanation of government growth, because the way the factors which they identify work will depend on cultural bias. Economic growth will only lead to bigger government if the relevant regimes are hierarchist or egalitarian, but it could lead to smaller government under an individualist culture. Similarly, whether the mass franchise leads to government growth will depend on how the culture handles the 'politics of envy'. Cultural bias, too, will determine whether entitlements once established in law are seen as sacred, what sort of technology is selected and how it is filtered. Hence all the elements reviewed up to now become at best intermediate variables. How they actually work, whether the sign is positive or negative, is determined by cultural bias.

Wildavsky's explanation is sketchy, and there are some obvious problems with it. There is a risk of teleology (wherever there is government growth, it must by definition be explained by egalitarianism). It shifts the problem into that of explaining why cultural bias should itself shift, without solving that problem [though Thompson *et al.* (1990: 69–75) have suggested that cultural change may occur through learning in response to surprises]. But the theory has an appealing simplicity and intellectual economy. There is nothing inexorable about government growth in this account. If cultural bias shifts, all the eleven growth factors will start to work in the opposite direction, so the cultural theory brings those explanations together into a new synthesis. The bold claim is that the literature to date has been looking at the wrong problem, trying to explain why government grows, rather than the underlying problem, why cultural bias shifts.

Post-industrialism as a new 'habitat'

Chapter One introduced the idea of using the development of 'post-industrial society' to explain the disappearance of a group of economic policy dinosaurs, as a result of the loss of habitat which it implies. Can a slowdown of government growth be linked to post-industrialism?

Industrialism might be linked to government growth in several ways. First, in a manufacturing-centred economy, public and private sector technology is more likely to be distinct. Scope for productivity increases in bureaucratic 'paperwork' will be relatively small. Second, the fairly homogeneous workforce of an industrial society will tend to have the electoral properties of Tocqueville's redistributive coalition. Third, some claim that there may be strong pressures for public spending growth to underpin mass consumption. Marxist theorists of Fordism claim that mass consumption of standard goods under Fordism is underwritten by high public spending on welfare (see Jessop 1988a: 4–5, 1988b: 4). But they offer no empirical systematic evidence that welfare spending turns down in 'post-Fordism', and to date there seems little sign of such a downturn.

As noted in Chapter One, the emerging 'post-Fordist' society is claimed to have two characteristics which are very different from the society it replaces, and both might check long-term government growth. One is a less homogeneous and more polarized labour force (Jessop 1988a: 7–9) destroying the Tocqueville coalition; the other is the 'flexible specialization' in production made possible by automation. Post-industrialism involves a services economy specializing in the very areas where public bureaucracies once were unchallenged specialists – office work, the management of information, high-level analysis and advocacy. Such a change can set the stage for a shift to private, even competitive, contracting for government work, and in that sense a reduction in the staff size of the public bureaucracy (though not necessarily of public spending). And the developing 'added-value' information services of the new era make possible a development of information networking through independent organization of services instead of through government.

The implications of such a shift for government spending and employment are far from clear (see Mulgan 1988). But the development of post-industrialism can also be argued to create a habitat in which government growth could go into extinction, according to several of the conventional explanations of government growth considered earlier. Specifically:

- The new socioeconomic structure boosts overall economic growth, reversing government growth according to the hypothesis of a curvilinear relationship between aggregate income levels and demand for public services (number 8 in Table 5.1).
- The more polarized labour force weakens the 'Tocqueville' electoral coalition, reversing the 'Tocqueville' theory of government growth built on a combination of mass franchise and pyramidal income distribution (number 9 in Table 5.1).
- The new technology of 'flexible specialization' transforms bureaucratic work in the traditionally labour-intensive government sector, wiping out or reversing the 'productivity lag' which helped to increase government employment under industrialism (number 6 in Table 5.1).
- The 'flexibilization' of production in post-industrialism accentuates the push towards industrial fragmentation in some areas. Such a development helps to set the taxability of the economy into reverse. The extractive capacity of government growth (number 11 in Table 5.1) will auto-destruct in those circumstances. It may be, too, that the climate for social mobilization as a link to government spending growth (number 4 in Table 5.1) changes into a climate for social *de*mobilization.

These hypotheses remain tentative and untestable. Those who assert that a shift from one accumulation regime to another is taking place do not identify clear criteria against which the change could be verified, and many of the economic features claimed to be associated with post-Fordism (like globalization of capital and monopolistic tendencies) have occurred previously. The approach is long on speculation and short on empirical backing, and some (like King 1990: 276) question whether flexible specialization constitutes a qualitative break with earlier production methods, given the retention of assembly-line methods in manufacturing. Whether their application to the work of government and *public* services – typically much less considered by 'post-industrialism' gurus – is less problematic will be considered further in Chapter Seven.

Conclusion

When public spending 'cutbacks' arrived in OECD countries from the 1970s, some observers thought new theories were needed for new times. Perhaps this is why a special literature on government cutbacks and policy termination grew up in the 1970s and 1980s (see Levine 1978; Jørgensen 1987; Dunsire and Hood 1989). But Gwen Gray (1984) argues that there is no need for new, special interpretations of what happened to public spending and employment in the 1980s. A special literature on policy termination and government cutbacks, she claims, is intellectually redundant.

It is true that a few of the many available explanations of the growth of government spending and employment (numbers 1–3 in Table 5.1) do imply that it is a one-way street. But *pace* Schumpeter, few of the conventional explanations of government growth see the process as inevitable and irreversible. Many of them suggest that growth will reverse if habitat changes sufficiently (numbers 4–7 in Table 5.1). Some of those 'extinction conditions' are extreme, but that does not apply to the idea that government growth is linked to technological change (number 6 in Table 5.1). And, as we have seen, 'post-industrialism', as a habitat which is less hospitable for long-established fiscal patterns, creates conditions in which at least half of the explanations of government spending growth considered on pp. 85–98 go into reverse.

Moreover, as we have seen, four other explanations of government growth (numbers 8–11 in Table 5.1) suggest that spending and/or employment growth will ultimately *auto*-destruct. Exactly the same conditions which prompt government growth will later cause growth to stop or reverse. The mechanical analogy is with the track of a windshield wiper or a tape player which reverses tapes automatically. And again, the conditions for auto-destruction are not extreme.

Accordingly, we do not need to invoke analogies with meteorites from outer space to account for a slowdown of government growth. To the extent that 'ideas' play a part in government growth or stabilization, Wildavsky's 'cultural bias' hypothesis (number 12 in Table 5.1) accommodates change in both directions and, like the idea of 'post-industrialism', subsumes many of the other explanations considered (numbers 4–11 in Table 5.1). Cultural bias can determine whether the 'sign' of intermediate variables like technology, economic growth and democratization is positive or negative for government growth.

The future shape of the government size graphs in Figs 5.1–5.4 remains to be seen. But if government spending and employment is set for decline, the main elements of an explanation suggested by existing theories of government growth involve some mixture of habitat, self-destruction and changing cultural bias, which would put a policy shift in this area (alongside the shift from Keynesianism to monetarism) in sector (j) of Fig 1.2. Certainly, we do not necessarily need new theories to explain government stabilization or contraction. We can readily use many of the established explanations of growth in government spending and employment to explain stabilization and cutbacks, and to do so has the attraction of simplicity, intellectual economy and logical consistency. It is like using theories of why wars occur to explain the 'problem' of why there should ever be peace (see Blainey 1973: 3–4).

6

Tax policy change: extinction or inertia?

For the first time in this century, the idea that the progressive income tax should not merely help pay the expenses of government but should also, perhaps even primarily, have the intention of redistributing income and wealth, has been repudiated by democratically-elected governments.
(Irving Kristol, quoted in *Sydney Morning Herald*, 28 April 1988)

Introduction: tax changes in OECD countries in the 1980s

Taxation is another sphere in which policy dinosaurs seemed to die out in many OECD countries in the 1980s. The policy dinosaur here is the tradition of nominally progressive income taxes, allied with a proliferation of 'tax expenditures' in the form of special tax deductions for politically favoured groups and activities. The change did not involve many wholly new taxes, or the abolition of old ones, nor major differences in overall tax revenue. Rather, it involved alterations in tax mix and structure. Consider the following three cases:

- In October 1986, US President Ronald Reagan signed into law an 829 page, 15 kilogram tax bill. The Tax Reform Act was described as the most sweeping reform of US income tax since the Second World War. It cut the top rate of business tax from 46 to 34 per cent and the top rate of personal tax from 50 to 28 per cent, while reversing the growth of tax expenditures which had spread dramatically over the 1970s. 'Far beyond the expectations of most experts and political pundits, the act ushered in the most sweeping tax changes in decades' (Mucciaroni 1990: 1).
- In the same month, a new Goods and Services Tax (GST) was introduced in New Zealand. The GST was jokingly dubbed 'Goodbye Second Term' by some wags who thought it would damage the Labour government's chances of re-election (in fact, the party was re-elected in 1987). It was spearheaded by Roger Douglas, New Zealand's controversial Finance Minister in David Lange's government, with his free-market doctrines of

'Rogernomics'. The GST was levied at 10 per cent, with only three exemptions. It was described as the most far-reaching tax of its kind in the world, and the biggest change in New Zealand's tax system in fifty years (Douglas and Callen 1987: 207). At the same time, top rates of income tax were cut from 66 to 48 per cent.

• In November 1988, Prime Minister Noboru Takeshita, leader of Japan's ruling Liberal Democrat Party, finally got approval from the lower house of the Japanese Parliament for a six bill tax reform package. This package was designed to replace the comparatively progressive income tax-based fiscal structure set up by the US Occupation of Japan under General Douglas MacArthur after the Second World War. It involved bringing in a highly controversial 3 per cent sales tax linked with a lowering of Japanese income and corporate tax rates and an easing of the inheritance tax which had been designed in the 1940s to produce greater social equality by wiping out large inherited family fortunes over three generations. Takeshita was not the first Japanese prime minister to try to reverse Japan's entrenched tax policy regime. His initiative followed a decade of failed attempts to change the tax structure by his predecessors, notably Masayoshi Ohira and Yasuhiro Nakasone. The change involved massive political effort and turmoil, including one marathon 26 hour Parliamentary sitting.

These three politicians were not the only ones in the OECD world to embark on apparently bold tax changes that rocked their respective political systems by reversing structures which had been established and developing for more than a generation. Over the 1980s, Margaret Thatcher's Conservative government in the UK cut the standard income tax rate from 33 to 25 per cent and raised Value-Added Tax from 8 to $17\frac{1}{2}$ per cent. And changes along similar lines were introduced in other countries, such as Germany, Canada and Australia (although the Australian Commonwealth government did not follow Japan and New Zealand in introducing a general sales tax, after an abortive 'tax summit' in 1985). At first sight at least, significant policy shifts seem to have occurred.

In a careful political-science survey of tax policy changes in OECD countries over the 1980s, Guy Peters (1991: 271) picks out three distinctive features about these changes. First, at about the same time, proposals for major tax policy changes reached the political agenda in many OECD countries and some Third World ones too. Second, these proposals had a remarkable similarity to one another. Third, in contrast to the fate of most radical policy ideas, many of the proposals were actually put into effect.

Gary Mucciaroni (1990) argues that 1980s US tax reform flies in the face of orthodox 'Chicago theory' explanations of policy development. He claims that, like some accounts of regulatory growth discussed in Chapter Two, the development of special tax deductions within the old progressive tax structure reflected a classic 'client politics' pattern of concentrated benefits and diffused costs. Each tax expenditure brought concentrated benefits to compact groups well placed for effective lobbying and was paid for by small extra levies on the remaining mass of taxpayers. The dominance of such a pattern is readily explicable in the orthodox framework of Chicago theory. But its collapse in the face of a mixture of 'majoritarian politics', 'interest group politics' and 'entrepreneurial politics' seems rather surprising for that approach. In similar vein, Peters (1991: 271) claims that many received accounts of tax politics 'appear better suited to explaining why the reforms were impossible, than for explaining how and why they did succeed'.

By now, that remark should sound a familiar note. As we have seen, similar claims have been made about the passing of other policy 'dinosaurs'. The political science literature on taxation in the early 1980s (such as Robinson and Sandford 1983) tended to stress the fragmented and *ad hoc* nature of tax policy change. Tax reform, it was claimed, tended to develop piecemeal, through horse-trading at the margins, not from any synoptic view of the tax system as a whole or the basic design principles to be applied. On the face of it, the comprehensive tax reforms adopted by so many countries in the 1980s seem to constitute a radical 'surprise' to such ideas, just as deregulation did for established ideas about regulatory 'capture'.

According to Peters, the international tax reform process in the 1980s came in two broad stages. The first stage was associated with key 'New Right' political leaders like Ronald Reagan and Margaret Thatcher in the early 1980s. It involved a cutting of income tax rates and a shift of revenue emphasis from 'direct' to 'indirect' taxes (that is, away from taxes levied on income and wealth and towards taxes on sales or transactions). Figures 6.1 and 6.2 show the proportion of total taxes taken by personal income taxes and general consumption taxes for five OECD countries and the OECD total between 1965 and 1989.

In many cases, the cutting of income tax rates was linked with price indexation of income tax 'brackets'. Tax brackets are the different categories into which income is divided in a progressive tax structure. A simplified example might be a case which imposed a 15 per cent tax on income between 0 and 29 on a given currency scale (in fact, there is invariably a cut-off below which no tax is paid in real-life tax structures), 25 per cent on income between 30 and 50, 40 per cent on income between 51 and 71, 60 per cent on income between 72 and 92, and 80 per cent on income above 93. In such a structure, increasing affluence brings with it increasing tax liability. Suppose the population is divided (again for simplicity) into five income groups, group A earning 29 currency units, B earning 50, C earning 71, D earning 92 and E earning 117. Assuming that there are no tax offsets or evasion, the proportion of income paid in tax will steadily rise with affluence: in this example, group A will pay 15 per cent of its income in tax, B 19 per cent, C 24 per cent, D 32 per cent and E 41 per cent.

Then suppose that prices rise at 10 per cent per year without any economic growth, and money incomes adjust with no change in relativities. Figure 6.3 indicates the effect on real post-tax incomes of our five hypothetical income groups after zero, six and ten years. All groups are worse off. The process is known as 'fiscal drag'. Egalitarians can note that failing to compensate for

Figure 6.1 Taxes on general consumption as % of total taxation 1965–89

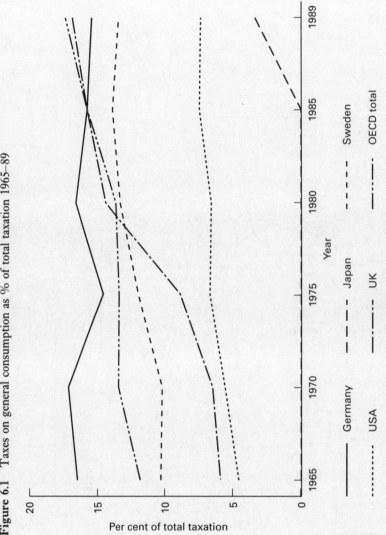

Germany ———   Japan – – –   Sweden – – –

USA ········   UK –··–··–   OECD total –·–·–

Source: OECD Revenue Statistics 1965–90 (Paris 1991), table 29, p. 86.

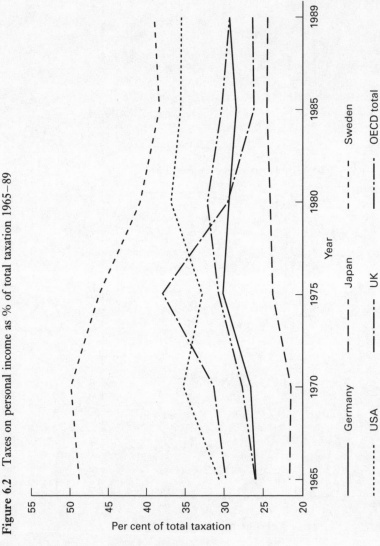

Figure 6.2 Taxes on personal income as % of total taxation 1965–89

Germany —————— Japan – – – – Sweden – – – –

USA ············ UK –··–··– OECD total –·–·–

Source: OECD Revenue Statistics 1965–90 (Paris 1991), table 11, p. 77.

Figure 6.3 Hypothetical effects of not changing tax brackets (progressive tax structure with 10 per cent yearly inflation)

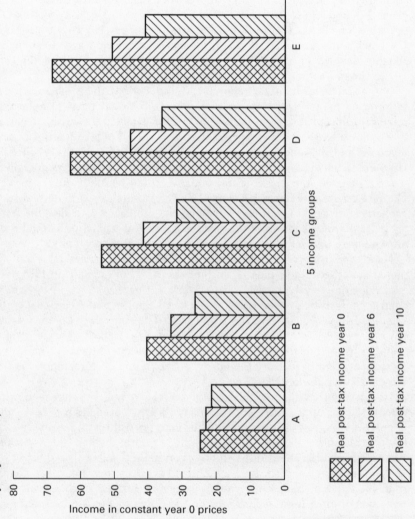

Income in constant year 0 prices

5 income groups

Real post-tax income year 0

Real post-tax income year 6

Real post-tax income year 10

inflation in such a structure will have a sharply levelling effect on post-tax incomes, and that tax revenue will rise dramatically (assuming that it draws tax equally from all groups, government's real income will nearly double in value). Group A gets off fairly lightly in percentage terms (though as the lowest income group it may be least able to bear even a light loss), but the other groups suffer heavy proportional falls (greatest for group D), and after ten years even the affluent group E's real post-tax income is starting to drop below group B's initial post-tax income. But political shocks are likely to shake the structure long before that time, putting pressure on government to change the tax bracket to offset the effects of inflation. In an era when inflation had roughly doubled in most OECD countries after the oil shocks of the early 1970s, the indexation movement was intended to limit its effects.

In the second round of tax reforms in the later 1980s, the emphasis went on to lowering the top corporate and individual income tax rates, to reduce the number of income tax brackets, and to cut tax expenditures arising from tax 'breaks' or offsets – that is, opportunities for paying less tax by making use of loopholes and allowances. In many countries, the use of such offsets had led to large and rapidly growing 'tax expenditures' (revenue foregone), as investment became diverted into 'tax-efficient' outlets secured by lobby groups in areas like real estate, retirement pension plans, life insurance, farming and more exotic tax-privileged investments. The effect was greatly to reduce the actual progressivity of the tax structure since, obviously, it tended to be the better-off who were best placed to take up such investment opportunities.

Hence nominal tax cuts represented by a reduction in general rates could be more than offset by widening the income tax base. For example, in 1985, New Zealand withdrew all tax concessions on new mortgage contracts, life assurance contracts or private pension schemes and taxed employers at 45 per cent on the value of fringe benefits given to employees. The Australian Commonwealth government also introduced a controversial Fringe Benefits Tax in 1986 to limit the fiscal attractiveness of in-kind benefits. Many of these tax reforms in most cases seem to increase the burden of tax borne by corporations and by those on lower and middle incomes.

Not all countries followed this general direction of policy change to the same extent. France, under Socialist government, briefly moved against the trend in the early 1980s, just as it did with public enterprise at that time, and in most respects remains at the low end of the scale of reform. Perhaps that is because France has traditionally laid the emphasis on indirect rather than direct taxes, so that there was less scope for New Zealand-type reforms. The USA, coming from the opposite tradition, seems to have gone furthest in the extent of its reduction of top rates of federal income tax. Some countries introduced quite new taxes, like the Japanese, Australian and New Zealand cases mentioned earlier.

How are these apparently radical tax changes to be explained? In principle, each of the possible explanations considered in Chapter One could be applied. Did new intellectual 'meteorites' hit the tax policy arena? Was there a swing back from the 1940s fashion for progressive income taxes as part of a general reaction to collectivism? Did the 'habitat' of tax policy change, either as a result of 'autonomous' socioeconomic development or because the institutional apparatus of tax policy destroyed its own habitat?

The 'intellectual meteorite' theory seems less plausible for tax policy reform than for regulatory reform. After all, justifications for cutting nominally high tax rates had been around in economics since Adam Smith. And it is doubtful if economists did such technically innovative work on tax reform as they did for deregulation. It is harder to identify key Nobel-prize-winning theories behind the process. Of course, it is often noted that the thrust of 1980s tax reform was broadly linked to the same 'New Right' intellectual ascendancy which spelt extinction for the other policy dinosaurs considered in this book. And certainly, the influential 'supply side' theory of early 1980s 'Reaganomics' was part of the policy background.

The underlying argument was that reducing government's demands would help to generate an economic renaissance by liberating entrepreneurs and sacrificing short-term equity for overall wealth creation would bring greater prosperity to the population at large. Prosperity would come, it was claimed, because the gains of those who 'got rich quick' would later 'trickle down' to those lower down the social scale. Extra demand and investment would create new jobs, rising incomes and more national income to be distributed to those at the bottom of the heap. Taking away the 'tax breaks' which artificially shaped resource flows into investment would raise efficiency, creating a 'level playing field' which would move more money into industrial investment and away from formerly tax-privileged areas like real estate.

The problem, as noted earlier, is that such arguments have been available for at least 200 years. So why did they suddenly become so much more persuasive in the 1980s? Could it then have been a Hirschmanesque reaction – a time when the political attractions of soaking the rich and sharing out the booty among everyone else waned as experience showed up the inherent limitations of that approach to taxation? Mucciaroni (1990: 8) argues that for the USA, there were significant 'self-destruct' elements in comprehensive tax reform: '. . . the very success of tax expenditure growth led to its demise because it undermined the broader purposes and long-term viability of the income tax'. His claim is that the spread of special tax deductions eventually split the business lobby. Some corporations came to see themselves as paying for the extra tax privileges of other firms. However, Mucciaroni also claims that the overall environment became 'colder' for the traditional pattern of progressive nominal tax rates linked with a proliferation of special tax deductions because of the onset of macroeconomic 'stagflation' among OECD countries in the 1970s, and that 'ideas' also counted in so far as the traditional pattern had been successfully portrayed as unfair and had lost its legitimacy by the 1980s.

Peters (1991: 286) also considers the possibility of explaining tax reform by declining citizen acquiescence to big government and high taxes. But he concludes that even if such a general change in popular attitudes could be clearly shown, the link between mass cultural change and real tax policy is problematic. He suggests that the changes may best be understood by reference to institutional factors such as the development of more accessible government structures, linked to new styles of interest groups and political entrepreneurship, and an overall climate of greater international economic competition.

Such ideas are, of course, general themes in political science. As we have seen, very similar explanations have been applied to the disappearance of other economic policy dinosaurs in the 1980s. But do we really need new-minted theories to explain the changes? And do those changes, as Peters and Mucciaroni claim, really confound orthodox accounts of tax policy development? The last chapter argued that many conventional explanations of government growth can also explain stabilization and cutbacks. Before we accept a similar claim about the inadequacy of orthodox explanations of tax policy development in the light of the 'flat tax' changes of the 1980s, we must examine some of those explanations more carefully. Three explanations will be explored here:

- Richard Rose and Terence Karran's (1987) 'inertia-driven' account of tax policy. It is a largely 'institutional' approach to tax policy dynamics, which stresses the forces of continuity in the process.
- Margaret Levi's (1988) 'predatory rule' thesis, which explains revenue trends and structures through the interests of self-regarding rulers.
- My own (Hood 1985) 'taxability' approach, which is designed to find the sources of tax 'selection' in the dynamics of sociotechnical change interacting with institutional capacity.

The 'political inertia' account of tax policy development

In an account of UK tax policy from the 1940s to the 1980s, Rose and Karran (1987) offer an 'inertia' interpretation of the process, which is a partial reaction against the well-known 'incremental' theory of policy-making developed by Charles Lindblom (1959, 1977). According to Lindblom's approach, policy is made, not by any process of synoptic planning (in which some 'directing intelligence' systematically works through the options against stable and clearly directed goals), but by a series of small adjustments to the *status quo*, involving a disjointed process of mutual accommodation and coalition-building. Rose and Karran (1987: 160) show that the year-on-year changes in taxation introduced in the UK over those four decades tend to be small in revenue terms, and that amendments to existing taxes are much more likely than repeal of current taxes or creation of new ones (ibid.: 113). Both of these conclusions fit with what incrementalists would expect.

But Rose and Karran's account of the tax policy process differs from the traditional incremental approach in several ways. They distinguish between intended short-term and unintended long-term consequences arising from compounding and accumulation. The incremental approach works well in explaining year-to-year tax policy changes, and the associated political horse-trading. But a different approach – the 'inertia perspective' – is needed to understand cumulative long-term change which can become irreversible (whereas the incremental approach stresses the extent to which year-to-year changes are reversible) and to understand aspects of tax policy which do not stem from conscious political decisions.

The inertia approach emphasizes the extent to which tax decisions in liberal democracies are consciously *avoided* by elected politicians, who mostly prefer to leave tax bureaucracies on auto-pilot and hence to limit their responsibility for the details of unpopular taxes. The approach also highlights the way that *cumulative* consequences of small year-to-year policy changes can result in outcomes which were entirely unintended by any of the individual policy-makers involved in the process – for example, in cumulative erosion of the tax base through successive deals with interest groups, which in time destroy the integrity of the tax system and counter-mobilize tax 'losers'. Also, whereas the incremental approach focuses on a process of small, regular changes, resulting in only moderate alterations in outcomes, the inertia approach focuses on the large, irregular changes that occur in the long run, and the variable, potentially destabilizing outcomes that such changes may bring.

Pace Peters' comments about the defects of established theories of tax policy, many aspects of the 'flat tax' reforms across the OECD in the 1980s in fact fit this theory quite well. First, as Rose and Karran predict, new taxes and abolitions of existing taxes were the exception, and changes largely consisted of amendments to existing taxes. They argue (Rose and Karran 1987: 17) that: '. . . most decisions will be confined to one category, fringe tuning. Politicians will be averse to imposing big tax increases and also to paying the price of big tax cuts, namely big cuts in popular programmes. Hence, a risk-averse politician will only take responsibility for measures that only make small changes in total tax revenue.' The changes of the 1980s fitted this prediction.

Indeed, as most commentators have noted, the changes that were made were broadly 'revenue neutral', and even the composition of tax revenue did not change abruptly. Figure 6.4 shows what happened to tax revenue as a proportion of GDP in the OECD as a whole and in some of the individual countries. Far from realizing the New Right dream of rolling back the state, those changes did not result in a major fall in tax revenue. Indeed, in several cases, they were linked with a rise in tax revenue. And, as Figs 6.1 and 6.2 show, the effect of changes in income tax rates and the introduction of new indirect taxes has not produced a *general*, sharply visible alteration in the relation between taxes on personal income and taxes on general consumption. Many of the key changes are qualitative, not captured in aggregate statistics.

Moreover, the tax reform of the 1980s fits Rose and Karran's expectation of large, irregular changes stemming from a long process of cumulation rather than the conventional incremental picture of minor year-to-year changes. Peters (1991: 284–5) suggests that by the early 1980s the cumulation of exemptions and deductions written into tax law, and the narrowing basis of taxable income, not only made taxes harder to operate but also made them seem increasingly unfair to the tax bureaucrats who collected them. In the workforce, regular employees who were 'tax captives' – paying their tax by obligatory deductions

Figure 6.4 Total tax revenues as % of GDP 1965-89

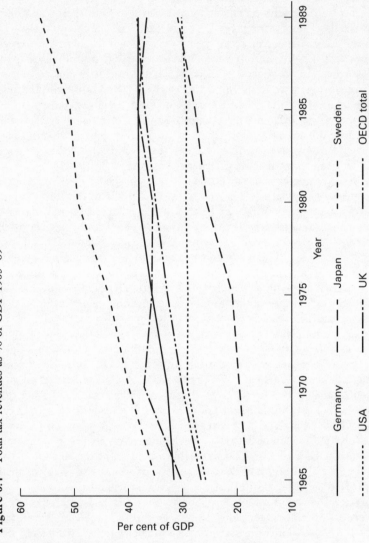

Source: OECD Revenue Statistics 1965-90 (Paris 1991), table 3, p. 73.

at source from their employers – stood in stark contrast to the 'tax escapees' on whom the tax authorities could not get a handle and who had more scope for claiming deductions.

But, though it carefully distinguishes between different kinds of change in taxation and successfully predicts the quantitative range of year-to-year revenue changes, the inertia approach does not say much about why the tide might turn from direct to indirect tax or from progressive tax with offsets to a flatter tax structure. Its strength lies in its ability to predict relatively slow changes in the tax revenue totals and composition. But, because it does not concentrate on the counter-inertia forces in the process, it does not shed much light on what determines the particular substantive direction that fiscal innovation will go in, rather than what the process is like (see Brittan 1988).

The 'predatory ruler' thesis

Margaret Levi (1988), in an amalgam of the Chicago theory tradition and Marxist political economy, has developed a theory of 'predatory rule' which purports to explain tax policy choices. The theory focuses on the 'rulers' – those who hold the position of chief executive in state institutions. Levi argues that such rulers are not simply handmaidens of some dominant group or class, as they are seen in most feminist or Marxist theories of 'the state'. Rather, they are rational self-interested actors. They have interests of their own to look after, which they will pursue wherever they can.

But what exactly are those interests? Are the rulers interested in minimizing their own tax liability, like the British monarch, who paid no income tax between 1937 and 1992? If so, we could explain the dynamics of tax development by reference to what suits the personal interests of the people at the top, for example in the tax treatment of the sort of part-time work that politicians typically do or the sort of work they do after politics. Such an analysis might well be revealing. But unlike some economics-of-politics theorists, Levi does not closely specify what the rulers' self-interest entails. She simply maintains that *whatever* the rulers' aims may be (whether they be personal, social or political), revenue is needed to realize those aims. Hence, she claims, self-interested rulers will tend to be 'predatory', that is, they will normally aim to extract as much revenue as they can from the population at large.

But rulers are not, of course, all-powerful in practice. They encounter significant limits to achieving their predatory aims. According to Levi, three main factors constrain the rulers' revenue-maximizing strategy and explain variations in state policies over time and between one country and another:

- *Relative bargaining power*, meaning the extent to which rulers monopolize control over coercive power and other key political resources. The more assets they control, the more 'predatory' they can be, dictating terms rather than offering concessions. For example, economic 'globalization' and the rise of powerful transnational corporations will be likely to reduce the relative bargaining power of national states over corporate tax levels.

- *Policy transaction costs*, meaning the costs of reaching agreements on policy and gaining compliance with tax policies. Levi (1988: 176) claims that relatively centralized representative institutions may give rulers more effective tax power, arguing that the development of a strong parliament in England in medieval and Renaissance times led to effective negotiation and high tax compliance compared to France during the same period, where monarchical power blocked the development of an effective Parliament. In the present day, Levi would presumably expect the EC to be fiscally weak relative to the USA.
- *Rulers' discount rates*, reflecting the extent to which rulers value the present relative to the future. If attention is concentrated on the short term, considerations about long-term effects of particular taxes will be laid aside, reflecting a high 'discount rate'. For example, during critical wars, rulers are likely to have high discount rates, caring little for the future. Similarly, rulers in those states where politicians have a high probability of ending up in an unmarked grave may also have high discount rates relative to those politicians who have a greater chance of dying in their beds.

Levi (1988: 184) claims: 'The creation of quasi-voluntary compliance is the key to what policies a ruler can and cannot enact.' Quasi-voluntary compliance is an alternative strategy to the use of raw coercion and the engineering of ideological compliance. Quasi-voluntary compliance combines the use of coercion against detected tax miscreants with widespread voluntarism in paying taxes among those who are liable. It involves the construction of 'institutions that encourage compliance without resort to coercion and other costly kinds of inducement and enforcement' (ibid.: 181).

Levi (1988: 69) argues that 'The achievement of significant quasi-voluntary compliance is always tenuous . . .'. Free-riding by those who want to escape from tax obligations is always liable to break out, and once it has developed on any significant scale, compliance is difficult to re-establish except in extraordinary circumstances such as war, revolution or depression that set the scene for a new 'conditional bargain' with the taxpaying populace. Levi (ibid.: 178–9) identifies long-term changes which alter state forms through their effects on relative bargaining power, policy transaction costs and rulers' discount rates. The result, according to Levi, is a long-term international trend towards taxation increasing in scale and becoming ever more sophisticated, broader in scope and more bureaucratic in form.

Levi's argument is nebulous. Making it operational and reaching determinate conclusions is problematic. Levi's bold claims for its explanatory power may simply reflect the fact that it is too ambiguous to be clearly falsifiable by any concrete case. Precisely because the 'theory' covers all the possible bases – politics and economics, the macro and the micro – it provides a language in which any specific case can be discussed. What it does *not* offer, despite its economics-of-politics pretensions, is a parsimonious basis for prediction. In addition, Levi (1988: 4) herself implies that her thesis does not fit the development of 'monetarism' in the 1980s. Evidently, she counts that era as 'the exception which proves the rule'. She suggests (though not very explicitly) that that policy reversal is a case of rulers *refraining* from gaining revenue for reasons other than the operation of relatively 'hard' constraints on their tax-raising capacity. It is an exceptional event which is not explained by a theory of 'normal' fiscal behaviour.

If the theory indeed cannot explain this important international tax policy shift, its usefulness is clearly rather limited for those trying to understand the determinants of contemporary tax reform, justifying Peters' comment that the tax policy literature better explains why that tax reform was impossible than why it happened. However, it seems excessively self-denying for Levi to suggest that the 'flatter taxes' policy of the 1980s is an ideologically driven 'deviant' case which cannot be explained by her theory.

After all, as noted earlier, in most cases the tax reforms meant a redistribution, not any lowering, of the total tax burden on citizens. Despite the pervasive rhetoric of 'tax cuts', Fig. 6.4 shows that there was no general or sharp decrease in tax revenues and that total tax revenue went up in several cases. Now this outcome is precisely what Levi's 'predatory rulers' would want, since it exactly fits her expectation of a trend towards increased scope and scale of taxation. The ever-increasing loopholes, offsets and allowances that had eroded the base of the old tax structure weakened the rulers' fiscal power. It would be rational for 'predatory' rulers to seek to reverse the process (provided, perhaps, that *they* could still personally escape from the full rigours of the taxation they imposed on those they governed).

Moreover, it would not be difficult to point to processes which could have made major impacts at least on the 'relative bargaining power' and 'transactions costs' of the rulers in maintaining the established tax regimes. In terms of bargaining power, as noted earlier, financial and economic 'globalization' may have lowered the leverage of rulers in taxing corporations, and raised the leverage of international corporations relative to domestic interest groups. And if taxes on companies were lowered, top income tax rates on individuals had to be lowered as well, otherwise wealthy individuals could simply turn themselves into corporations for legal purposes to lower their tax liability.

Similarly, there are ways in which transactions costs might have shaped the process. Traditionally, fiscally productive *ad valorem* taxes on general sales were hampered by in-kind transactions, many small retail units and limited accounting controls. The greater monetization of economies as large agri-business took over from small peasant farmers and rural populations declined, allied with the move to larger-scale retail and distributive units, and the development of more sophisticated automated accounting systems, radically lowered the information-gathering costs of taxing the populace through the indirect tax 'handle'.

Indeed, it might even be argued that the new international fiscal structure reflects the advent of a new 'conditional bargain' between rulers and key interest groups. Peters (1991: 285–6) argues that across the OECD countries and particularly in the USA, there was a move towards greater openness and accessibility in political structures removing barriers to majoritarian politics.

The developments he has in mind might include the televising of major political institutions and processes, decentralization and the growth of 'leaks' about government decision-making.

Peters suggests that such developments opened the way for a new kind of 'policy entrepreneur' in tax policy, gaining political 'profit' by aggregating small claims against entrenched interest groups (in the same way that policy entrepreneurship has been suggested to lie behind other policy reversals discussed in this book). Even if this bold claim is not accepted, it might still be argued that the steady multiplication of tax 'escape routes' (through tax exemptions) had a delegitimizing effect on the whole fiscal system, as well as eroding revenue, and that the changes might be interpreted in part as a 'relegitimizing' process associated with what Levi calls a new 'fiscal constitution'. As she puts it

> I argue that rulers can increase compliance by demonstrating that the tax system is fair. A perception of exploitation – that is, an unfair contract – promotes noncompliance ... Favoritism toward special interest groups, programs that they disapprove of, declining return for their taxes, the failure of some to comply can all violate taxpayers' norms of fairness. The consequence will be a decrease in quasi-voluntary compliance.
>
> (Levi 1988: 53)

So it can perhaps be argued that this approach, too, has some limited potential for explaining the flat-tax reforms of the 1980s, even though it was not designed to do so.

A changing-context approach? The 'taxability' approach

Rose and Karran's (1987) explanation of tax policy development rests heavily on long-term institutional dynamics, while Levi (1988) focuses on the self-interest of the ruler. But – just as habitat changes often figure large in extinction science – the 'habitat' of tax policy may also shape developments. In earlier work (Hood 1985), I tried to explain long-run UK tax policy development in the forty years up to the early 1980s as a process in which administrative adaptation rather than pressure group activity on its own governs the policy dynamic. The claim is that long-term fiscal adaptation can be seen as a sort of natural selection process, in which environmental forces determine which fiscal forms stay in the game. Both existing taxes and new tax policy 'mutants' are continually being 'tested' for their survival capacity against a changing socioeconomic backdrop. If policy dinosaurs disappear, it must mean that they have come to fail those tests. The argument is that the process of 'testing' takes place according to three implicit criteria. Those three criteria are political acceptability, viability of revenue base and 'administerability'.

- *Political acceptability.* A tax which arouses widespread political discontent over a politically significant period of time will not survive. This condition overlaps with Levi's ideas about 'quasi-voluntary compliance', and for the same reason. To modify the old dictum: you can coerce a few people all of the time or many people some of the time but not many people all of the time. The British poll tax, introduced in 1988–89 as a replacement for the traditional house property tax, is perhaps the clearest recent example in OECD countries of a tax which failed this test. But the conditions for political acceptability themselves need to be spelt out carefully if this condition is not to be teleological. As a first approximation, it can be suggested that the degree of tax refusal is some function of extensiveness (number of opponents), intensiveness (how strongly the opponents oppose) and threatfulness (how much damage the opponents are capable of inflicting with the resources available to them). A tax which meets extensive resistance may be politically viable if the intensiveness and threatfulness of resistance is limited, and a tax which meets intensive resistance may be viable if extensiveness and threatfulness are limited. But tax resistance which scores high on threatfulness, or which combines extensiveness and intensiveness (as in the case of the poll tax), will be difficult to overcome.

• *Viability of revenue base*. Even if it passes the political acceptability test, a tax which is not yoked to a fertile economic base risks withering away (though, of course, there are examples of taxes introduced for policy reasons other than that of producing revenue). The weakness of taxes imposed on the 'luxuries' of the rich (like taxes on yachts, racehorses, swimming pools, fast cars) tends to lie in this area rather than in political unacceptability. And socioeconomic change can change this condition too. For example, a world of candles, oil lamps and open fires will be a more fertile sphere for taxes on matches than a world of electric light and central heating plants. Similarly, the long-term decline in tobacco smoking may come to weaken the revenue base of tobacco taxes.

• *'Administrability'*. Even if it is politically acceptable and built on a potentially fertile economic base, a tax which is not 'administrable' (readily enforceable, smoothly operable) will fail. Winston Churchill's abortive tax on betting when he was British Chancellor of the Exchequer from 1926 to 1930 is a clear example of a tax which passed the first two conditions but not the third (see Hood 1976: 169–80).

Both long-established and newly invented taxes can founder on any one of these three reefs. Or, to change the metaphor, the flock of 'golden geese' must not be too fierce or numerous to be exploited. Nor is it enough for the 'golden goose' to be plump or fecund enough to be useful for revenue purpose. And it is not enough for the goose to be readily 'pluckable'. *All* of these conditions must be simultaneously fulfilled. So the claim, consistent with Levi's emphasis on 'quasi-voluntary compliance', is that 'administrability', though not a *sufficient* condition for tax viability, is always a *necessary* one.

Like 'political acceptability', the conditions for 'administrability' need to be defined to avoid teleology. 'Administrability' refers to the ease with which taxes can be collected with relative economy of effort from people who would not choose to pay taxes if they had a real opportunity to do otherwise. Drawing on administrative design ideas which go back at least as far as Jeremy Bentham,

I identified five basic elements in tax 'administrability'. They are listability, conduitability, standard clarity, reinforceability and cross-sanctions.

First, *listability* (or 'cadastrability') is the property of being applicable to a readily identifiable population of taxable units, if possible from sources which are available in advance and cannot be easily contaminated by evasive action. (A 'cadaster' is the traditional term for a tax register.) For example, traditional taxes on those appointed to public office (as in Frederick the Great's Prussia and many other European states in the past) would score high on 'listability'. On the other hand, taxes on livestock (particularly those, like pigs, with high reproductive rates) would score very low, given the difficulties of keeping track of such animals from any central point. A poll tax on a fairly mobile population in an inner-city suburb (like the British poll tax of 1988/9–93) comes closer to the 'livestock' end of the 'listability' spectrum than to the 'public officeholders' end.

Second, *conduitability* is the property of being assessable and collectable through a relatively small number of surveillable channels or 'bottlenecks' at which oversight can economically be applied. (A 'conduit' is a channel or drain.) For example, if employment is concentrated into a few big companies, the companies' own records and administrative staff can be used as the 'conduit' for income taxes. Hence a tax on new cars is potentially easily 'conduitable' through a relatively small number of motor manufacturers, but a tax on used cars (if not imported) is less easily conduitable, given a multitude of small dealers, private sales and part-time operators in the business.

Third, *standard clarity* is the property of being relatable to values that can be ascertained relatively economically and 'objectively'. For example, a tax based on records of actual prices paid (as in capital gains taxes based on stock market records) is high on 'standard clarity'. A tax based on assessment of the value of items which have not been sold will score low on this measure. The used-car tax example used earlier is obviously a case where standard clarity would be problematic. Even if payment of the tax were made a condition of legal transfer of ownership (which is the way that such taxes are normally set up, requiring buyers to pay in order to be able to prove ownership of the relevant property in law), there is a clear incentive for buyers and sellers to collude to under-declare the real price paid for each vehicle.

Listability, conduitability and standard clarity are the basic elements of fiscal 'administrability', or the 'pluckability' of the golden goose. To this basic trio, I later added reinforceability and cross-sanctions (Hood 1986: 74–81).

Reinforceability is the property of cross-checking oversight from different vantage points, used for different purposes, which will tend to reinforce one another. Reinforceability is a Benthamite design principle (Bentham 1931: 415–16). For example, a system which prevents a dead person's property from being legally inheritable before a process of probate by a public authority can be used to reinforce checks on tax paid by that person during life. In the same way, in our used-car tax example, the legal transfer of ownership title could be used as a point for checking that annual licence or registration taxes had been paid.

Cross-sanctions refers to an incentive structure which makes tax evasion automatically result in the denial of other benefits. ['Cross-sanctions' comes from Bernstein (1955: 245–6), building on the work of Landis (1938: 244).] For example, where payment of stamp duty on transfers is needed before a law court can recognize ownership, a strong 'cross-sanction' exists, and the same applies to our example of the tax on sale of used cars. However, to avoid the likely problem of under-declaration of true prices paid (as discussed earlier), some additional cross-sanction would be needed. One possibility would be to give aggrieved used-car buyers legal rights of redress against sellers, but to link the amounts for which they could claim compensation to the purchase price declared to the tax authorities.

A perfect or 'ideal' tax, in terms of 'administrability', would possess all five properties at once. In reality, few real-life tax designs do so, even for quite successful and long-lasting taxes, and the last two conditions of 'reinforceability' and 'cross-sanctions' seem less critical than the first three in practice. Many taxes seem to get along fairly satisfactorily without them. Moreover, greater 'enforceability' may at some point come at the expense of at least one of the other tests of fiscal survival, particularly political acceptability.

For example, the introduction of mandatory high-integrity universal state identification systems in countries which have no tradition of such identification, like Australia and the UK, would certainly make their tax systems more 'administrable' by increasing the 'listability' condition and limiting the ever-present problem of people who evade income taxes by concealing their true identity from employers. But the popular backlash which developed in Australia over the 'Australia card' initiative in 1987–88 (a government plan to introduce a mandatory high-integrity identity card system for the adult population), causing a newly re-elected Labor government to ditch the plan in 1988, is an example of the way in which administrability and political acceptability can conflict.

Further, the scope of 'design' in fiscal arrangements is shaped by overall socioeconomic structures, which both create and destroy administrability niches (cf. Hinrichs 1966). For example, many radio sets in the 1920s were fairly easily 'listable'. The equipment, as can be seen from examples which survive as collectors' pieces, was large and fixed, usually bought from specialist suppliers, and (except for the 'crystal sets' attached to the wire springs of the mattresses of those days) typically needed elaborate outside aerials to pick up a satisfactory radio signal. In these conditions, a licence tax on radio sets (as imposed by many states) was relatively 'administrable'. By the 1970s, when radios had become miniaturized and could almost be bought with the groceries in the supermarket, the listability element had completely disappeared, so that licence taxes for radio sets were finally abandoned in the UK in 1970 (Hood 1985: 25). Television sets are probably heading in the same direction as far as miniaturization and multiple patterns of non-specialist supply are concerned, but the advent of cable and satellite TV introduce new possible tax handles.

Identifying the conditions for fiscal 'niches' to develop or disappear has parallels with 'niche theory' in biology (cf. Schubert 1976: 185). And clearly such an approach has the potential to explain (even to predict) why fiscal 'dinosaurs' die. Specifically, there are five hypotheses which can be drawn from this approach to identify conditions under which taxes survive or die.

First, the greater the resistance or opportunism faced by any tax design, the more important the five elements outlined above will be to its viability; so if developments take place which weaken general tax compliance, the pressure will go on to any cracks in the administrative design. Second, among the factors governing the degree of resistance or opportunism is the overall economic growth rate, which determines whether the division of resources between taxpayers and government is perceived as a positive-sum same game (in which both sides can gain at the same time) or a zero-sum game (in which one side's gain is the other side's loss). When growth slows, tax resistance is likely to rise. Third, as noted earlier, a tax design can be viable even when it does not have *all* of the five properties. But a tax design which comes to meet *none* of them will not be viable for long, and is likely to disappear. Fourth, the five properties develop from the socioeconomic 'habitat' of tax policy. Changes in the economy and society can both create and destroy any of those properties. So a tax design which is viable in one period may cease to be so at a later date, and vice versa. Fifth, a fully 'administrable' tax design may still fail on criteria of political acceptability or revenue fertility. But a tax which meets the two other criteria will not ordinarily succeed unless it is also 'administrable' in these terms.

Analysing tax policy dynamics in these terms gives a narrower perspective than Levi's 'grand-theoretic' approach, and a more environmentally driven approach to tax dynamics than Rose and Karran's 'inertia' analysis. It was originally conceived to explain long-term tax policy changes in the UK alone. It concentrates on the operational testing of tax 'life forms', rather than on the way that new tax 'mutants' come on the scene (for example, in the international diffusion of tax-reform ideas which undoubtedly played a part in the tax changes of the 1980s).

Nevertheless, looking at tax policy dynamics in this way seems at least as good as Levi's approach in explaining (and even predicting) tax 'rejects', such as the UK poll tax referred to earlier. And it can help us to understand how taxes are shaped by their 'habitats', by pinpointing socioeconomic factors which may have worked through the putative 'taxability filter' to produce general shifts in tax design of the kind observed in the 1980s. From this perspective, key socioeconomic changes that may have worked through the enforceability filter to destroy the habitat of the tax dinosaurs are changes in employment structure and distribution, change in lifestyle patterns and shifts in retail and distribution patterns.

Changes in employment structure may have significantly altered tax habitats. A decline in massive employment organizations (through the effects of big corporations and public authorities increasingly sub-contracting functions once performed in-house and dividing themselves into primary and secondary employment units) will reduce income tax 'conduitability'. Related increases in self-employment, part-time employment, second jobs and 'boutique-scale' production (many of them associated with increasing feminization of the labour force), will also weaken listability and conduitability in the employment habitat of the income tax structure. Along with those changes went growth in the service sector (for example, in childminding, management consultancy and contract cleaning). When linked with welfare-state structures in which the income threshold of eligibility for state-welfare benefits was close to the threshold of liability for payment of income tax, such changes inevitably made income tax much more troublesome to operate.

Moreover, changes in lifestyle patterns may also have serious effects on tax habitat. The diffusion of 'middle-class' lifestyle patterns in the developed countries may have swamped the capacity of tax bureaucracies to cope with the tax offsets applying to traditional middle-class lifestyles such as home ownership or financially complex asset or income structures. An avalanche of tax-driven investment, the development of more complex and opaque pay structures (with bonuses, in-kind benefits, etc.), and a general growth of 'tax-wise' financial sophistication allied to the substantial growth of the financial services industry, may have tested traditional offset structures to destruction.

Finally, changed patterns of retailing and distribution may produce new tax 'niches' for Levi's predatory rulers to occupy, by increasing scope for conduitability and standard clarity. In some ways, the retailing revolution in developed countries is recreating the fiscal control properties of a traditional economy which bases its tax regime on controlling and monitoring the flow of goods through a relatively small number of readily controllable seaports. Major changes in retail and distribution patterns, with retail sales concentrated into fewer, larger units, make *ad valorem* sales taxes more administratively viable. A notable feature of the changing tax 'habitat' is dependence on computerized accounting systems to check fraud by employees, which make it far more difficult for today's 'mega-shopkeepers' to falsify their sales records for the tax authorities, than it would have been for their corner-store grandparents.

Changes in these three aspects of tax habitat may suggest that the (partial) extinction of the dinosaurs and their (partial) replacement by new life forms is explainable by something other than ideological meteorites coming from out of the blue. The habitat changes are compatible with ideas about the development of post-industrial or post-Fordist socioeconomic structure, which were referred to in Chapter One, because changes in employment structure, the development of more flexible units of production and the wider diffusion of middle-class lifestyle patterns are all elements of those ideas.

But it is also quite plausible to attribute at least some of those developments to 'self-induced' changes, in which the tax structure destroys itself by encouraging reactions which undermine its design foundations. For example, Max Weber discussed how the Roman Empire's tax system encouraged the development of a subsistence economy, undermining the empire's own fiscal foundations (Gerth and Mills 1948: 210). And in contemporary times, at least part of the development of less fiscally surveillable forms of employment and reward could be seen as a rational response to the establishment of deduction-at-source mass income tax regimes operated through employers. And the spread of tax-efficient investments using tax offsets is even more clearly an area in which the old income tax structure may have been its own undoing, as Mucciaroni argues. Indeed, focusing on the self-destructive dynamics of the traditional tax structure may help to explain why tax policy change was not uniformly developed through OECD countries, because we would expect those changes to be most dramatic in those countries which put the heaviest emphasis on the progressive income tax (with offsets for successful 'rent-seeking' groups) as a major source of revenue. It would help to explain why France and other 'Latin' countries were not in the forefront of the tax revolution compared to countries like Japan, the USA, Germany and the UK.

Conclusion

As with government spending growth, it is debatable whether 1980s tax policy in the OECD countries is a clear case of general policy extinction. As we have seen, total tax burdens did not fall in general, and major differences remain in the tax profiles of different OECD states (see Steinmo 1989).

But to the extent that cutting of top tax rates and the shift to consumption taxes qualify as a major shift, do they defy conventional analyses of tax policy development, as Peters claims? The three analyses of tax policy dynamics considered here give us very different perspectives on the tax policy changes of the 1980s. From Rose and Karran's inertia perspective, we would expect to find the dinosaurs still alive in many ways, in that continuity and inheritance dominate current policy (see also Rose 1990). But the possibility of abrupt, discontinuous change is recognized by their theory and distinguishes it from the well-known Lindblom variant of incrementalism. Such changes stem from the unanticipated long-term effects of successive short-term expedients, and in that sense involve a self-destructive dynamic. For Levi, it seems that 1980s tax reform may need to be explained by ideological meteorites rather than by normal predatoriness on the part of rulers. But, as we have seen, it is possible to explain at least part of those changes without dispensing with Levi's 'predatory rule' assumptions. Policy change from this perspective stems from changing coalitions of interest, for example in Peters' ideas about new tax policy entrepreneurship or in the growing power of international corporations reducing national governments' bargaining power. In my own approach, tax viability is heavily determined by 'habitat' (though habitat can itself be altered by self-destructive processes). Habitat alterations associated with socioeconomic changes in the developed countries in the past twenty years or so can explain the weakening of the traditional tax regime from this perspective.

If we put these three approaches (summarized in Table 6.1) together, it would suggest that tax policy changes, like privatization, might belong in sector (l) of Chapter One. We find no specific cultural or 'power of ideas' interpretation in the conventional tax policy literature (in contrast to the literature on government growth or regulatory reform).

Table 6.1 Three approaches to explaining tax policy change

Approach	The political inertia thesis (Rose and Karran)	The theory of predatory rule (Levi)	The enforceability filter thesis (Hood)
Emphasis	Institutional deadweight	Ruler self-interest	Tax administrability
Account of policy dynamics	Long-term cumulative effects of short-run changes can be unexpected and destabilizing	'Conditional bargains' and voluntary compliance unravel; discount rates and transaction costs change	Autonomous and self-induced changes in tax policy habitat alter enforceability conditions
Applicability to 1980s tax changes	Can explain predominance of amendment to existing taxes and overall tax revenue growth	No, according to Levi; but could flatter taxes in fact fit the predatory rule hypothesis?	Can explain erosion of direct and growth of indirect taxes by reference to background changes
Limitations	Main focus on inertia	Vague and unfalsifiable	Main focus on enforcement

Of course, all three approaches have their limitations. For example, the inertia approach and the enforceability filter approach do not explain the motivation behind levying a new tax and the predatory rule approach does not explain the use of taxes for purposes other than raising revenue (such as policy on unleaded petrol). None of them focuses as such on international policy diffusion, which seems to have been a major part of the story of tax design in the 1980s. Peters (1991: 287) argues that: 'Once the process of tax reform began in one country, it became easier (or even necessary with corporate taxation) for other countries to adopt similar reforms. Some of this international effect was the result simply of the diffusion of a policy innovation . . . while a portion of the change may also be a result of the need to maintain competitiveness.'

But, as has already been stressed, diffusion cannot itself explain reversal. All it can explain is why a reversal, once it has begun somewhere, comes to be spread and reinforced – why a tide flows (in Douglas', 1989, metaphor), rather than why it turns. And, despite Peters' claim that 1980s tax reform defied conventional accounts of tax policy change, each of the three tax-policy specific approaches has considerable power to explain why this particular group of policy dinosaurs came under pressure. The sudden, irregular change is compatible with what the 'inertia model' would expect; the changes could be seen as a result of changing 'transactions costs' and 'relative bargaining power' in

Levi's predatory-rule model; and they could also be interpreted as the result of socioeconomic changes working through the tax 'enforceability filter' in my own model. In this case, as with others that we have looked at, existing theories may have more power to understand tax policy extinction and the emergence of new fiscal life forms than they are credited with by those who talk of theory-defying policy revolutions.

7

Economic rationalism in public management: from Progressive Public Administration to New Public Management?

> What has been taking place in almost every government in developed political systems . . . is a new emphasis on the organizational designs for public management . . . This internationalization of public management parallels the internationalization of public and private sector economies.
>
> (Aucoin 1990: 134)

The end of the progressive public administration style?

Many public administration watchers identified an international change of style taking place in their subject during the 1980s. A new hyped-up language of managerialism and economic rationalism was applied to the organization of public services. A new breed of accountants and management consultants started to colonize the public sector in many countries, to the point where 'accountability' began to be jestingly defined by sceptics as putting accountants in charge of everything. In some cases, too, high public office was achieved by a new generation of 'econocrats' who had been schooled in a much more restrictive and 'dry' neoclassical approach to their subject than their predecessors (see Pusey 1991).

In several OECD countries, the ideas of 'progressive-era' public administration (PPA) seemed to be heading for the dinosaurs' graveyard. In their place came a new set of apparently related doctrines, presented as a movement for 'economic rationalism' and labelled by some as the 'New Public Management' or 'NPM' (see Aucoin 1990; Hood 1991a; Pollitt 1993). David Osborne and Ted Gaebler's (1992) bestseller, *Reinventing Government*, popularized many of these new doctrines and hailed them as 'revolutionary'.

By 'PPA' is meant those ideas about public management which came into favour in the 'progressive era' of the late nineteenth and early twentieth century. The term 'progressive' is here used broadly to denote a general current of turn-of-the-century thinking about government and public services, rather than specifically to refer to political parties of that name. But PPA doctrines have earlier roots, for example in the German Cameralist tradition dating back to the sixteenth century (see Small 1909) and even Chinese Confucian ideas of nearly 2000 years before (see Creel 1964: 162, fn. 46). Although frequently challenged, this approach to public management is historically deep-rooted and recurrent.

For PPA, the central issue of public management is how to limit corruption and the waste and incompetence that goes with it. As Barry Karl (1963: 18) puts it: '. . . it seemed clear enough that the cost of government was directly proportional to the dishonesty of politicians'. Implicitly, the underlying assumptions of turn-of-the-century progressivism are:

• Politicians are inherently venal. They will use their high public office wherever possible to enrich themselves, their friends and relations.
• Private business is monopolistic or oligopolistic. That is, markets in many areas are dominated by one or a few big corporations, and the 'perfect competition' of introductory economics textbooks is the exception, not the rule.
• One of the largest businesses in the economy – if not *the* biggest one – is organized crime. And crime is, by definition, outside the ordinary limitations of the law of contract and delict.

What is the best policy for honesty in these circumstances? Should public organizations copy private business? Should public services be provided by contracts with private businesses? The progressive argument is that, in such conditions, such practices will lead to high-cost, low-quality services. Waste and poor-quality performance will result, either because the system will be riddled with corrupt favouritism and harassment, or because the public contract 'market' will be controlled by organized crime, or both.

From this stark view of the world, progressives put heavy stress on two basic doctrines of organizational design. First, they held that the public sector should be sharply distinct from the private sector in terms of continuity, ethos, methods of doing business, organizational design, the type of staff recruited and how they are rewarded and promoted. The aim was to put public administration in the hands of a dedicated 'Jesuitical corps' – a favourite and recurring metaphor, used by Beatrice Webb (see Barker 1984: 34) and others – insulated as far as possible from the corrupt world outside. Public servants should 'love the state as priests love the church' (as Sir Arthur Helps once put it: see Schaffer 1973: 39) and not as stockbrokers love the stock exchange.

The other basic PPA doctrine is that politicians and senior public officials must be kept in a procedural straitjacket to limit the damage they can do. That is, their ability to exercise discretionary power needs to be restricted by an elaborate structure of quasi-independent institutions and general rules of procedure. Such rules include popular recall and referendum to vote out errant officials or legislate over their heads (cf. Walker 1987; Cashman 1988: 52–3), as well as public service 'statutes' and general rules of procedure, particularly for handling money, staff and contracts. The institutions and rules are designed to prevent favouritism, harassment and corruption and to maintain arm's-length relations between politicians and the entrenched custodians of particular public 'trusts', like independent central banks or anti-corruption investigatory bodies.

Not all OECD countries embraced PPA doctrines to the same extent. Perhaps the German tradition takes the approach furthest, in that it combines a highly rule-bound approach to public service with a tradition of public bodies independent from direct control by executive politicians (notably the famous Bundesbank). But a move in the same direction also took place in many other countries. An example is the Australian progressive-era tradition of statutory boards with independent power relative to executive politicians: such boards included Public Service Boards intended to insulate the public service from political jobbery and harassment (see Halligan and Wettenhall 1990). The US adoption of 'merit hiring' (that is, depoliticized selection for much of the federal civil service beginning after President Garfield was murdered by a frustrated would-be civil servant in 1881) and development of the federal regulatory commissions as independent public bodies also clearly reflects the PPA agenda.

Explanations of the ascendancy of the PPA model

Conventional interpretations of the long-term development of public management structures fell into two main groups. Perhaps the most common approach was to see the adoption of the PPA style as part of a one-way historical process towards social 'modernization' – the institutional equivalent of real estate development. In that perspective, administrative history is seen as an inexorable march towards modernization. Historians like Benjamin de Witt (1968) interpreted US progressivism as a successful assault on outmoded privilege in business and politics by the standard-bearers of modern democracy (cf. Olson 1979: 7).

More generally, in the early twentieth century, Max Weber was the doyen of this approach. In a classic essay written about 1911, Weber characterized 'modern bureaucracy' in terms which had several affinities with the PPA model (including lifetime career service, fixed pay rather than pay related to performance, and a stress on procedural rules). A famous passage in the essay describes such a structure as superior to any other method of organization in just the same way as machine production is superior to handcraft (Gerth and Mills 1948: 214). It was perhaps natural to regard PPA as part of that wave of history.

In similar vein is the tradition of 'Fabian public administration', epitomized by Sydney and Beatrice Webb, who founded the London School of Economics and Political Science in 1895. From that perspective, the highest possible point of administrative evolution involves collectivist allocation rather than markets, and direction by an ascetic élite corps rather than by managers hired on the open market (see Barker 1984). This approach to public administration was old-fashioned by the 1960s (even at the LSE). But the Weberian tradition of understanding administrative change as modernization remained strongly entrenched, and PPA was often seen as the hallmark of modernity in public administration.

The main alternative to understanding PPA as the reflection of wave-of-history 'modernization' is to interpret it more critically as a product of particular interests. Though there are many interpretations of progressivism, the movement is frequently understood as reflecting the rise of a 'new middle class' of affluent professionals whose power was based on expertise rather than on inherited wealth alone (Olson 1979: 8–9). The new middle class argued for public regulation to counter big business corruption and for professional public administration based on a dichotomy between 'politics' and 'administration' to counter the patronage power of 'machine politics'; that is, politicians offering public service jobs and benefits to the newly enfranchised lower classes in return for their votes (see Cashman 1988: 45–8). For Marxists, this famous and recurring policy–administration dichotomy reflects the power of business interests attempting to distance the administrative system from direct exposure to the electoral power of the working class and its representatives (see Dearlove 1979).

By the early 1980s, perhaps the strongest 'interest-based' alternative to the Weberian/Fabian interpretation of PPA as the last step in functional modernization was the 'economics of bureaucracy' approach, of which a landmark text was William Niskanen's famous *Bureaucracy and Representative Government* (1971). We have already encountered this approach in various guises in earlier chapters. It suggests that public administration structures are best understood as a reflection of successful 'rent-seeking' political interests, not as a functional adaptation to the 'modernization needs' of a society. Looked at in this way, PPA is simply a convenient cover story for the 'producerist' interests of public bureaucrats and their interest-group allies in the legislature. PPA practices such as lifetime employment, regular salaries paid irrespective of performance, captive markets and independent public power can be read as a way of shielding shirk-prone bureaucrats and professionals both from the rigours of market competition and from real subordination to political control. But if PPA did indeed serve those entrenched interests so well, how can we account for the rise of 'New Public Management'?

The dinosaur-killer: New Public Management

Such now conventional accounts of public administration development received a major jolt in the 1980s when several OECD countries started moving towards what came to be known as 'New Public Management' (NPM) in place of the PPA model. The term 'NPM' was coined to label a shift in public management styles. It was intended to cut across the particular language in which PR consultants dressed up public management reforms within each country (such as the French *'Projet de Service'*, the British 'Next Steps', the Canadian 'Public Service 2000') and highlight their common features. The analogy is with equally general terms like 'new politics', 'new right' and 'new industrial state', which were invented for a similar reason.

Ostensibly, the NPM model strikes directly at the heart of the two basic doctrines of PPA described above. One of its themes is the doctrine of lessening or removing organizational differences between the public and private sector, to reduce avoidable public sector inefficiency. The doctrine is that methods of doing business in public organizations need to be shifted away from heavy emphasis on general rules of procedure and be focused more on getting results.

The particular doctrines of public management encompassed by NPM have been variously described by different commentators (such as Aucoin 1990; Hood 1991a; Pollitt 1993). Christopher Pollitt (1993) identifies two phases of the development of NPM. He distinguishes between an early 'neo-Taylorian' phase concerned with tightening labour discipline and cutting costs by measurement of work output in the style pioneered by Frederick Winslow Taylor in the 1890s, and a later 'quality' phase concerned with arresting the perceived decline in public service standards by specifying and monitoring performance targets.

Though the commentators' interpretations differ in detail, there is much overlap in their accounts of what NPM entailed. General themes are the idea of a shift in emphasis from policy-making to management skills in the upper reaches of public sector organizations, from a stress on process to a stress on output, from orderly hierarchies to an intendedly more competitive basis for providing public services, from fixed to variable pay and from a uniform and inclusive public service to a variant structure with more emphasis on contract provision.

Six dimensions of the change from a PPA to an NPM approach are shown in Table 7.1, which summarizes in simplified form some of the shifts in received doctrine. The first three doctrines in Table 7.1 involve reducing the degree of insulation of the public from the private sector (which, the reader will recall, is one of the cardinal PPA design principles for public management). The other three doctrines involve reducing the emphasis on the other cardinal PPA design principle, the doctrine of public management according to system-wide rules of procedure. The doctrines are:

• More emphasis on *disaggregating* public organizations into separate self-contained units. Rather than large-scale uniform structures, NPM doctrine holds that better management requires setting up separately managed units for each 'product'. The aim is to divide the public sector into separately managed or 'corporatized' units with their own designer logos and corporate identity, operating with 'one-line' budgets, mission statements, business plans and managerial autonomy. The new disaggregated structure replaces the PPA style of providing many public services through 'semi-anonymized' organizations within a single aggregated unit, with detailed service-wide rules, common service provision in a number of key areas, close central control of pay bargaining and staffing levels.

Table 7.1   Six components of NPM and performance assumptions

	No.	Doctrine	Assumed link to performance	Replaces	Operational significance
Public service distinctiveness	1	'Unbundle' the public service into corporatized units organized by product	Make units 'manageable'; focus blame; create anti-waste lobby by splitting provision and production	Belief that public service needs to be uniform and inclusive to be accountable without underlaps and overlaps	Erosion of single service employment; arm's-length dealings; devolved budgets
	2	More contract-based competitive provision, with internal markets and term contracts	Rivalry will cut costs and push up standards; contracts will make performance standards explicit	Flexibility, independence and lower transaction costs require loosely specified employment contracts and open-ended provision	Distinction of primary and secondary public service labour force
	3	Stress on private-sector styles of management practice	Need to apply 'proven' private sector management tools in the public sector	Stress on public service 'ethic'; fixed pay and hiring rules; model employer stance; centralized staffing structure, jobs for life	Move from double imbalance PS pay, career service, unmonetized rewards, 'due process' employee entitlements
Rules vs discretion	4	Put more emphasis on visible 'hands-on' top management	Accountability requires clear assignment of responsibility, not diffusion of power	Paramount stress on policy skills and rules, not active management	More 'freedom to manage' by discretionary power
	5	Make performance standards and measures explicit, formal and measurable	Accountability means clearly stated aims; efficiency needs 'hard look' at goals	Qualitative and implicit standards and norms	Erosion of self-management by professionals
	6	Greater emphasis on output controls	Need for greater stress on results	Stress on procedure and control by 'collibration' (opposed maximizers)	Resources and pay based on performance; blurring of funds for pay and for activity

Source: Adapted from Hood (1991a: 4–5).

- More emphasis on formal *competition*, both among public sector organizations like schools, hospitals and universities, and between public and private organizations (even independent organizations like charities), through 'market testing' and franchising. Such competition has been more noticeable for 'delivery' of public policy than for policy advice, more in the area of social and welfare services than in areas like law enforcement and tax collection, and more in local and national organization than international organization. It replaces the traditional PPA structure in which public sector organizations typically have permanent captive markets in the interests of professional continuity and the avoidance of 'corrupt practices in soliciting contracts.
- More emphasis on the adoption within the public sector of private-sector management practices. Examples include: a management style combining commercial confidentiality with extensive use of PR, projecting diffuse images and slogans rather than precise factual reporting; the abandonment of traditional public sector aspirations to be a 'model employer' setting an example to, rather than taking its cue from, private sector employers in matters like pay and conditions of employment (notably anti-discrimination rules); and a move away from the traditional 'double imbalance' public administration pay structure, in which lower-level staff are relatively highly paid compared to their private-sector counterparts and top-level staff are relatively low-paid (see Sjölund 1989). For financial reporting, NPM accounting ideas are designed to make the costs of products transparent and the costs of individuals (such as personal salaries and particular types of discretionary expenditure) opaque, whereas PPA accounting ideas were designed to do the opposite, making the costs of individuals and other key input activities transparent, but doing so by leaving the costs of products opaque.
- More emphasis on *hands-on management*. The move here is away from the traditional progressive-era style of 'hands-off' management in the public sector, with relatively anonymous bureaucrats at the top of public sector organizations, fenced in by personnel management rules designed to prevent favouritism by managers. In its place comes a new style in which top managers are more visible and publicity-seeking, cultivate an image of active control and have greater discretionary power.
- More emphasis on setting *explicit and measurable* (or at least checkable) performance standards for public organizations in terms of the range, level and content of services to be provided. Involved here is a shift away from the tradition of 'high-trust' relations within public organizations towards a 'low-trust', arm's-length style (Fox 1974: 72–84, 102–119; Sako 1991), moving away from the traditional emphasis on long-term commitment and diffuse obligations. Implicitly, the accountability metaphor underlying PPA is that of trustee and beneficiary (John Locke's metaphor for government), in which the trustee has irreducible fiduciary duties to the beneficiary and the beneficiary does not set the trustee's goals directly. But the accountability metaphor underlying NPM is that of a principal dealing with a potentially untrustworthy agent, aiming to spell out goals with maximum precision and

setting up monitoring and incentive schemes to induce the agent to follow the principal's wishes. This shift to a low-trust management style is ironic, given the professed admiration for high-trust Japanese corporate management ideology in many OECD countries during the 1980s, at much the same time that NPM ideas were spreading through the public sector of those countries. It came to be commonplace to speak of the chain-of-command dimension of public sector organization in the legal/economic language of 'principals' and 'agents' and to conceive different units of the public bureaucracy as separate 'firms', not parts of the same public service expected to cooperate with one another, often on a high-trust, word-of-mouth basis.

- More emphasis on controlling public organizations by pre-set *output measures* instead of the traditional style of *ad hoc* 'orders of the day' coming from the top, or by the subtle balancing of incompatible desiderata in the 'collibration' type of control described in Chapter One. Together with this tendency at the level of organizations and their sub-units, goes a move towards public sector pay based on individual job performance as assessed by superiors. Such a shift reverses the PPA doctrine of the classified public service, with a common and uniform pay matrix based on general rank or educational qualifications.

The movement from PPA to NPM was not confined to countries under right-wing government (and some right-governed countries like Japan did not move far towards NPM), and it was certainly not simply an Anglo-American phenomenon of the Reagan/Thatcher era. The Antipodean countries, South Africa and Hong Kong put at least equally high emphasis on the development of NPM (see, for instance, Nethercote 1989; Sturgess 1989; Scott *et al.* 1990). And NPM was not confined to the English-speaking countries. For example, Sweden placed particularly strong emphasis on some aspects of NPM during the 1980s; and Denmark, the Netherlands and France are also countries in which NPM themes were prominent in the 1980s, for example in developing variable pay systems (Hegewisch 1991: table 3).

However, NPM certainly did not triumph everywhere (see Derlien 1992). As with privatization, there are interesting variations in the extent to which the PPA model went into 'extinction' across the OECD world. It is notable that some of the traditional OECD 'showcase' economies – Japan, Germany and Switzerland – seem to have put less emphasis on adopting NPM-type reforms (on the six dimensions indicated in Table 7.1) in the 1980s than countries like Sweden, New Zealand or the UK. For example, the NPM tendency to decentralize personnel management (hiring, grading, job classifications, etc.) to operating units away from central personnel agencies was not a marked tendency in Japan, where the National Personnel Authority retained its powers over entrance exams, discipline and the public service pay matrix in the 1980s (though ministries always controlled promotion and specific recruitment of successful examinees). And whereas 'pay for performance' doctrines took a strong hold in countries like Sweden, Denmark, New Zealand and the UK, there was no equivalent movement in Germany or Japan.

Explaining PPA's extinction and the rise of NPM: how much of a surprise?

Given the lack of a systematic database on such developments, any 'scoring' of variations has to be impressionistic. But the 'high NPM' group within the OECD would be likely to include Sweden, Canada, New Zealand, Australia and the UK, with France, Denmark, the Netherlands, Norway and Ireland also showing some marked shifts in the direction of NPM. At the other end, the 'low NPM' group would be likely to include Germany, Greece, Spain, Switzerland, Japan and Turkey.

Nevertheless, the weakening of PPA and the rise of NPM seems to be sufficiently widespread to be considered as a possible 'policy extinction' in the terms of this book. And some commentators, like Osborne and Gaebler (1992), certainly portray NPM's rise as an epoch-making change which heralded the extinction of the old PPA order. How can we explain that change and how much of a 'surprise' does it pose for traditional ways of understanding the development of public administration?

At first sight, it does seem to be a surprise in several ways. For the Fabian public administration tradition, the partial demise of the PPA model looks like an unanticipated (and unwelcome) backward step in evolution. But, as noted earlier, that tradition was virtually dead in academia before NPM came on to the scene, though it certainly lingered on in the world of practice. More serious for conventional academic understanding of public administration development was the apparent abandonment of some of the features of 'modern' bureaucracy stressed by Weber, notably the stress on rule-bound administration, the notion of lifetime careers and fixed pay for service. At first sight, NPM seems to be a significant departure from the Weberian script of 'modernization' in that sense. And, perhaps more seriously still, the demise of PPA seemed to challenge the economics-of-politics understanding of bureaucratic development (as in the case of regulation), just as that approach had been formally expounded. If senior bureaucrats are really as powerful as the economics-of-politics model assumes, and PPA suits their private 'rent-seeking' interests so well, how could it be that the PPA model seemed to collapse in so many countries with such apparent ease and lack of resistance?

An intellectually driven revolution?

Something, it seems, disturbed the 'expected' path of administrative change – whether the path expected was a steady approach to the Fabian heaven, the Weberian railroad track to institutional modernization at the end of which lies turn-of-the-century Prussian bureaucracy, or the economics-of-politics expectation of producerist power entrenched behind the PPA ideology. What exactly was that 'something'? Was it intellectual power that caused NPM to challenge the older PPA public administration style?

The prescriptive ideas behind NPM seem to come from two different – and potentially conflicting – sources. One element was the 'new institutional economics' which has figured in many of the earlier chapters. Ideas about alternative approaches to public sector management were drawn from the post-Second World War development of public choice, transactions cost theory and principal-agent theory – from the early work of Duncan Black (1958) and Kenneth Arrow (1963) to theories of managerial discretion which developed in the 1960s and 1970s (cf. Leibenstein 1976) and associated ideas of strategic behaviour in organizations.

Out of the new institutional economics came a set of public management doctrines built on ideals of: *contestability* rather than monopoly; *user choice* rather than 'producerist' styles of provision; financial *transparency* rather than fiscal opacity and hidden cross-subsidies; close concentration on micro-level analysis of the material aspects of *incentive structures* in public sector organizations rather than reliance on a generalized bureaucratic 'ethos' of *noblesse oblige* by individuals who are assumed to have a quasi-religious vocation (the 'Jesuitical corps' which PPA aims to foster). Such doctrines offered a conception of 'good public management' quite different from that embodied in PPA.

The other source of NPM ideas was the latest of a set of successive waves of business-type 'managerialism' which have swept through the public sector, in the tradition of the international scientific management movement (see Merkle 1980; Hume 1981; Pollitt 1993). In fact, there seem to have been numerous contending and contradictory managerialist tendencies in play, notably a management accounting stream and a 'corporate culture' stream, epitomized in Tom Peters' and Robert Waterman's bestseller *In Search of Excellence* (1982). From the managerialist perspective, the new principles of good management were held to be portable across organizations, policy fields and the public/private sector divide (Martin 1983), rather than particular to each specific area of policy expertise. Management was seen as a function which is paramount over technical or professional expertise in the public sector, with managers needing high discretionary power to achieve results ('free to manage'). It was also seen as central and indispensable to better organizational performance, through managers' heroic role in shaping corporate cultures (Peters and Waterman 1982) and in active measurement and adjustment of organizational outputs.

As with other policy shifts considered earlier, those who successfully championed the cause of NPM naturally put their victory down to the superior power of such ideas. NPM from this perspective is simply a technically better product than the flawed PPA design which it replaced, and rests on a stronger basis of logic, argument and evidence. For Osborne and Gaebler (1992: 322–30), the new approach to public management represents a new 'global paradigm', and transition to the new paradigm is inevitable 'just as the transition from machine rule to Progressive government was inevitable' (ibid.: 325).

However, as with privatization, there are at least three problems with interpreting the demise of PPA and the rise of NPM as a case of the power of ideas. First, as with privatization, there were no 'crucial experiments' in which NPM defeated PPA by a knock-out in clear controlled conditions on a level playing field. An 'experimental' approach was invariably rejected by the NPM partisans. In the normal style of administrative reform rhetoric, NPM advocates repeatedly used a collection of anecdotes to argue for a general 'cloning' of the new approach, on the grounds that the facts of the case were clear and there was no time to waste in experimentation.

Second, the basic doctrines were not in fact particularly new. The analytic approaches of the post-Second World War institutional economics were undoubtedly innovative, and in that sense offered some refreshment to older liberal themes. But NPM's basic doctrines in fact added little of substance to the utilitarian doctrines of public management developed by Jeremy Bentham and his followers 150 years earlier on exactly the same principles of contestability, transparency, consumer-centrism and 'incentivation' (cf. Hume 1981). Ideas like performance indicators, competitive provision, franchising supply, pay for performance, did not appear for the first time in the 1980s. It was more the packaging which was new than the ideas inside.

Third, NPM lends itself just as plausibly to be interpreted as a 'cargo cult' or a new PR gloss on an old theme rather than a fundamentally new paradigm. It is easy to show that the 'managerialist' ideas which it espouses have been a recurring theme in US public administration over a long period. A 'cargo cult' is an anthropological term denoting the endless rebirth, despite repeated failures and disappointments, of ideas about a particular path to salvation. 'Cargo' was the word used in Melanesian 'pidgin English' to denote the material trappings of the Europeans, and 'cargo cults' are sects who believe that the practice of particular types of ritual will deliver 'cargo' into the hands of the believers (Lawrence 1964; Worsley 1968). Indeed, instead of 'surprise' leading to a change of approach, the *same* beliefs keep on re-emerging. In public management, like the repeat weddings of some much-married film stars, hope tends to triumph over experience.

Specifically, the beguiling idea that all the messy problems of public administration can be solved by the practice of the managerial ritual believed to be typical of private sector business, is something that has recurred for over a century in the USA despite repeated failure and disappointment. Because the ideas chime so well with stereotyped beliefs about ossified bureaucracies, rigid attitudes and self-serving officials, experience of failure prompts believers to try to change the facts rather than the theory. Indeed, George Downs and Philip Larkey (1986) describe a recurring cycle of euphoria and disillusion in the emergence of simplistic and stereotyped recipes for better public management in the USA, which shows striking similarities with the well-documented cargo cults of Melanesia. Though NPM certainly involved skilful presentation, its rise did not rest on logical proof or experimental evidence, and indeed, like privatization, it seems to have been heavily practice-led rather than theory-led.

NPM as a product of interests – and PPA self-destruction?

As with progressivism, it is perhaps understandable that NPM proponents should interpret their success as part of a 'wave of history' ridden by public-spirited visionaries. Like progressivism, it has also been interpreted in terms of changing interests, for example as a business-led move to reshape democratic politics towards what some have termed 'South-American style business democracy' (Pusey 1991: 11).

For Marxists, it is of course easy – perhaps too easy – to interpret any policy change as a product of business interests. But the shift from PPA to NPM does not seem quite so easy to explain from the viewpoint of economics-of-bureaucracy theory. Indeed, it seemed to defy Niskanen's (1971) explanation of bureaucratic growth and power. Why should senior bureaucrats connive at reform measures which could unravel their power base, in the form of a monopoly of knowledge (denied to politicians) about the true cost structure of public service provision? Were the NPM reforms a sign that elected politicians were more powerful relative to bureaucrats than the Niskanen model allows for?

Patrick Dunleavy (1985, 1991: 174–209), in a now well-known argument, claims that the apparent paradox results from the fact that Niskanen's model is mis-specified and fails to follow its own economics-of-bureaucracy logic thoroughly. In what he calls the 'bureau-shaping' model, Dunleavy argues that top-level bureaucrats – the ones who are assumed to count in conventional economics-of-bureaucracy approaches – have no necessary interest in expanding the total size of their budgets or even their total staff. On the contrary, he argues, such expansion is likely to bring only extra work (and perhaps tedious industrial relations conflicts) for the people at the top, without significant personal benefits, as long as top public sector salaries are controlled on a uniform basis.

By and large, what counts for the top bureaucrat is what Dunleavy calls the 'core' budget; broadly, what each agency spends on itself, rather than the parts of its budget which it hands on to other agencies or clients. Dunleavy argues that the true self-interest of top-level bureaucrats lies in aiming for high-status and satisfying work in collegial élite units, distancing themselves from front-line supervision in favour of a 'super-control' position which offers more job satisfaction and less tedious routine. Once bureaucrats adopt such preferences, there is nothing against their interests in enthusiastically cutting service delivery budgets down the line, or in breaking up and 'deprivileging' the middle-level world of public service delivery, as long as the power and status of central agencies is retained or augmented. On the contrary, such a movement will serve the self-interest of the people at the very top, 'for example, by shedding troublesome direct managerial responsibilities and gaining increased staff and time resources for intellectually more attractive tasks such as planning and guidance' (Dunleavy 1991: 207). In short, just as 'patrol avoidance' is a common feature of police behaviour, 'management avoidance' will be central to understanding the behaviour of top bureaucrats. The bureau-shaping theory is a theory of management avoidance or shirking front-line supervisory responsibilities.

Dunleavy's logic is compelling, and once the economics-of-politics perspective has been re-specified in this form, some aspects of NPM's rise

* Suggesting there is a variety of strains of policy changes around the world.

Economic rationalism in public management 137

– particularly 'unbundling' of public bureaucracies and heightened competition
at the level of 'delivery' services and routine office work – becomes much less
of a surprise. Indeed, it is exactly what would be predicted, and management
avoidance will be likely to be cumulative from this viewpoint (once corporate
executive units have been split off from policy units, the executive units will in
turn split into oversight and delivery units, and so on *ad infinitum*). Never- *
theless, the notion that the NPM movement stems from a shift of bureaucrats'
utility curves raises as many questions as it answers. For example, some bureaucracies (notably the Australian Commonwealth bureaucracy in the 1980s)
have set their face against the splitting-off of delivery agencies from policy
agencies that took place in the UK and New Zealand, raising the issue of
whether the bureau-shaping theory is 'Britocentric'. Even in the UK, does the
development of NPM in the area of top bureaucrats' interests – such as
market-testing central government functions and open competition for particular top jobs – go further than the bureau-shaping theory would predict?
And how can we explain why top bureaucrats in so many OECD countries
apparently acted 'irrationally' (or altruistically) for so long – that is, in developing the old PPA style of vertically and horizontally integrated 'giantist'
bureaucracy which (according to Dunleavy's logic) benefited the people down
the line rather than the people at the top? Why did it take them so long to see
the light? Why did the old PPA model ever come into existence at all, and why
did it not become extinct far earlier?

Clearly, to answer that question, we are driven to the conclusion either that
something must have changed historically in the interest groups involved in
bureaucratic politics, or that PPA destroyed itself. There are exponents of both
positions. Some commentators assert that the topmost positions in the bureaucracy came to be occupied by a 'new class', which perceived its interests in
ways different to its predecessors. Two Australian observers, Anna Yeatman
(1987: 350–51) and Michael Pusey (1991), have developed such an analysis, in
the tradition of James Burnham's (1942) analysis of managers as a 'new class',
discussed in Chapter Three, or of Milovan Djilas' (1957) famous 'new class'
analysis of the former Communist regime in Yugoslavia. Pusey's claims that
the upper echelons of the Australian public service are increasingly occupied
by a 'new class' of econocrats. Drawn from élite schools and backgrounds,
growing up among the consumer affluence of the long boom after the Second
World War, they differ sharply from their predecessors who in many cases
developed 'public service' ideals from close experience of the rigours of ordinary life in the depressed 1930s or the Second World War. And their education in narrow neoclassical economics (uncontaminated by the humanities or
even of the other social sciences) in élite universities makes them natural
sympathizers with New Right ideas. It may be, too, that such a background
would better equip them to see where their narrow self-interest lay than their
liberally educated predecessors.

Such an historical shift would certainly help us to understand why PPA
went into extinction when it did, and why the rational bureau-shaping ana-
lysed by Dunleavy started to develop in the particular period that it did. But

it is not clear that the shift at the top towards bureaucrats from ever-more privileged social backgrounds with more neoclassical economics training applies in all cases. In the UK and France, for example, it is doubtful if the trend in that direction was as strong as it was in Australia or New Zealand, in that the upper reaches of the civil service have always been disproportionately drawn from those with élite educational backgrounds, and there is little sign of long-term change. If a 'new class' interpretation is applicable here, it would need to refer to those who colonized the public management from the outside as well as from inside – the privatization 'complex', the management consultants, accountants and IT specialists who form the contemporary equivalent of the 'efficiency experts' who championed PPA eighty years or so earlier.

The other possible explanation of the shift is that PPA destroyed itself in some way. There is no developed interpretation in the current NPM literature along these lines, but the idea that the PPA model self-destructed is implicit in several commentaries. Perhaps the most explicit one is Martin Painter's (1990) idea of rejuvenation and decay, which was mentioned in Chapter One. As noted there, Painter argues that 'merit' and 'efficiency', the watchwords of turn-of-the-century PPA, reflected contemporary ideas of office discipline and social progress, and were enshrined in institutions which came to be dominated by particular interests, such as public service labour unions. But by the 1970s, the measures adopted in the name of 'merit' and 'efficiency' were seen to work *against* those values, particularly by those who saw traditional closed-shop career progression as unfairly loading the scales against female talent and by those who saw turn-of-the century measures to deflect graft and fraud as an obstacle to the realization of management efficiency on the basis of organizational devolution. Such an interpretation of the rise of NPM in fact appears to be a hybrid, incorporating elements of self-destruction, rising interests and habitat changes which helped the new coalitions along.

Weberianism in a new habitat?

If the extinction of PPA and the rise of NPM is not necessarily a major surprise for a reconstructed economics-of-bureaucracy approach (perhaps allied to a 'new class' interpretation), must we still conclude that NPM's rise dealt a mortal blow to conventional Weberian views about the path to administrative 'modernization'?

In some ways – particularly its preference for performance pay and hands-on management – NPM does seem to be at odds with the Weberian notion of administrative 'modernization'. But in other ways, it could be seen as marking a new frontier in the development of Weberian bureaucracy. A case in point is NPM's emphasis on measurement and calculation, what Michael Power and Richard Laughlin (1992) call the 'accountingization' of public administration. The extension of calculation and measurement (NPM's performance indicators) in place of traditional taken-for-granted or unspoken yardsticks is very much in the spirit of Weberian modernization. And the same goes for the increasing stress on formal contracts (or quasi-contracts) as the basis for action in public management, replacing an older tradition of taken-for-granted and unspecified arrangements. Indeed, far from being a move away from Weberian notions of the shift to ever greater explication of formal rules and norms, the 'contractorization' of public administration under the banner of NPM could be seen as a further development of Weberian bureaucracy.

Indeed, another way of interpreting the shift from PPA to NPM is that the new sociotechnical order developing in the long peace in the developed countries since the Second World War – the rise of 'post-industrialism' or 'post-Fordism', much discussed in earlier chapters – created a new 'habitat' for public administration which allowed Weber's vision of bureaucracy to break out of the technological constraints in which it had been fettered in the early years of the century.

Specifically, it could be claimed that 'informatization' (an inelegant imported term which has been coined to denote the diffusion of computers interlinked through telecommunication networks as part of the new core technology of public administration) has created possibilities for realizing the Weberian vision of calculation, measurement and rule-following as the core of bureaucratic activity beyond Weber's wildest dreams. The limited scope for such activities in the 'steam age' when Weber was writing his classic account of bureaucracy has been transformed by the development of information technology.

That is, the clerkly bureaucrats of Weber's day have increasingly turned into microchips, in forms made familiar by ATM machines and cheque-writing computers. Weber wrote of individual bureaucrats, using a 'Fordist' metaphor, as 'a single cog in an ever-moving mechanism' (cf. Gerth and Mills 1948: 228). Today we would use the electronic metaphor of nodes in a network, and over large parts of public management it would not even be a metaphor. The same development is even further removing traditional barriers between 'public sector work' and 'private sector work'. It could be argued to move us closer, not further away from, the Weberian idea that public and private bureaucracy have essential similarities in their handling of work (as well as increasing the scope for contracting out work which once might have been specific to public bureaucracy).

Such developments removed the need for routine information-handling tasks to be performed in the same physical location, or even in the same organization, as that containing the 'general staff' at policy level, but Weber's specification of bureaucracy does not preclude such a development. And informatization underpins a greater development of performance indicators and cost-centring, through control and monitoring arrangements which would have been infinitely more laborious and costly to operate in a pre-IT age. But all this development is exactly in the spirit of Weberian bureaucracy, not contrary to it. When John Taylor and Howard Williams (1991: 172) argue that as a result of 'informatization', 'A new public administration is being forged and new information flows, and the computer networks which facilitate and mediate them, are fundamental to the innovation process', we might conclude that informatization is moving us closer to, not further away from, the Weberian vision of impersonal (and inflexible) rule-bound handling of cases and ever more minute control systems. On this line of argument, habitat change is transforming modern public management to 'out-Weber Weber'.

Summary and conclusion

Compared to much of the literature discussed in earlier chapters of this book, accounts of the fall of PPA and the rise of NPM remain less developed and sparser. We still lack clear measuring rods for comparing public management styles, and the distinction between 'surface' change and 'deep' change will always be difficult in public organizations. Clearly, too, the PPA model of public management did not die out to the same extent everywhere, so if a policy 'dinosaur' is really going into extinction here, the process is still far from complete. And even now, many commentators see less a trend change in public management than a rapid succession of ephemeral fads and fashions which sweep through the subject and have their brief heyday of attention before going into oblivion. For example, the late Dick Spann (1981) saw public management ideas as a wheel of fashion, where everything is short term, nothing lasts for much longer than yesterday's fad for platform soles or kipper ties, every fashion, however bizarre, will be back some day. Certainly, it could be argued that the shifts and different variants within NPM – from cost-cutting 'macho management' to 'quality' concerns, from a stress on equipping politicians to manage to an attempt to separate 'management' from 'policy', from defending the public sector to a simple reflection of 'New Right' ideology – would be consistent with Spann's interpretation.

But if the interpretation offered earlier is correct, not *everything* in the NPM movement is 'up for grabs'. Certainly, particular glosses and slogans within NPM have varied in the way that Spann would expect. But the general shift away from the two cardinal doctrines of PPA – the belief in public sector distinctiveness and the stress on procedural rules limiting managerial discretion – seems to be a much more enduring trend than the sceptical 'wheel of fashion' interpretation would suggest. And such an interpretation would not anyway help us to understand why NPM developed at the particular time that it did. It only tells us that fashions change, not why this year's fashion should be tailcoats rather than doublets, or the other way round. Indeed, it would hardly be surprising if the traditional PPA model was approaching the 'endangered species' stage, since (Keynesian macroeconomic policy apart) most of the policy extinctions considered in earlier chapters are products of the same progressive-era thinking about policy and institutions which produced the public administration model to be challenged by NPM.

As with the policy extinctions considered in previous chapters, it is hard to conclude that PPA's extinction was brought about by the meteoric power of new ideas or evidence. Many of the ideas were recycled versions of doctrines which had had their day before. As with privatization, in many cases practice seems to have preceded formal articulation of doctrine. Before Osborne and

Gaebler's *Reinventing Government* (1992), the literature on public service managerialism consisted largely of sceptical academic commentaries. As a set of ideas, there are good grounds for arguing that NPM looks more like the latest version of a recurring 'cargo cult', particularly in the Anglo-Saxon countries, than the product of irrefutable logic or of some Baconian *experimentum crucis*. Cultural change (argued by Wildavsky, as we saw in Chapter Five, to be crucial in shaping government growth) and rhetorical power may well have been important, but these elements belong, as we saw in Chapter One, in an area where ideas cannot be distinguished from interests.

The two most developed sets of explanations of the shift to NPM in the literature of political science and public administration focus on changes in 'habitat' (Osborne and Gaebler's idea of demand changes in 'post-industrialism' and Taylor and Williams' idea of 'informatization' as the central force shaping NPM) and on changes in interests (Dunleavy's idea of 'bureau-shaping' and Yeatman and Pusey's idea of a 'new class' at the top). But self-destruction, tentatively discussed by Painter, seems to be tied in with the development of the new NPM interest coalition, because one of the major puzzles about the shift (like the Reformation in Northern Europe) is why the old PPA structures collapsed so easily in the face of a relatively inchoate alternative. If a mixture of self-destruction, changing habitat and changing interests lay behind PPA's demise, it would suggest a similar pattern to that identified for privatization and tax reform – putting it in sector (1) of Fig. 1.2.

Even the extent to which the extinction of PPA really comes as a 'surprise' to conventional ways of understanding long-term public management developments is debatable. For the Fabian public administration tradition, as we have seen, NPM's rise is certainly an (unwelcome) surprise; but this tradition does not count as serious political science today. However, as we saw in the last section, many aspects of NPM are not a surprise from the viewpoint of Weberian ideas about the development of 'modern' public administration. They simply represent a development of accountingization beyond what Weber could have imagined, and the automation of many processes of fitting cases to categories that were done manually in Weber's day. And though NPM is a surprise for the standard Niskanen model of bureaucratic development, we saw earlier that Dunleavy has shown how that model can be developed following its own logic to make developments like corporatization and contracting out predictable rather than surprising, from the viewpoint of the self-interested senior bureaucrats. Indeed, the real puzzle may be why the PPA model lasted so long rather than why NPM developed to challenge it.

8

Conclusion: explaining economic policy shifts

It is undoubtedly irksome to many economists that the science of economics, strictly considered, should not offer answers to many important questions that *appear* to be economic in nature but in fact belong to moral and political theory.

(Kristol 1983: 201)

Our capacity to comprehend large-scale political and social change remains utterly undeveloped.

(Hirschman 1993: 174)

Did the policy 'dinosaurs' actually die?

This book began with a loose comparison between the dinosaurs' extinction 64 million years ago and the waning of several once-familiar doctrines of economic policy during the 1980s. At first sight, the extinction analogy seems beguiling. But, as was noted at the start, it can also be tendentious. After all, are these policy 'dinosaurs' really dead? Exactly what sort of 'extinction' – if any – is involved here?

The extinction of a species is harder to establish than the death of an individual. 'Living fossils' – surviving versions of species thought to be extinct – sometimes come to light, like the coelacanth. Species believed to be on the edge of extinction can come back from the brink, like the Hawaiian goose or the Arabian oryx. Some extinct species can be recreated, like the aurochs and the tarpan. And a species can go into extinction in one form, but live on in another. After all, many scientists say that birds are directly descended from dinosaurs. If so, an 'extinct species' has turned into one of the most common and most successful life forms of today.

Similar problems arise in interpreting policy reversals. What one observer counts as a clear case of extinction can be seen by another as no more than a temporary eclipse or a minor repackaging. For instance, observers like Sir Christopher Foster (1992) have interpreted utility privatization in the UK Thatcher style as a major policy break. Others, like Christine Whitehead

(1988: 236), argue that the changes amount to less than meets the eye. Whitehead's argument is that the utility regulatory regimes introduced after privatization largely amount to a continuation of pre-privatization policies. Much the same political goals apply, such as universal pricing and access to service. And the goals themselves are basically achieved by the same means, notably the cross-subsidization of some customers by others. Apparently new policies are often tailored to historically ingrained patterns (cf. King 1992: 219, 240).

Readers will have seen two other limitations in the analogy between these economic policy shifts and the dinosaurs' demise. First, instead of the finality implied in extinction, writers like Albert Hirschman (1982) and Henri Pirenne (1914) see a historical pattern of long-term cycles and recurrence for phenomena such as the size of government and the preference for collective or individual solutions to policy issues. For instance, by the 1980s, the idea of poll tax had been dead in England for several centuries (seventeenth-century poll taxes had been highly unpopular and a poll tax had led directly to the 1381 Peasants' Revolt, the biggest medieval uprising in England). If such a life form can stage a sudden, albeit short-lived, comeback in the UK in the late 1980s (with somewhat similar political results as 600 years before), it is hard to believe that any economic policy idea can ever be gone for good. There are few unambiguous public policy counterparts to the diplodocus or the stegosaurus.

Indeed, many of the 'New Right's' favourite policy ideas of the 1980s seemed to involve a rediscovery of near 'extinct' eighteenth-century ideas and practices – such as 'workfare', private law enforcement, franchising of public services, variable payment of public officials. [The outright sale of public office was almost the only major extinct policy nostrum of the eighteenth century which did not come back into favour in the 1980s, despite general enthusiasm for privatization (see Hood 1991b).] If policy shifts are seen as part of a cyclical pattern in long-term historical perspective, we can expect that the policy 'dinosaurs' may be back one day. Indeed, several of the successor policies to the 'dinosaurs' may already be passing their peak, for example with the return to deficit financing across many of the OECD countries during the slump of the early 1990s.

The other obvious problem with the 'dinosaur' analogy is that even the *temporary* disappearance of the old policy orthodoxies is by no means beyond dispute. For instance, as we noted in Chapter Two, along with the much-hyped shift to pro-competitive regulation in a few key areas such as banking and the supply of telecommunications equipment, formal regulation has in fact *grown* sharply in the EC and OECD countries in fields like environmental and health and safety policy, in what is often seen as an unstoppable drift to 'juridification', that is, the subjection of more and more areas of social life to formal regulation (Teubner 1987). The much-discussed US model of airline deregulation has not been widely or rapidly followed by other countries.

Similarly, we noted that public enterprises kept on proliferating in new forms – particularly at lower levels of government, for intergovernmental policy areas and for new policy ventures (such as the operation of student loans in the UK and for the privatization of East German industry by the *Treuhandanstalt* after the 1990 German unification) – at the very same time that other old-style public enterprises like telecommunications utilities were being transformed into privately owned companies. Indeed, corporatization of public administration in the 'NPM' movement (as discussed in Chapter Seven) in many ways recreates the old arm's-length public enterprise model in new forms – and with it, presumably, all the associated and well-documented problems of oversight and control over such corporations, which were typically given as reasons for the shift to privatization in the trading sector.

The same point applies to government growth. It is not clear from OECD data that public spending and employment in most countries has yet staged any more than (at most) a temporary deceleration, or reached a plateau between peaks, in the peak-and-rising plateau pattern of public expenditure growth detected by Peacock and Wiseman (see Chapter Five). And many aspects of the 'PPA' model of public management still seem to be alive and well in some powerful OECD states like Japan and Germany. Indeed, even in countries where NPM seems to have gone furthest, some commentators question whether the new 'managerially correct' rhetoric goes much more than skin deep and whether it is capable of enduring major political shocks. The once-heretical idea of 'post-managerialism' is already being discussed in some countries.

It is certainly important to temper any over-casual acceptance of the debatable idea of once-for-all policy extinction. But it seems equally difficult to argue that *nothing* changed in the world of public policy over the period from the later 1970s. Hype may have far exceeded the substance of change, as often happens in the world of public policy. Nevertheless, the policy changes that did occur are hard to dismiss as trivial: the doubling or trebling of unemployment rates across most of the OECD world to levels which would have been considered politically intolerable in the 1950s and 1960s; the widespread abandonment of 'classical' regulation in areas like telecommunications and finance which were once considered central to economic and military sovereignty; dramatic cuts in top income tax rates in many countries; the privatization of public enterprises in some countries on a scale unprecedented in normal peacetime conditions this century; the fairly general slowdown in government expenditure growth; and the move in several countries to overturn the PPA public administration style which had carefully been built up over a century. Even if the metaphor of extinction may be too strong for these changes, they still need to be explained.

How surprising were the policy shifts?

None of these policy shifts were widely predicted in mainstream social science, and most of them were not predicted at all. In that sense, they did come as a major surprise, and exposed a serious weakness in social theory. Nor is that weakness just a failure to spot the precise turning-points, like the average

But what kind of social theory would be able to make such predictions?

Potential policy turning points were always acknowledged as long as there were alternative contestable paradigms.

uninformed investor on the stock exchange. There was a more serious failure across much of the literature even to acknowledge the possibility of policy turning-points, let alone to predict correctly when and where they would occur.

Nor was this failure confined to what economists see as the 'soft' social sciences of political science and sociology. Although (or perhaps because) many of the main players in all of the six cases were 'econocrats' and economics had a great deal to say about policy content, none of the six policy extinctions was *predicted* by economists, and indeed in most cases they seemed to fly directly in the face of economists' *explanations* of how public policy works, notably the producer capture theory of regulation and the various rent-seeking theories of public spending and public enterprise.

In that sense, 1980s policy shifts taught social science a painful but salutary lesson – to beware of casual belief in one-way policy trends which were 'above' or 'beyond' politics. Nevertheless, there is a difference between inability to predict and inability to 'retrodict'. The financial journalist who failed to pre- *who does predict a* dict yesterday's stock crash or boom may still be able to explain it after *crash?* the event. In general, social scientists (like financial journalists) are better at retrodiction than at prediction; and the argument in earlier chapters has been that in most of the six areas we do not need to summarily discard established explanations of what shapes policy. Some of the policy shifts are less 'surprising' in retrospect than others. As we have seen, the flattening of growth in government spending, the move to 'flatter taxes', and even perhaps the rise of NPM, are not inconsistent with all established explanations of policy development.

The more surprising changes, in terms of established theory, seemed to be the advent of regulatory reform, the onset of privatization and the apparent abandonment of full employment as a macroeconomic policy objective. But these changes were surprising in different ways. The regulatory shift was surprising because it seemed to fly in the face of a fairly developed body of theory, offering a challenge to the 'Chicago' interpretation of regulation to modify its model to make dergulation 'endogenous'. The privatization shift was surprising, not because it seemed to falsify pre-existing theory, but because there was no well-developed explanatory theory of public enterprise in the first place, and in this case the challenge was to construct such a theory. The rise of unemployment and the associated shift in macroeconomic policy involved elements of both kinds of surprise. It challenged those theories which expected 'corporatist' states to perform much better on unemployment than 'non-corporatist' states, and revealed some of the casual logic in the 'party matters' and 'political business cycle' literature.

Why did these 'extinctions' occur?

As we saw in Chapter One, general explanations of why policies might suffer reversal or extinction do not fit very easily into the orthodox categories into which modern political scientists like to fit ideas about the state and public policy (such as the conventional litany of Marxism, pluralism and New Rightism). Cutting across those conventional categories, Chapter One identified four main explanations of policy 'extinction', and briefly identified some possible hybrids (in Fig. 1.2).

It seems hard to argue for any of the 'pure types' – areas (a) to (d) in Fig. 1.2, or ideas, habitat, interest changes or institutional self-destruction working alone. All of the cases discussed here seem to have been hybrid in these terms. Indeed, as the summary in Table 8.1 indicates, each of those four basic types of explanation can be, and commonly are, applied to each of the six policy areas examined in this book. For each of those areas, there are explanations highlighting the power of 'ideology', rhetoric or intellectual development. For each, there are explanations pointing to the interests who stood to benefit from the policy shifts, and the entrepreneurial activity which put together the new coalitions. For each, there are explanations fitting the policy shifts to economic and sociotechnical changes. And, albeit much less developed in many cases, there are at least traces of explanations which interpret policies and institutions as their own worst enemies in a process of self-destruction rather than self-reinforcement. None of these explanations can be dismissed out of hand.

None of these changes took place in an 'ideas vacuum'. In every case, a relatively coherent body of new (or at least repackaged) doctrines was coming on to the policy ideas market from the think-tanks and the policy shops, devised and endorsed by powerful economists. Such ideas provided a vigorous critique of existing policy as well as suggesting an operational basis for alternative policy designs, and many well-informed commentators stress the force of those ideas in developing the new policy paradigms which succeeded the old 'dinosaurs'. It is now commonplace to argue that the six policy reversals discussed in this book are part of a single 'New Right' assault on older orthodoxies, many of which date from the progressive era, and which in that sense can be considered as policy 'cousins' with a common political genesis.

In every case, too, we can identify emerging or established interests – such as the corporate consumers of regulated producers, the privatization 'complex', Dunleavy's 'bureau-shapers' or Yeatman's 'new class' – which stood to make material gains from the extinction of the old policies and their succession by new 'life forms'. Although all of the policy shifts were presented as advancing the general welfare, there were winners and losers in every case.

Some kind of 'habitat change' can also be identified in the social backdrop of policy. In most cases, the background sociotechnical habitat seems to have been changing in a way which in some sense produced a 'colder' climate for the operation of traditional policy approaches and a 'warmer' one for the development of interests favouring different policy designs, for instance in the move away from a large-employer structure changing the sociotechnical 'niches' in which traditional income tax regimes were located. Similarly, many commentators have seen shifts in sociotechnical structure as at least helping to weaken the technological (and national) insulation of many traditional 'public service' and public enterprise sectors, with information handling, storage, retrieval and

Table 8.1 Explanations of policy reversal in six policy areas

Policy area	Climate-changing ideas	Shift of interests	Habitat change	Policy self-destruction
Regulation	'Politics of ideas' (Derthick and Quirk)	Counter-mobilization by 'losers' (Keeler; Bendor and Moe)	Technological interpretations, e.g. of telecoms deregulation	Capture life-cycles (Bernstein); wealth dissipation (Peltzman)
Public enterprise	'Ideological' interpretations of privatization (Wiltshire)	Privatization as an entrepreneured 'policy boom' (Dunleavy, Dobeck)	Global competition, technology eroding natural monopoly, development of financial markets (Vickers and Wright)	Reactive public mood swings (Hirschman); self-destruction of control framework (Foster)
Macro-economic policy	Changing economic theory fashions (Whiteley)	Middle-stratum voters learning to favour high unemployment (Scharpf)	Post-Fordism destroying social base of Keynesianism; globalization destroying administrative base of PBCs	'Tragic' government *vs* unions game (Scharpf)
Public spending and employment	Changing cultural bias (Wildavsky)	Positional goods changing support for public provision (King)	Technology puts Baumol's labour-intensive theory of government growth in reverse	Self-destruct of redistributive coalition and extractive capacity
Tax policy	'New Right' ideology accounts	Business lobby divides as growth of tax breaks prompts counter-mobilization (Mucciaroni); new tax policy enterpreneurs (Peters)	'Tax niches' theory (Hood); tax culture change theory (Peters)	Self-destruct of conduits and value clarity on which tax base built
Public management	Power and/or packaging of NPM ideas (Aucoin)	'Bureau-shaping' behaviour (Dunleavy); New Class (Pusey, Yeatman)	Post-industrial sociotechnical context (Osborne and Gaebler; Taylor and Williams)	Auto-value degradation in ageing institutions (Painter)

analysis – once special skills of public bureaucracies, with their development of large-scale filing and recording systems – becoming part of the core technology of the private sector in developed countries, and the development of the service sector alongside manufacturing and agriculture producing new capacities for private delivery of public services. Changes in income distribution and the composition of the workforce may also have helped to weaken the 'Tocqueville coalition' for government growth and expand the middle-level group of floating voters not committed to either a 'Keynesian' or 'monetarist' game in Fritz Scharpf's account of macroeconomic policy. Social changes like the growth of business travel and of telecommunication-linked services may have played a part in producing more concentrated consumer muscle in areas of traditional pro-producer regulation. It is fashionable to decry 'contextualism' in political science (March and Olsen 1989), that is, the notion that politics is narrowly determined by social and technological change. But it seems hard to ignore the effect of long-term changes in technology and related social behaviour in accounting for policy change.

Finally, all of the policy shifts considered here took place as some form of reaction against the perceived shortcomings of existing policy, and in that sense elements of 'policy as its own worst enemy' may be identified. As noted in Chapter One, the emphasis in much of the current policy literature on the way that policy structures and institutions renew themselves and maintain their own client communities seems to look at only one side of the coin and to ignore the opposite process of self-destruction. As it develops, a policy can come to weaken the social foundations on which it rests, like ivy killing the tree on which it grows. As we have seen, several accounts apply a 'self-destruct' interpretation to the demise of old-style progressive public administration, public enterprise and regulation. Just as the failings of earlier regulatory regimes are said to have prompted nationalization in some cases, so the behaviour of public enterprises is seen to have paved the way for privatization (cf. Foster 1992). And tax systems can clearly destroy their own habitat, for instance if income taxes cause a growth of self-employment, unmonitorable cash transactions and in-kind payment systems, or if the growth of offsets splits the business lobby, as Mucciaroni (1990) argues.

Accordingly, it seems likely that a policy dynamic in which all four elements are strongly present – involving area (m) in Fig. 1.2 – is a particularly good bet for extinction. Getting into area (m) for a public policy could be seen as the opposite of winning the jackpot on a fruit-machine. That is, it would require a number of different elements to line up simultaneously for a devastating event to occur, and the (low) probability of that conjuncture is such as to ensure that major established policies do not go into extinction every day.

But the interesting questions, of course, are more fine-grained than that. Three issues in particular are worth raising in conclusion, though they cannot be answered definitively here. First, are there more parsimonious conditions for extinction than sector (m) of Fig. 1.2? Can policies go into extinction with less than all four factors present, or with some operating much more strongly than others? Second, are there different forms of each of the four basic types themselves? Third, are there different routes by which a process of extinction can get to the intersection of the circles in Fig. 1.2?

First, it seems intuitively plausible that not all of the four mechanisms would need to be equally present, or indeed present at all, to provide conditions for policy extinction. It would seem logical to expect that some forces could compensate or substitute for others. For example, if habitat conditions change sharply enough, policy might turn around relatively easily without a coherent body of preconceived ideas. Similarly, the more policy 'self-destructs', the less need there is for autonomous habitat change. And we could imagine conditions of habitat change or policy self-destruction which prompted the *same* dominant interest groups to favour policy reversal, without requiring new interest groups to come into existence through policy entrepreneuring or counter-mobilization. Hence the 'extinction mix' could differ from one case to another.

Indeed, the discussion of the six cases in previous chapters suggests that not all of them involved the same mix of factors. Any conclusion must be highly tentative, in that differences may be as much a function of the predilections of different observers programmed to see different things, as inherent properties of the cases themselves. But the case of regulatory reform does stand out as an area in which 'habitat change', certainly in the sense of the technology of 'post-industrialism', seems hard to detect. Some commentators have stressed the effects of technological change in telecommunications as part of the backdrop to regulatory reform, but many of the leading areas of deregulation, such as airlines and railways, had not been transformed by 'post-industrialism' at the time that regulatory reform took place. Hence the argument for putting regulatory reform into sector (k). In the cases of changing macroeconomic policy and the slowdown in government growth, it seems difficult to identify specific cases of policy entrepreneurship or the mobilization of new interests, and these factors have not been stressed by commentators in those fields. Hence we might locate those cases in sector (j). And in the cases of privatization, tax policy change and the rise of NPM, it is less clear that well-articulated new ideas about how to conduct policy were fundamental to the process, in that (unlike the development of new regulatory theory or the assault on Keynesianism) rationales of the policy changes either developed after the shift had begun or involved no radically new ideas. In the areas of tax policy and privatization, intellectual developments were more at the level of technology than new fundamental propositions about human behaviour. The basic ideas had been around for a long time, and were not associated with dramatic Nobel prize winning ideas in the same way that applied to deregulation and monetarism. For NPM, relatively unrationalized practice seems to have preceded synthetic theory. Hence there is a case for placing these policy shifts in sector (l), as is shown in Fig. 8.1.

If there is anything in this analysis, it would suggest that there is more than one recipe for policy extinction. And the four basic elements themselves are not homogeneous. For each of them, we can identify a 'harder' and a 'softer' version. As we saw in Chapter One, there is a 'hard' version of the power of

Figure 8.1 Routes to policy reversal revisited

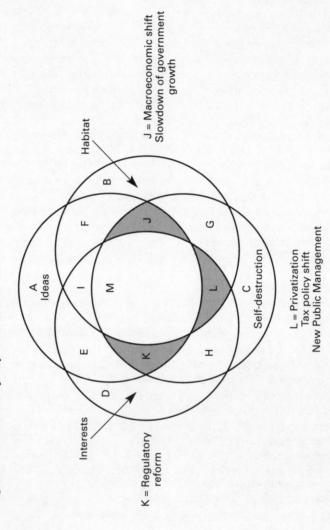

A
Ideas

Habitat

Interests

Self-destruction

J = Macroeconomic shift
Slowdown of government
growth

L = Privatization
Tax policy shift
New Public Management

K = Regulatory
reform

ideas, which sees policy change as springing from the impact of crucial experiments and irrefragable logic. But there is also a 'softer' version seeing policy change as shaped by cultural changes or by persuasive arguments and metaphors which fit the times and the emerging interests in society, and hence become established as received ideas. Regulatory reform and the shift from Keynesianism to monetarism seem to be the most plausible cases for the 'power of ideas' in its 'hard' sense. But in general the power of ideas in this sense seems to be much more difficult to sustain than the power of ideas in a softer sense. Unambiguous and replicable 'crucial experiments' of a Baconian kind were missing in every case and consciously avoided by the reformers in most of them. While the extreme metaphor of economists' ideas as 'climate-changing' meteorites seems relatively implausible, a 'softer', rhetorically based version of the 'power of ideas' is much harder to dismiss – and much harder to disentangle from the other extinction mechanisms.

The power of interests has a 'hard' and 'soft' sense too. The 'harder' element involves changes in the configuration of political interests prompted by political dynamics which are genuinely autonomous of environment or the climate of ideas, such as counter-mobilization against dominant coalitions or the 'creative destruction' achieved by policy entrepreneurs mobilizing new interest groups through innovative policy packages. Such ideas have certainly been developed to explain the shift in regulatory and tax policy, and are at least implicit in some of the literature on government spending growth. At the 'softer' end is policy change brought about by shifts in the policy stances of already established interest groups, for example of public enterprise chiefs on the issue of privatization or of top bureaucrats on 'bureau-shaping'. But this 'softer' aspect of interest change is inherently difficult to separate from the other mechanisms of policy extinction: if interests shift their policy stance, is it because of the power of persuasion, a changing context or a sense that institutions and policies have destroyed the very conditions or values which they were established to promote?

Habitat change, too, can operate in both a 'hard' and a 'soft' sense. At the 'hard' end, technological development shapes policy in the same way that the invention of the stirrup is said to have revolutionized warfare, and many of the claims about the policy effect of 'post-Fordism' or post-industrialism relates to the power of the new information technologies to develop 'flexible specialization', with profound effects for the role of government. Such forces may well have had an impact on government employment (possibly reversing the 'Baumol' explanation of government growth in at least some areas) and perhaps on the style of public management more generally. It may have had an impact on some areas of regulatory reform (notably telecommunications and finance), but certainly not on all of them; and it seems difficult to relate the other policy extinctions considered here to habitat change in this sense.

The 'softer' aspect of habitat change is the effect of changing social behaviour on policy, such as the changing nature of employment, demography, income levels and distribution, or family structure. Many of the policy shifts here seem to relate to this aspect of habitat change; but it is particularly hard to separate habitat change in this sense from self-destruct processes, particularly for taxation, where it is debatable how far social habitat changes are exogenous to policy (in that they stemmed from autonomous processes of social development which would have taken place irrespective of the direction of existing policy) or caused by it.

Finally, policy can also operate as its own worst enemy in both a 'hard' and a 'soft' sense. At the 'harder' end comes policy self-destruction brought about through the development of processes of reactive evasion, which undermine the social control system on which policies are built (for example, with control systems which become worn-out and blunted in use). Tax policy shifts and privatization are cases where such a process of habitat self-destruction has some *prima facie* plausibility, and some, like Sharpf, would argue that Keynesianism and political business cycle behaviour would also inevitably destroy their social habitat as a result of the expectations which develop among players as to how the government will play the game, and the effect of their strategic responses built upon those assumptions.

At the 'softer' end of policy self-destruction belongs the development of a political reaction in the style depicted by Hirschman, in which the basic values downplayed by the policy start to come back into popular or political favour and the values which are emphasized lose their attraction. 'Better the devil you know than the devil you don't know', goes the old saying. But in public policy it sometimes seems to be the reverse. But again, at this 'softer' end of the process, policy self-destruction starts to blur into the other three extinction mechanisms, in that we need very detailed historical knowledge to separate them.

Hence we could think of each of the four circles in Fig. 8.1 as divided into an inner and outer circle, the inner circle representing the 'hard' or 'core' sense of each element, and the outer circle representing the 'soft' sense. Clearly, there is likely to be much more overlap among the outer circles than among the inner circles; and if such a hard/soft distinction can be made, it would suggest that there are at least forty-nine rather than thirteen possible routes to policy extinction.

Finally, are there different possible paths to extinction, in the sense that the same policy can go into extinction for different reasons in different contexts or that a policy can work itself into the central intersections of Fig. 8.1 from different starting-points? Logically, the intersections could be entered from different points and follow different paths, even if the ultimate profile is the same, just as different flies might end up sticking to the same fly-paper but get there through very different flight-paths. For example, two opposite 'roads to policy ruin' might be: on the one hand, an 'intellectual' route to extinction, starting largely in the realm of ideas [sector (a)], but moving to 'ripeness' by taking in other sectors later; and, on the other, a 'policy in search of a rationale' dynamic, in which a policy shift begins as a result of habitat changes or the decomposition of existing policy, acquiring clear-cut vested interests or a coherent intellectual justification only later. The regulatory shift might well be argued to fit the former flight-path, and many observers (like Foster) would argue that privatization fitted the latter.

But even that analysis implies that a particular policy field (such as macroeconomic policy or public management) is likely to display similar 'extinction paths' everywhere, and that assumption needs to be questioned too. Clearly, for those who believe that an inexorable process of 'globalization' is taking place in the contemporary world (see Giddens 1987: 16, 34–6; Albrow 1990; Luard 1990), policies might be expected to go into extinction everywhere for the same reason. The term 'globalization' denotes the processes by which particular societies are coming to be incorporated into a single world society, for example in economics, security and culture. If this beguiling line of analysis is accepted, we might see policy extinctions everywhere as part of the same 'global' process towards a convergent policy style, consisting (in crude terms) of an amalgam of a French-type tax style (with heavier emphasis on sales taxes than on progressive income taxes), a German-type macroeconomic policy style (placing heavier emphasis on control of inflation than on checking unemployment), a US-type regulatory and public management style (placing heavier emphasis on regulation than on public enterprise and on the use of private-sector methods than on a deep-rooted 'public service ethic') and a Swiss-type approach to government size (placing heavier emphasis on checking the growth of government than satisfying all the demands on the public purse).

However, even if a similar pattern of policy extinction appeared to take place in several countries, we cannot necessarily conclude that those extinctions occurred everywhere for the same reason and with the same effect. In fact, it often happens that reforms which look similar when viewed from a distance turn out to have been adopted for quite different purposes and with different effects.

We referred to Hans Mueller's (1984) interpretation of civil service reform in Prussia and England in Chapter One, as a possible case in point. And much the same may apply to current reform themes, such as privatization or performance pay, when we look carefully at local conditions. For instance, whereas it is often argued that the British move to privatization reflected factors such as disillusionment with the experience of a generation of nationalization, coupled with a new ascendant right-wing ideology and an urgent search for ways to relieve growing fiscal stress, the Japanese move (particularly on privatization of telecoms) is sometimes seen as a response to outside (US) pressure to 'open up' NTT, although it can also be interpreted as a vote-winning tactic to woo urban voters at the expense of NTT's unionized workers who tended to support the opposition Socialist Party. In the case of NPM, we have seen that the doctrines have been adopted by labourist or social democratic governments in some countries as part of a strategy to ward off right-wing attacks on the 'inefficient' public sector and hence to keep a statist welfarist system going, whereas in other contexts they have been adopted by radical right governments as a poor second to privatization and as part of an ultimate strategy of 'bureaucide' and demolition of the welfare state.

Indeed, many questions remain unanswered about the apparent disappearance of the economic policy 'dinosaurs' across the OECD world in the 1980s. Anything approaching 'extinction science' in this area is still in its earliest stages, as Hirschman's comment implies. Historians will still be debating these issues fifty years hence. Like the case of the dinosaurs, there is no unchallengeable account of policy extinction – which is what makes the field interesting. But, unlike the case of the dinosaurs, there is no general agreement that the six policy fields considered here have all witnessed a clear-cut case of 'extinction'. Even if they have, it seems likely that policy extinction, like policy genesis, may involve a common end-state but can be approached by many different combinations of the basic available routes.

References

Abromeit, H. (1986) Privatisation in Great Britain, *Annals of Public and Cooperative Economy*, 57: 153–79.

Adam, C., Cavendish, W. and Mistry, P.S. (1992) *Adjusting Privatization*. London, James Currey.

Aglietta, M. (1976) *A Theory of Capitalist Regulation*. London, New Left Books.

Albrow, M. (1990) Introduction. In M. Albrow and E. King (eds) *Globalization Knowledge and Society*. London, Sage.

Alt, J.E. and Chrystal, K.A. (1983) *Political Economics*. Brighton, Wheatsheaf.

Arrow, K. (1963) *Social Choice and Individual Values*, 2nd edn. New Haven, CT, Yale University Press.

Aucoin, P. (1990) Administrative reform in public management, *Governance*, 3: 115–37.

Austin, G. (1992) Scale bias and state building, *LSE Working Papers on Economic History*, No. 6/92. London, London School of Economics.

Ayres, I. and Braithwaite, J. (1992) *Responsive Regulation*. New York, Oxford University Press.

Barker, A. (ed.) (1982) *Quangos in Britain*. London, Macmillan.

Barker, R. (1984) The Fabian state. In B. Pimlott (ed.) *Fabian Essays in Socialist Thought*. London, Heinemann.

Bauer, M. (1988) The politics of state-directed privatisation: the case of France, 1986–88, *West European Politics*, 11(4): 49–60.

Baumol, W.J. (1967) The macro-economics of unbalanced growth, *American Economic Review*, 57: 415–26.

Baumol, W.J. (1968) Entrepreneurship in economic theory, *American Economic Review*, 58.1(2): 64–71.

Baumol, W.J. and Oates, W.E. (1985) *The Theory of Environmental Policy*. Englewood Cliffs, NJ, Prentice-Hall.

Bell, D. (1973) *The Coming of Post-Industrial Society*. New York, Basic Books.

Bendor, J. and Moe, T.M. (1985) An adaptive model of bureaucratic politics, *American Political Science Review*, 79: 755–74.

Bendor, J. and Moe, T.M. (1986) Agenda control, committee capture and the dynamics of institutional politics, *American Political Science Review*, 80: 1187–207.

Bentham, J. (1931) *The Theory of Legislation* (ed. C.K. Ogden). London, Routledge and Kegan Paul.

Bernstein, M.H. (1955) *Regulating Business by Independent Commission*. Princeton, NJ, Princeton University Press.

Berry, W.D. and Lowery, D. (1987) Explaining the size of the public sector, *Journal of Politics*, 49: 401–40.

Black, D. (1958) *The Theory of Committees and Elections*. Cambridge, Cambridge University Press.

Blainey, G. (1973) *The Causes of War*. London, Macmillan.

Borcherding, T.E. (ed.) (1977) *Budgets and Bureaucrats*. Durham, NC, Duke University Press.

Borcherding, T.E. Pommerehne, W.W. and Schneider, F. (1982) Comparing the efficiency of private and public production: The evidence from five countries, *Zeitschrift für Nationalökonomie*, Suppl. 2: 127–56. Berlin, Springer.

Bös, D. (1986) *Public Enterprise Economics*. Amsterdam, Elsevier.

Bradley, K. and Nejad, A. (1989) *Managing Owners*. Cambridge, Cambridge University Press.

Breyer, S.G. (1982) *Regulation and Its Reform*. New Haven, CT, Yale University Press.

Brittan, S. (1988) Review of *Taxation by Political Inertia* (by Rose and Karran). *Financial Times*, 28 January.

Buchanan, J.M. and Wagner, R.E. (1977) *Democracy in Deficit: The Political Legacy of Lord Keynes*. New York, Academic Press.

Burnham, J. (1942) *The Managerial Revolution*. London, Putnam.

Cashman, S.D. (1988) *America in the Age of the Titans: The Progressive Era and World War I*. New York, New York University Press.

Christensen, J. (forthcoming) Denmark: Institutional constraint and the advancement of individual self-interest in HPO. In C. Hood and B.G. Peters (eds) *Rewards at the Top*, pp. 70–89. London, Sage.

Coll, S. (1986) *The Deal of the Century: The Breakup of AT&T*. New York, Atheneum Press.

Cook, P. and Minogue, M. (1990) Waiting for privatization in developing countries, *Public Administration and Development*, 10: 389–403.

Corbett, D. (1965) *Politics and the Airlines*. London, Allen and Unwin.

Creel, H.G. (1964) The beginnings of bureaucracy in China, *Journal of Asian Studies*, 23(2): 155–83.

Dearlove, J. (1979) *The Reorganization of British Local Government*. Cambridge, Cambridge University Press.

Delorme, R. and André, C. (1983) *L'Etat et L'Economie*. Paris, Seuil.

Dempsey, P.S. (1989) *The Social and Economic Consequences of Deregulation*. New York, Quorum.

Derivery, D. (1975) The managers of public enterprises in France. In M. Dogan (ed.) *The Mandarins of Western Europe*, pp. 210–25. London, Sage.

Derlien, H.-U. (1992) Observations on the state of comparative administration research in Europe: Rather comparable than comparative, *Governance*, 5(3): 279–311.

Derthick, M. and Quirk, P. (1985) *The Politics of Deregulation*. Washington, DC, Brookings.

Deutsch, K. (1961) Social mobilization and political development, *American Political Science Review*, 55: 493–514.

Djilas, M. (1957) *The New Class*. New York, Praeger.

Dobek, M. (1993) Privatization as a political priority, *Political Studies*, XLI(1): 24–40.

Doron, G. (1979) Administrative regulation of an industry: The cigarette case, *Public Administration Review*, 39: 163–70.

Douglas, J. (1989) Review article: The changing tide, *British Journal of Political Science*, 19: 399–424.

Douglas, M. (1982) Cultural bias. In *In the Active Voice*, pp. 183–254. London, Routledge.

Douglas, M. (1987) *How Institutions Think*. London, Routledge.

Douglas, M. (1990) Risk as a forensic resource, *Daedalus (Proceedings of the American Academy of Arts and Sciences)*, 119(4): 1–16.

Douglas, M. and Wildavsky, A. (1983) *Risk and Culture*. Berkeley, CA, University of California Press.

Douglas, R. and Callen, L. (1987) *Toward Prosperity*. Auckland, Bateman.

Downs, A. (1957) *An Economic Theory of Democracy*. New York, Harper and Row.

Downs, G.W. and Larkey, P.D. (1986) *The Search for Government Efficiency*. Philadelphia, PA, Temple University Press.

Dunleavy, P.J. (1985) Bureaucrats, budgets and the growth of the state, *British Journal of Political Science*, 15: 299–328.

Dunleavy, P.J. (1986) Explaining the privatization boom, *Public Administration*, 64: 13–34.

Dunleavy, P.J. (1991) *Democracy, Bureaucracy and Public Choice*. Hemel Hempstead, Harvester Wheatsheaf.

Dunleavy, P. and O'Leary, B. (1987) *Theories of the State*. London, Macmillan.

Dunsire, A. (1990) Holistic governance, *Public Policy and Administration*, 5(1): 3–18.

Dunsire, A. and Hood, C.C. (1989) *Cutback Management in Public Bureaucracies*. Cambridge, Cambridge University Press.

Edelman, M. (1964) *The Symbolic Uses of Politics*. Urbana, IL, Illinois University Press.

Evans, P.B., Rueschmeyer, D. and Skocpol, T. (eds) (1985) *Bringing the State Back In*. Cambridge, MA, Harvard University Press.

Feigenbaum, H.B. and Henig, J.R. (1993) Privatization and democracy, *Governance*, 6(3): 438–53.

Flora, P. (1986) *Growth to Limits*. Berlin, de Gruyter.

Foster, C.D. (1992) *Privatization, Public Ownership and the Regulation of Natural Monopoly*. Oxford, Blackwell.

Fox, A. (1974) *Beyond Contract*. London, Faber and Faber.

Freudenberg, W.R. (1992) Nothing recedes like success?, *Risk – Issues in Health and Safety*, 1 (Winter): 1–35.

Frey, B.S. and Schneider, F. (1982) Politico-economic models in competition with alternative models: Which predict better?, *European Journal of Political Research*, 10(3): 241–54.

Friedman, M. (1977) From Galbraith to economic freedom, *IEA Occasional Paper No. 49*. London, Institute of Economic Affairs.

Fukuyama, F. (1989) The end of history, *The National Interest*, 16: 3–18.

Galbraith, J.K. (1967) *The New Industrial State*. London, Hamish Hamilton.

Gerth, H.H. and Mills, C.W. (1948) *From Max Weber: Essays in Sociology*. London, Routledge and Kegan Paul.

Giddens, A. (1987) *Social Theory and Modern Sociology*. Stanford, CA, Stanford University Press.

Gould, F. (1983) The growth of public expenditures: Theory and evidence from six advanced democracies. In C.L. Taylor (ed.) *Why Governments Grow: Measuring Public Sector Size*, pp. 217–39. Beverly Hills, CA, Sage.

Gray, G. (1984) The termination of Medibank, *Politics (Australia)*, 19(2): 1–17.

Greene, K.V. (1973) Attitudes towards risk and the relative size of the public sector, *Public Finance Quarterly*, 1: 205–218.

Hall, P. (1986) *Governing the Economy*. Cambridge, Polity Press.

Hall, P. (1990) Policy paradigms, experts and the state: The case of macro-economic policy making in Britain. In S. Brooks and A. Gagnon (eds) *Social Scientists, Policy and the State*, pp. 53–78. New York, Praeger.

Hall, P. (1992) The movement from Keynesianism to monetarism: Institutional analysis and British economic policy in the 1970s. In S. Steinmo, K. Thelen and F. Longstreth (eds) *Structuring Politics*, pp. 90–113. Cambridge, Cambridge University Press.

Halligan, J. and Wettenhall, R. (1990) Major changes in the structure of government institutions. In J. Power (ed.) *Public Administration in Australia: A Watershed.* Sydney, RAIPA/Hale and Iremonger.

Hammond, T.H. and Knott, J.H. (1988) The deregulatory snowball: Explaining deregulation in the financial industry, *Journal of Politics*, 50: 3–30.

Hancher, L. and Moran, M. (eds) (1989) *Capitalism, Culture and Regulation*. Oxford, Clarendon Press.

Hardin, G. (1968) The tragedy of the Commons, *Science*, December: 1243–8.

Hart, O. (1989) An economist's perspective on the theory of the firm, *Columbia Law Review*, 89(7): 1757–74.

Hegewisch, A. (1991) Public and private sector trends in remuneration policies and contract flexibility in Europe. Paper presented at seminar *International Comparisons of Public Sector Pay in 10 Countries: 1990 Results from the Price Waterhouse/ Cranfield Survey*. London, Public Finance Foundation.

Henig, J.R., Hamnett, C. and Feigenbaum, H.B. (1988) The politics of privatization: A comparative perspective, *Governance*, 1(4): 442–68.

Hennestad, B.W. (1990) The symbolic impact of double bind leadership: Double bind and the dynamics of organizational culture, *Journal of Management Studies*, 27: 265–80.

Herber, B.P. (1967) *Modern Public Finance*. Homewood, IL, Richard D. Irwin.

Hibbs, D.A. Jr (1977) Political parties and macroeconomic policy, *American Political Science Review*, 71: 1467–87.

Hibbs, D.A. Jr (1982) Economic outcomes and political support for British governments among occupational classes: A dynamic analysis, *American Political Science Review*, 76: 259–79.

Hills, J. (1986) *Deregulating Telecoms*. London, Pinter.

Hinrichs, H.H. (1966) *A General Theory of Tax Structure Change During Economic Development*. Cambridge, MA, Harvard Law School.

Hirsch, F. (1977) *Social Limits to Growth*. London, Routledge and Kegan Paul.

Hirschman, A.O. (1982) *Shifting Involvements*. Oxford, Blackwell.

Hirschman, A.O. (1991) *The Rhetoric of Reaction*. Cambridge, MA, Belknap Press.

Hirschman, A.O. (1993) Exit, voice and the fate of the German Democratic Republic: An essay in conceptual history, *World Politics*, 45(2): 173–202.

Hogwood, B.W. and Peters, B.G. (1983) *Policy Dynamics*. Brighton, Wheatsheaf.

Hood, C.C. (1976) *The Limits of Administration*. Chichester, John Wiley.

Hood, C.C. (1978) Keeping the centre small, *Political Studies*, 26(1): 30–46.

Hood, C.C. (1985) British tax policy change as administrative adaptation, *Policy Sciences*, 18: 3–31.

Hood, C.C. (1986) *Administrative Analysis*. Brighton, Wheatsheaf.

Hood, C.C. (1991a) A public management for all seasons?, *Public Administration*, 69: 3–19.

Hood, C.C. (1991b) Privatisation good, sale of office bad?, *Contemporary Record*, 4(3): 32–5.

Hood, C.C. and Jackson, M.J. (1991) *Administrative Argument*. Aldershot, Dartmouth.
Hood, C.C. and Schuppert, G.F. (eds) (1988) *Delivering Public Services in Western Europe*. London, Sage.
Hume, L.J. (1981) *Bentham and Bureaucracy*. Cambridge, Cambridge University Press. ✗
Ikenberry, G.J. (1990) The international spread of privatization policies. In E.N. Suleiman and J. Waterbury (eds) *The Political Economy of Public Sector Reform and Privatization*, pp. 88–109. Oxford, Westview.
Jessop, B. (1988a) Conservative regimes and the transition to post-Fordism, *Essex Papers in Politics and Government* No. 47. Department of Government, University of Essex.
Jessop, B. (1988b) Regulation theories in retrospect and prospect, *Zentrum für Interdisziplinäre Forschung*, Research Group 'Staatsaufgaben', Preprint Series No. 1. Bielefeld, University of Bielefeld.
Jorgensen, T.B. (1987) Financial management in the public sector. In J. Kooiman and K.A. Eliasson (eds) *Managing Public Organizations*, pp. 189–204. London, Sage.
Jouvenel, B. de (1963) *The Pure Theory of Politics*. Cambridge, Cambridge University Press.
Kalecki, M. (1943) Political aspects of full employment, *Political Quarterly*, 14(4): 322–31.
Karl, B.D. (1963) *Executive Reorganization and Reform in the New Deal*. Cambridge, MA, Harvard University Press.
Katzenbach, E.L. (1958) The horse cavalry in the twentieth century, *Public Policy*, 8: 120–49.
Katzenstein, P. (1985) *Small States in World Markets*. Ithaca, NY, Cornell University Press.
Kay, J.A. and Thompson, D.J. (1986) Privatization: A policy in search of a rationale?, *Economic Journal*, 96: 18–32.
Keeler, T.E. (1984) Theories of regulation and the deregulation movement, *Public Choice*, 44: 103–145.
Kesselman, M. (1992) How should one study economic policy-making?, *World Politics*, ✗ 44(4): 645–72.
Keynes, J.M. (1936) *The General Theory of Employment, Interest and Money*. New York, Harcourt, Brace and World.
King, D.S. (1989) Voluntary and state provision of welfare as part of the public–private continuum. In A. Ware (ed.) *Charities and Government*. Manchester, Manchester University Press.
King, D.S. (1990) Economic activity and the challenge to local government. In D.S. King and J. Pierre (eds) *Challenges to Local Government*, pp. 265–87. London, Sage.
King, D.S. (1992) The establishment of work-welfare programs in the United States and Britain: Politics, ideas and institutions. In S. Steinmo, K. Thelen and F. Longstreth (eds) *Structuring Politics*, pp. 217–50. Cambridge, Cambridge University Press.
Kingdon, J.W. (1984) *Agendas, Alternatives and Public Policies*. Boston, MA, Little, Brown.
Kolko, G. (1977) *The Triumph of Conservatism*. New York, Free Press.
Kristol, I. (1983) *Reflections of a Neoconservative*. New York, Basic Books.
Landis, J.M. (1938) *The Administrative Process*. New Haven, CT, Yale University Press.
Lane, F.C. (1966) *Venice and History*. Baltimore, MD, Johns Hopkins University Press.
Laver, M. (1983) *Invitation to Politics*. Oxford, Robertson.
Lawrence, P. (1964) *Road Belong Cargo*. Manchester, Manchester University Press.

Leibenstein, H. (1976) *Beyond Economic Man*. Cambridge, MA, Harvard University Press.

Letwin, O. (1988) *Privatising the World*. London, Cassell.

Levi, M. (1988) *Of Rule and Revenue*. Berkeley, CA, University of California Press.

Levine, C.H. (1978) A symposium: Organizational decline and cutback management, *Public Administration Review*, 38: 316–25.

Lewin, L. (1991) *Self-interest and Public Interest in Western Politics*. Oxford, Oxford University Press.

Lewis, E. (1988) Public entrepreneurship and the teleology of technology, *Administration and Society*, 20(1): 109–126.

Lindblom, C.E. (1959) The 'science' of muddling through, *Public Administration Review*, 19: 79–88.

Lindblom, C.E. (1977) *Politics and Markets*. New York, Basic Books.

Luard, E. (1990) *The Globalization of Politics*. London, Macmillan.

Luhmann, N. (1985) *A Sociological Theory of Law* (tr. E. King and M. Albrow). London, Routledge and Kegan Paul.

MacAvoy, P. and Robinson, P. (1983) Winning by losing: The AT&T settlement and its impact on telecommunications, *Yale Journal of Regulation*, 1(1): 1–42.

MacDonagh, O. (1961) *A Pattern of Government Growth*. London, MacGibbon and Kee.

Macrae, N. (1984) *The 2024 Report*. London, Sidgwick and Jackson.

Majone, G. (1989a) *Evidence, Argument and Persuasion in the Policy Process*. New Haven, CT, Yale University Press.

Majone, G (ed.) (1989b) *Deregulation or Re-regulation*. London, Pinter.

March, J.G. and Olsen, J.P. (1989) *Rediscovering Institutions*. New Haven, CT, Yale University Press.

Marmor, T.R. and Fellman, P. (1986) Policy entrepreneurship in government: An American study, *Journal of Public Policy*, 6(3): 225–53.

Martin, S. (1983) *Managing Without Managers*. Beverly Hills, CA, Sage.

Maslow, A.H. (1954) *Motivation and Personality*. New York, Harper.

McCloskey, D.N. (1985) *The Rhetoric of Economics*. Madison, WI, Wisconsin University Press.

Meltzer, A.H. and Richard, S.F. (1981) A rational theory of the size of government, *Journal of Political Economy*, 89: 914–27.

Merkle, J. (1980) *Management and Ideology*. Berkeley, CA, University of California Press.

Meyer, M.W., Stevenson, W. and Webster, S. (1985) *Limits to Bureaucratic Growth*. Berlin, de Gruyter.

Minogue, K. (1986) Loquocentric society and its critics, *Government and Opposition*, 21: 338–61.

Mucciaroni, G. (1990) Public choice and the politics of comprehensive tax reform, *Governance*, 3(1): 1–32.

Mueller, H.E. (1984) *Bureaucracy, Education and Monopoly*. Berkeley, CA, University of California Press.

Mulgan, G. (1988) New times: The power of the weak, *Marxism Today*, December: 24–31.

Naisbitt, J. (1982) *Megatrends*. New York, Warner.

Nethercote, J.R. (1989) Public service reform: Commonwealth experience. Paper presented to the *Academy of Social Sciences of Australia*, 25 February, University House, Australian National University.

Niskanen, W.A. (1971) *Bureaucracy and Representative Government*. Chicago, IL, Aldine Atherton.

Noll, R. (1987) The political foundations of regulatory policy. In K. McCubbins and T. Sullivan (eds) *Congress*, 462–92. Cambridge, Cambridge University Press.

Nordhaus, W.D. (1975) The political business cycle, *Review of Economic Studies*, 42: 169–90.

Nordhaus, W.D. (1989) Alternative approaches to the political business cycle, *Brookings Papers on Economic Activity*, 2: 1–29.

North, D. (1990) A transaction cost theory of politics, *Journal of Theoretical Politics*, 2: 355–67.

OECD (1990) *Public Management Developments 1990*. Paris, OECD.

Olson, K.W. (1979) *Biography of a Progressive: Franklin K. Lane 1864–1921*. Westport, CT, Greenwood Press.

Olson, M. (1965) *The Logic of Collective Action*. Cambridge, MA, Harvard University Press.

Olson, M. (1982) *The Rise and Decline of Nations*. New Haven, CT, Yale University Press.

Osborne, D. and Gaebler, T. (1992) *Reinventing Government*. Reading, MA, Addison-Wesley.

Painter, M. (1990) Values in the history of public administration. In J. Power (ed.) *Public Administration in Australia: A Watershed*, pp. 75–93. Sydney, RAIPA/Hale and Iremonger.

Parker, D. (1985) Is the private sector more efficient?, *Public Administration Bulletin*, 48: 2–23.

Parkinson, C.N. (1965) *Parkinson's Law or the Pursuit of Progress*. Harmondsworth, Penguin.

Parris, H. (1965) *Government and the Railways in Nineteenth-century Britain*. London, Routledge and Kegan Paul.

Peacock, A. (1979) Public expenditure growth in post-industrial society. In B. Gustafsson (ed.) *Post-Industrial Society*, pp. 80–95. London, Croom Helm.

Peacock, A. and Wiseman, J. (1961) *The Growth of Public Expenditure in the UK*. Oxford, Oxford University Press.

Peltzman, S. (1980) The growth of government, *Journal of Law and Economics*, 23(2): 209–288.

Peltzman, S. (1981) Current developments in the economics of regulation. In G. Fromm (ed.) *Studies of Public Regulation*. Cambridge, MA, MIT Press.

Peltzman, S. (1989) The economic theory of regulation after a decade of deregulation, *Brookings Papers on Economic Activity* (Microeconomics): 1–41.

Peters, B.G. (1991) *The Politics of Taxation*. Oxford, Blackwell.

Peters, T. and Waterman, R. (1982) *In Search of Excellence*. New York, Harper and Row.

Piore, M.J. and Sabel, C.F. (1984) *The Second Industrial Divide*. New York, Basic Books.

Pirenne, H. (1914) *Les periodes de l'histoire social du capitalisme*. Brussels, Hayez.

Pirie, M. (1988) *Privatisation: Theory, Practice and Choice*. Aldershot, Wildwood House.

Pollitt, C. (1993) *Managerialism and the Public Services*, 2nd edn. Oxford, Blackwell.

Pommerehne, W.W. and Kirchgässner, G. (1988) Gesamtwirtschaftliche Effizienz, gesellschaftliche Unverteilung und Wachstum der Staatstätigkeit: Ein Überblick. In H. Zimmerman (ed.) *Die Zunkunft der Staatsfinanzierung*. Stuttgart, Wissenschaftliche Verlagsgesellschaft.

Pommerehne, W.W. and Schneider, F. (1983) Does government in a representative democracy follow a majority of voters' preferences: An empirical examination. In H. Hanusch (ed.) *Anatomy of Government Deficiencies*, pp. 61–88. Berlin, Springer.

Power, M. and Laughlin, R. (1992) Critical theory and accounting. In N. Alveson and H. Willmott (eds) *Critical Management Studies*, pp. 113–35. London, Sage.

Pusey, M. (1991) *Economic Rationalism in Canberra*. Cambridge, Cambridge University Press.

Quirk, P. (1988) In defense of the politics of ideas, *Journal of Politics*, 50: 31–41.

Rhoads, S. (1985) *The Economist's View of the World*. Cambridge, Cambridge University Press.

Riker, W.H. (1962) *The Theory of Political Coalitions*. New Haven, CT, Yale University Press.

Riker, W.H. (1982) *Liberalism Against Populism*. Oxford, Freeman.

Robinson, A. and Sandford, C.T. (1983) *Tax Policy-making in the United Kingdom*. London, Heinemann.

Robson, W.A. (1948) *Public Administration Today*. London, Stevens.

Rose, R. (1984) *Understanding Big Government*. London, Sage.

Rose, R. (1989) Privatization. In G. Fels and G.M. von Furstenberg (eds) *A Supply-side Agenda for Germany*, pp. 247–77. London, Springer.

Rose, R. (1990) Inheritance before choice in public policy, *Journal of Theoretical Politics*, 2(3): 263–91.

Rose, R. and Karran, T. (1987) *Taxation by Political Inertia*. London, Allen and Unwin.

Rose, R. and Peters, B.G. (1978) *Can Government Go Bankrupt?* New York, Basic Books.

Sandbrook, R. (1988) Patrimonialism and the failing of parastatals. In P. Cook and C. Kirkpatrick (eds) *Privatisation in Less Developed Countries*, pp. 162–79. Brighton, Wheatsheaf.

Sako, M. (1991) The role of 'trust' in Japanese buyer–seller relationships, *Ricerche Economiche*, 45: 449–74.

Sato, S. (1985) The experience of Japan. In Asian Development Bank (ed.) *Privatisation*, pp. 111–66. Manila, Asian Development Bank.

Saunders, P. (1986) Explaining international differences in public expenditure. *Working Papers in Economics* No. 90. Sydney, Department of Economics, University of Sydney.

Schaffer, B. (1973) *The Administrative Factor*. London, Frank Cass.

Scharpf, F.W. (1987) The political calculus of inflation and unemployment in Western Europe, *Journal of Public Policy*, 7: 227–58.

Schmidt, M.G. (1982) Does corporatism matter? In G. Lehmbruch and P.C. Schmitter (eds) *Patterns of Corporatist Policy Making*, pp. 237–58. London, Sage.

Schubert, G. (1976) Politics as a life science. In A. Somit (ed.) *Biology and Politics*, pp. 155–95. Paris: Mouton and Maison des Sciences de l'Homme.

Schumpeter, J.A. (1944) *Capitalism, Socialism and Democracy*. London, Allen and Unwin.

Schumpeter, J.A. (1952) *Capitalism, Socialism and Democracy*, 2nd edn. London, Allen and Unwin.

Scott, G., Bushnell, P. and Sallee, N. (1990) Reform of the core public sector: New Zealand experience, *Governance*, 3: 138–67.

Self, P. (1985) *Political Theories of Modern Government*. London, Allen and Unwin.

Sharkansky, I. (1979) *Wither the State?* Chatham, NJ, Chatham House.

Shonfield, A. (1984) *In Defence of the Mixed Economy*. Oxford, Oxford University Press.

Shubik, M. (1984) *A Game-theoretic Approach to Political Economy*. Game Theory in the Social Sciences, Vol. 2. Cambridge, MA, MIT Press.

Sjölund, M. (1989) *Statens lönepolitik 1966–1988*. Stockholm, Allmänna Förlaget.

Small, A.W. (1909) *The Cameralists*. Chicago, IL: Chicago University Press.

Spann, R.N. (1981) Fashions and fantasies in public administration, *Australian Journal of Public Administration*, 40: 12–25.

Starr, P. (1990) The new life of the liberal state. In E.N. Suleiman and J. Waterbury (eds) *The Political Economy of Public Sector Reform and Privatization*, pp. 22–53. Oxford, Westview.

Steinmo, S. (1989) Political institutions and tax policy in the United States, Sweden and Britain, *World Politics*, 41(4): 502.

Steinmo, S., Thelen, K. and Longstreth, E. (eds) (1992) *Structuring Politics*. Cambridge, Cambridge University Press.

Stigler, G.J. (1971) The theory of economic regulation, *Bell Journal of Economics and Management Science*, 2(1): 1–21.

Strange, S. (1988) *States and Markets*. London, Pinter.

Sturgess, G. (1989) First keynote address. In B. Carey and P. Ryan (eds) *In Transition: NSW and the Corporatisation Agenda*, pp. 4–10. Sydney, Macquarie Public Sector Studies Program/Association for Management Education and Research.

Taylor, J.A. and Williams, H. (1991) Public administration and the information polity, *Public Administration*, 69(2): 171–90.

Teubner, G. (1987) Juridification. In G. Teubner (ed.) *Juridification of Social Spheres*, pp. 3–48. Berlin, de Gruyter.

Thelen, K. and Steinmo, S. (1992) Historical institutionalism in comparative politics. In S. Steinmo, K. Thelen and F. Longstreth (eds) *Structuring Politics*, pp. 1–32. Cambridge, Cambridge University Press.

Therborn, G. (1987) Does corporatism really matter?, *Journal of Public Policy*, 7(3): 259–84.

Thompson, M., Ellis, R. and Wildavksy, A. (1990) *Cultural Theory*. Boulder, CO, Westview.

Tocqueville, A. de (1946) *Democracy in America*. Oxford, Oxford University Press.

Toynbee, A. (1972) *A Study of History* (abridged ed.). Oxford, Oxford University Press.

Tufte, E.R. (1978) *Political Control of the Economy*. Princeton, NJ, Princeton University Press.

Tufte, E.R. (1980) Review of Rose and Peters (1978), *American Political Science Review*, 74: 567–8.

Veljanovksi, C. (1987) *Selling the State*. London, Weidenfeld and Nicholson.

Vickers, J. and Wright, V. (1988) The politics of industrial privatisation in Western Europe, *West European Politics*, 11(4): 1–30.

Von Beyme, K. (1984) Do parties matter?, *Government and Opposition*, 19(1): 5–29.

Wagner, A. (1887) *Finanzwissenschaft*, Parts I and II. Leipzig, C.F. Winter.

Walker, G. de Q. (1987) *Initiative and Referendum*. Sydney, Centre for Independent Studies.

Walker, J.L. (1974) Performance gaps, policy research and political entrepreneurs, *Policy Studies Journal*, 3: 112–16.

Waltz, K. (1979) *Theory of International Relations*. Reading, MA, Addison-Wesley.

Weidenbaum, M.L. (1981) The problem of balancing the costs and benefits of regulation: Two views. In J.F. Gatti (ed.) *The Limits of Government Regulation*, pp. 143–9. New York, Academic Press.

Weir, M. and Skocpol, T. (1985) State structures and the possibilities for 'Keynesian' responses to the great depression in Sweden, Britain and the United States. In P.B. Evans, D. Rueschemeyer and T. Skocpol (eds) *Bringing the State Back In*, pp. 107–163. Cambridge, Cambridge University Press.

Wettenhall, R.L. (1963) Administrative boards in nineteenth century Australia, *Public Administration (Sydney)*, 22(3).

Wettenhall, R.L. (1966) The recoup concept in public enterprise, *Public Administration*, 44: 391–414.

Wettenhall, R.L. (1970) *The Iron Road and the State*. Hobart, University of Tasmania.

Wettenhall, R.L. (1988) Why public enterprise?, *Canberra Bulletin of Public Administration*, 57: 44–50.

Whitehead, C.M. (ed.) (1988) *Reshaping the Nationalized Industries*. Oxford, Transaction.

Whiteley, P. (1986) *Political Control of the Macroeconomy*. London, Sage.

Wildavsky, A. (1980) Policy as its own cause. In *The Art and Craft of Policy Analysis*, pp. 62–85. London, Macmillan.

Wildavksy, A. (1985) The logic of public sector growth. In J.E. Lane (ed.) *State and Market*, pp. 231–70. London, Sage.

Wilensky, H.L. (1981) Democratic corporatism, consensus and social policy: Reflections on changing values and the 'crisis' of the welfare state. In OECD (ed.) *The Welfare State in Crisis*, pp. 185–95. Paris, OECD.

Wilensky, H.L. and Turner, L. (1987) *Democratic Corporatism and Policy Linkages*. Berkeley, CA, Institute of International Studies, University of California.

Williams, R.J. (1976) Politics and the ecology of regulation, *Public Adminstration*, 54: 319–31.

Wilson, G. (1984) Social regulation and explanations of regulatory failure, *Political Studies*, 32(2): 203–225.

Wilson, J.Q. (1980) The politics of regulation. In J.Q. Wilson (ed.) *The Politics of Regulation*, pp. 357–94. New York, Basic Books.

Wilson, J.Q. (1989) *Bureaucracy*. New York, Basic Books.

Wiltshire, K. (1988) *Privatization: The British Experience*. Melbourne, Longman.

Witt, B. de (1968) *The Progressive Movement*. Seattle, WA, Washington University Press (reprint of 1915 edn).

Worsley, P. (1968) *The Trumpet Shall Sound*, 2nd edn. London, MacGibbon and Kee.

Wright, M. (ed.) (1980) *Public Spending Decisions*. London, Allen and Unwin.

Yeatman, A. (1987) The concept of public management and the Australian state in the 1980s, *Australian Journal of Public Administration*, 46: 339–53.

Index